D1271605

AFRICAN SPACES

AFRICAN

designs for living
in upper volta

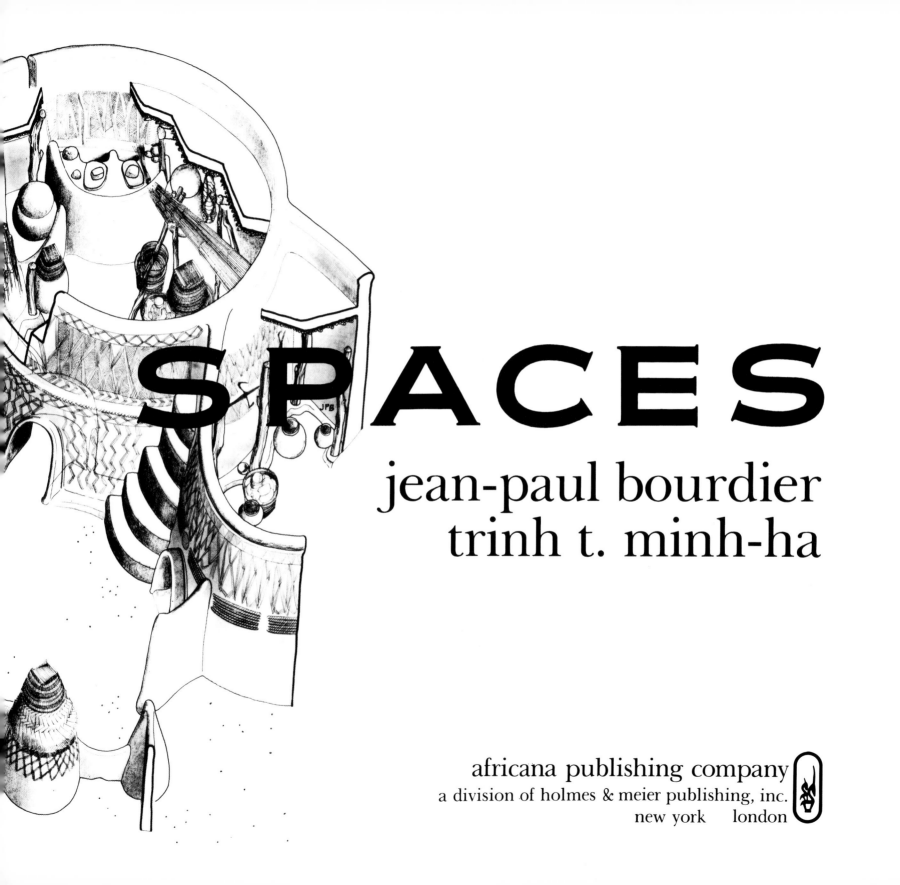

SPACES

jean-paul bourdier
trinh t. minh-ha

africana publishing company
a division of holmes & meier publishing, inc.
new york   london

First published in the United States of America 1985
by Africana Publishing Company,
a division of Holmes & Meier Publishers, Inc.
30 Irving Place
New York, N.Y. 10003

Great Britain:
Holmes & Meier Publishers, Ltd.
One Hallswelle Parade
London NW11 ODL

Copyright © 1985 by Jean-Paul Bourdier
All rights reserved

Book design by Stephanie Barton

Manufactured in the United States of America

Library of Congress Cataloging in Publication Data

Bourdier, Jean-Paul.
  African spaces.

  Bibliography: p.
  Includes index.
  1. Dwellings—Upper Volta. I. Trinh, T. Minh-Ha
(Thi Minh-Ha), 1952-   . II. Title.
GT377.U66B68 1985   728.3′73′096625   84-12362
ISBN 0-8419-0890-7

Publisher's note: At the time of going to press, the name of Upper Volta had
just been changed to Burkina Faso.

LIBRARY
ALMA COLLEGE
ALMA, MICHIGAN

CONTENTS

ACKNOWLEDGMENTS

We have benefited from the help, support, and interest of a great number of people over the four years it has taken us to complete this work and would like here to express our feelings of gratitude to all of them.

We would like, first of all, to thank the many villagers who welcomed us into their homes, allowing us free access to their dwelling spaces and providing us with assistance in our field survey.

We started research on the subject a few months after our arrival in 1977 in Senegal (where we both taught for three consecutive years—Jean-Paul at the School of Architecture and Urbanism, and Minh-ha at the National Conservatory of Music and Drama in Dakar). At this time we were devoid of any means either to finance our fields trips or to convince those around us (colleagues, people in high administrative positions, a few nongovernmental organizations) of the worthiness of such a study and the necessity for it in an African university context. It was only thanks to the generosity of Jean-Michel de Dion and his confidence in the project that this work was initially made possible.

After the first field work was carried out, we received financial support from various sources and are particularly grateful to Monsieur le Secrétaire d'Etat à la Recherche Scientifique et Technique du Sénégal and to Mr. Tochterman from the Unesco Division des Etablissements Humains et de l'Environnement Socio-culturel in Paris.

We would like to extend our thanks to Monsieur Le Ministre de l'Enseignement Supérieur et de la Recherche Scientifique de Haute-Volta, the director of the Centre Voltaïque de la Recherche Scientifique, and all the administrators of regions we visited or spent time in, who facilitated our stay in Upper Volta and encouraged us in our work.

We gratefully acknowledge the no less important help of René-Maurice Gueye, director of the Ecole d'Architecture et d'Urbanisme de Dakar; Pierre Goudiaby, president of the Ordre des Architectes de Dakar; architects Jean-Paul Castanet, Moussa Fall, and Cheikh Ngom; the Chefs de Mouvement des Chemins de Fer Sénégalais et Maliens; the BLACT; and the directors of various companies in Dakar: Bourgi, Maurel et Prom, SAIB, and Buhant Teisseire.

We also wish to thank, for their editorial assistance, Margaret Sevcenko, Jonathan Beck, Harriett Boyce, and especially Kate Rothrock, who worked on the entire manuscript; as well as Naomi L. Lipman and Jack Lynch of Holmes & Meier Publishers, Inc.; for their critical remarks and friendly help at vari-

ous stages of the work, Denis Fogelgesang, Jacques Bouby, Henri Barral, Marie-Jean Demanie, and Fifi Bocoum; for the typing of the manuscript, Maureen Jurkowski; for library assistance, Mamadou Sall from the IFAN; and finally, for the translation of the German materials, Bernard Wentz.

Parts of this study have been published in the following magazines, which we gratefully acknowledge: Chapters 1 and 7 in *African Arts* (November 1982 and August 1983); Chapter 10 in *Landscape* (December 1983); parts of the conclusion in *Mimar: Architecture in Development* (published by Concept Media, Singapore; No. 4, 1982) and in *Progressive Architecture* (August 1982).

The publication of this book has been made possible in part by a grant from the Aga Khan Program for Islamic Architecture at Harvard University and the Massachusetts Institute of Technology

Photographs and drawings by Jean-Paul Bourdier

Photographs 1, 2, 4, 31, 59, 62, 68, 75, 95 by Trinh T. Minh-ha

Field survey done with the assistance of:
Ndongo Athj
Innocent Bimenyimana
Makhtar Faye
El Hadj Malick Gaye
Sharon Murray
Mame Dioulame Seye
Ndary Touré

AFRICAN SPACES

INTRODUCTION

The diversity and elaborateness of African vernacular architecture remain widely unknown, both to the general public and to architects. The built environment of hundreds of ethnic groups throughout Africa presents, however, an astonishing variety of design principles and adapted building techniques that belie the widespread image of the primitive hut so readily attributed to rural Africa. A fuller understanding of the fundamental constituents of architecture, such as type, space, form, and function, may be gained through the documentation of traditional habitations, which constitute not only a geographical and social phenomenon but also a striking religious manifestation, reflecting and interacting with the collective perception of space, attitudes, behaviors, and ritual practices of a society. Such documentation requires a survey of built forms and spatial systems whose significance will emerge only through the parallel study of their essential functional qualities along with the characteristic social or spiritual activities that allow them to integrate into the overall cultural pattern.

The architecture of rural West Africa may, broadly speaking, be distributed into three main types. Climate, soil, and lifestyle figure among the dominant factors that determine the form of houses and the choice of building materials, and each of the types in question may be considered to correspond to a specific climatic zone.

In the Sahel belt, south of the Sahara, the climate is semi-desertic, the vegetation grassland steppe, and the population mainly composed of nomadic shepherds who follow their herds to the areas where trees are scarce but seasonal grass grows in abundance. Their dwellings are, therefore, temporary, free-standing structures, easily dismantled. They are erected follow-

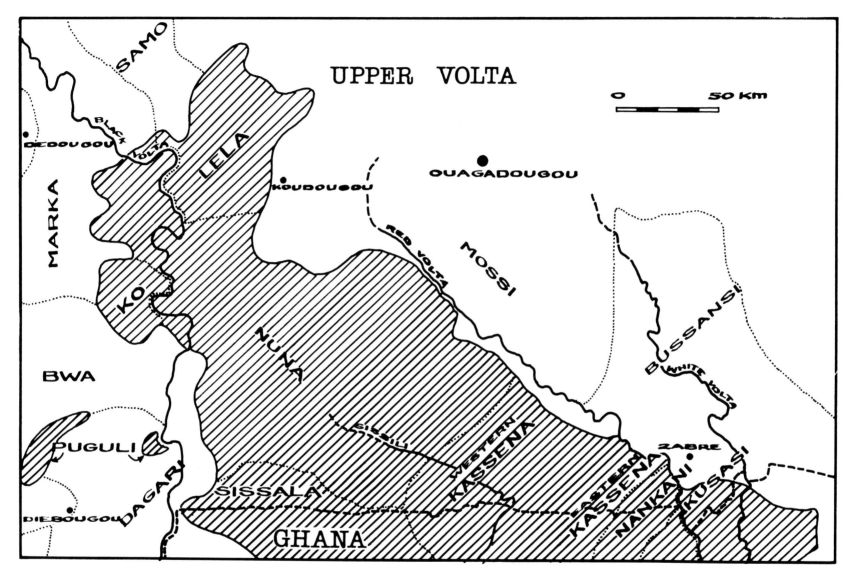

D.1. Area inhabited by the Gurunsi
in Upper Volta.

ing aerodynamic forms (such as the Tuareg tents or the Fulani semispherical shelters) with a minimum of wooden supports, and covered with a thatch of grass or reeds, woven and plaited mats, skins or heavy cloths. Farther south, in the Sudan region, longer annual rainfall with a high degree of variability makes possible crop production and fosters the growth of a savanna woodland vegetation. Consonant with his sedentary mode of life, the Sudanese farmer opts for a more permanent dwelling. The availability of clayey soils and to some extent wood also accounts for the presence of adobe habitations, covered either with conical thatched roofs or with earthen domes or equipped with flat adobe terraces supported by rafters. The use of flat adobe roofs allows for various assymetrical building shapes and their diverse patterns of association—as shown in the drawings in this study. Finally, in the humid forest zone spreading along the coastline from southern Senegal to Nigeria, the heavy pre-cipitation and density of forest growth affect differently the built environment of the inhabitants. Here, dwellings are erected either with woven cleft wood or bamboo walls, facilitating air circulation, or with earthen walls reinforced by an armature of bamboo or palm-frond wattles to protect against rain deterioration. Further protection is provided by thatched conical or saddleback roofs with projecting eaves to deflect rainwater. Roof shapes in turn influence the form and arrangement of dwelling spaces. Thus, with the exception of the impluvium type of house, where adobe parallelepipedic units are nested below a single thatched, two-sloped circular roof, dwelling spaces remain separate freestanding structures, since waterproof connections are difficult to achieve between conical thatched roofs and do not lend themselves to an expandable house plan when made between thatched saddleback roofs.

The country of Upper Volta is situated in the very center of the Sudan-Sahel zone. The eight ethnic groups whose architectures are examined in the following chapters are among its oldest populations and occupy in its central southern region the area found roughly between the Red and Black Voltas (D.1). They constitute a relatively homogeneous cultural entity commonly known as the "Gurunsi," a generic name which, in the new Republic of the Upper Volta, covers the Lela, the Nuna (numerically the most important), the Ko, the Puguli, the Sissala, the Kassena, the Nankani, and the Kusasi. The latter four groups extend to northern Ghana, where they are bordered by the Gonja, the Dagomba, and the Mamprusi, their southern neighbors. The Gurunsi area in Upper Volta is flanked on the north and east by the centralized Mossi kingdoms (Yatenga, Ouagadougou, Tenkodogo) and on the west by the territories of the Dagari, the Bwa, the Marka, and the Samo.

Like most of Upper Volta, Gurunsiland is composed of Precambrian rocks. It presents a morphology of peneplain with monotonously flat surfaces, except towards the valleys of the Voltas and the Sissili. The soils are ferruginous, laterite is common, and the water table is very deep. Since the impermeable rocks induce a rapid runoff, rivers are alternately dry and in sudden flood, while wells yield very little water at any depth. The Gurunsi country is drained in the north and west by the Black Volta and in the center and south by the Red Volta and the Sissili. Only the Black Volta flows year-round. During the wet season, its swollen affluents may cause villages to remain isolated for many hours after a rain, but dwindle, during the dry season, into a succession of small, stagnant pools. The Red Volta and the Sissili are important drainage systems only between June and September.

The climate, typical of the Sudan zone, consists of two main seasons: one relatively cool and dry, the other hot and wet. The

5

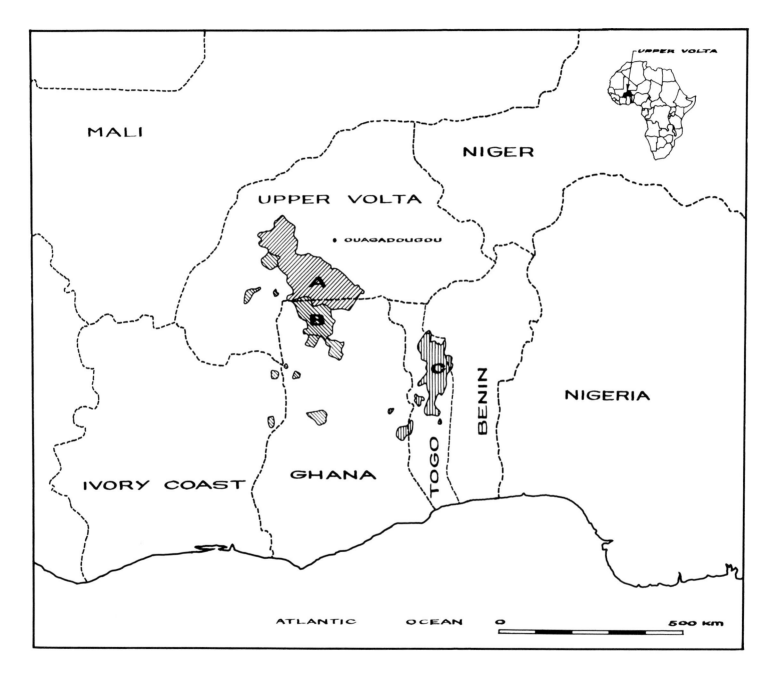

D.2. The three groups (A, B and C)
of Gurunsi languages as seen by
Manessy (1969).

former begins in approximately mid-November with the advent of the harmattan and ends in mid-April, followed by an alternately dry and humid transitional period from mid-April to mid-June. The rainy season extends from mid-June to mid-September, with the maximum precipitation in August, and is also followed by a transitional period from mid-September to mid-November. The natural vegetation in this area is savanna woodland. The most widely encountered trees include locust bean *(Parkia biglobosa)*, shea *(Butyrospermum parkii)*, kapok *(Bombax costatum)*, tamarind *(Tamarindus indica)*, and *Kenyaya senegalensis*, a kind of acacia. Toward the north of Lelaland, one may also add baobabs *(Adansonia digitata)* and the *Borassus aethiopium* of the palm family. Agriculture remains the Gurunsi's predominant activity. Plants cultivated include several varieties of sorghum *(Sorghum vulgare)*, millet *(Pennisetum typhoides)*, maize, rice, okra, fonio, beans, onions, and less frequently, cotton and peanuts. Cattle raising maintains a secondary but important role. It was certainly more important in the nineteenth century, before the Zabarima invasions (discussed below), since habitations are designed with central courts serving as cattle kraals at night, and cows are required in sacrifices as well as in matrimonial and judicial compensations.

The Gurunsi people number about 350,000, or 5.5 percent of Upper Volta's total population.[1] The languages they speak belong to the Gur or Voltaic family and are grouped under two subdivisions: (1) the Mole-Dagbane, which includes the Kusasi speaking Kusal and the Nankani speaking Nankane or Gureñe, and (2) the Grusi, which comprises the Kassena speaking Kasem, the Nuna speaking Nuni, the Lela speaking Lyele, the Ko speaking Winye, the Puguli speaking Phwo, and the Sissala speaking Isala. Gabriel Manessy, on the basis of a comparative study of twenty-one Gurunsi languages,[2] hypothesizes the division of an older Gurunsi tongue into three dialect clusters A, B, and C (D.2), with the six languages of the Grusi subdivision distributed in clusters A and C. These original clusters are supposed to have progressively split up into more distinct units, each with its own organization and constituting what nowadays have been termed different languages of the same family.[3] The actual situation is, however, far more complex than the picture such classifications could convey, for further ramifications within each language group often occur. Examples may be found among the Nuna of the circle of Leo, who divide into the Bassenyera, the Bwona, the Gwora, the Menkyera, and the Sankura, or among the Lela, who speak three subdialects in three different parts of the area (Didyr, Reo, and Batondo).[4]

Some Gurunsi societies, on the other hand, do not consider themselves to belong to any of the eight groups mentioned. Such is the case, for example, of the inhabitants of Koumbo, a village at the boundary of the Nuna and Kassena territories, who claim to be neither Nuna nor Kassena, but Kwana. This is also true of the Lela from Batondo, who call themselves Nebwale.[5] Numerous other examples could be cited which reconfirm that the generic tag Gurunsi refers, not to a single group, but to an aggregate of linguistic communities aware both of their originality and, as we shall see, of their cultural affinities. How then, one may ask, has the term Gurunsi come into use to designate this plurality, and in what way can its use be justified?

The term has been traced back to a map published in *Mission from Cape Coast Castle to Ashantee* by Edward T. Bowdich, who was sent in 1817 as ambassador to Kumasi by the governor of Cape Coast to conclude, on behalf of Great Britain, a treaty of peace and friendship with the kings of Ashanti and Juaben. The map shows a town spelled "Gooroosie," situated northeast of Dagwumba (Dagomba) and Gamba (Mamprusi) and southeast of the Mossi kingdom of Kookoopala (Koupela), which is approximately where the Nankani stand in relation to their neighboring Dagomba, Mamprusi, and Mossi. Years later, S. W. Koelle, a Protestant missionary stationed in Freetown, Sierra Leone, indicated a Guresa-speaking group east of the Mossi and Kasem (Kassena) peoples on the map accompanying his *Polyglotta Africana* (1854). The German explorer H. Barth also mentioned a Gurunga group in his "Information Regarding the Provinces of Gurma, Mósi and Tombo" (1849–1855) as one of the "several smaller tribes, the degree of whose affinity is not easy to determine, especially as the names are more or less corrupted by the traders."[6]

These sources suggest that the term Gurunsi, which appeared successively as Gooroosie, Guresa, and Gurunga, may first have been attributed to the Gureñe-speaking people, the Nankani. Its use appears to have gradually been extended to the other ethnic groups, since 1886 with Gottlob Adolph Krause, then with J. G. Christaller (1889–1890), K. Von François (1888), Capitaine Binger (1888), H. Delafosse (1912–1924), and L. Tauxier (1909–1924).[7] Nowadays, the only people in Upper Volta who appear to claim the term and call themselves Gurensi (variant of Gurunsi) are the Nankani. In our survey, opinions were found to vary widely from one local source to another. Except for the Eastern Kassena and the Kusasi, who occupy areas immediately east and west of the

9

Nankani and, therefore, often reject the term Gurunsi,[8] the six other groups accept it as a collective name parallel to their more specific ethnic identifications.

The word Gurunsi is generally believed to be a foreign appellation used to refer to the peoples in question by one of their politically more centralized neighbors: the Mossi, the Mamprusi, the Dagomba, or the Zabarima. Several local sources attribute it to the Songhaï-speaking Zabarima, who raided the area in the late 1880s. Each source, however, interprets its meaning differently: one account explains it as equivalent to "uncircumcised," another as "fetishist."[9] Both are traits that distinguish the Gurunsi from their neighbors mentioned above—the sociological content—rather than direct translations of the word. Similar information was given by Lieutenant Marc, a colonial administrator in Mossiland, according to whom the word derives from the Songhaï term *grounga*, which means "uncircumcised." Louis Tauxier, who took this information literally and double-checked it, naturally rejected it as false, finding that *grounga* does not exist in Songhaï.[10]

Discarding Lieutenant Marc's hypothesis, Tauxier asserts that Gurunsi is the plural of Gurunga, a Mossi word that has always been used by this group to designate their neighbors west of the Red Volta, probably since the twelfth century. A. W. Cardinall and M. Fortes, who studied the Gurunsi population of nothern Ghana, reached a similar conclusion. The name Grunshi or Gorensi, they observed, was a term of contempt derived from the Mole-Dagbane peoples, either the Mossi, the Dagomba, or the Mamprusi.[11] It carried the connotation of "slave" or "social inferior." Among the Mossi, to treat someone as "Gurunsi" is equivalent to regarding that person as savage, uncivilized, or, worse, thievish.[12] It is not unusual to encounter cases where this derogatory term is used by members of one Gurunsi group to refer to members of another Gurunsi group—not, however, as an insult arising out of ignorance or antagonism, but as "an institutional form of an intertribal joking relationship."[13]

Despite the differences separating them, the Gurunsi people have many cultural traits in common. Whether the people have always seen themselves as a cultural unit claiming to be "all Gurunsi" (J. Zwernemann), or simply accept this notion vulgarized by the colonial administrators and officially recognized by the governments since independence, is a question that remains to be answered. For the many foreign observers who have studied the area, the Gurunsi figure among the autochthonous inhabitants of the region and the oldest civilizations of Africa.[14] Linguistically regrouped, they are generally viewed as a plural whole.

The Gurunsi recognize two forms of power at the origin of a dichotomy termed the segmentary system and the system of centralized power. The former is the organization type that originally prevailed in Gurunsi societies (apparently the only one known to the Ko and the Lela until the colonial period[15]). Each local group—an agglomeration of several extended families belonging to different lineages but cultivating the same land—is headed by a "priest-king," or custodian of the earth, called *tengsoba* by the Mossi, *tiyatu* by the Nuna, and *tegatu* (*tega* "earth" + *tu,* a suffix which designates lordship in the sense of owner as well as chief or master) by the Kassena. The *tegatu*-ship belongs to the lineage whose ancestor was the first settler of the territory currently occupied by his descendants. Placing

11

himself under the protection of the local Earth God, whose hierophanes, known as *taèwa* in Kasem, may be a sacred hill, swamp, or wood, this founding ancestor (the *tegatu*) plays the role of mediator between the people and the divinity who gave them the resources to live, and is also designated by the term *taèwatu*. He is in charge of all sacrifices necessary to the well-being of the community: fertility of the earth, fecundity of women, immunity against diseases. No land can be cleared for a new field, no compound erected, no grave dug without the intervention of the *tegatu,* whose ritual collaboration is indispensable. When a man first arrives in an uninhabited country, he obtains land from the *tegatu* nearest the site of the new settlement, and may or may not be himself appointed *tegatu* of this site by the latter. Such power is not founded on a relationship of authority; the custodian of the earth is obeyed but does not really give orders. All actions taken by this man are understood as coming from a mediator who intercedes with the earth spirits on behalf of the local group.

Parallel to this segmentary system is the institution of the *pio* or *peo* (in Nuni) whose conception of power is fundamentally different, and is generally believed to have been imported by foreign rulers (Mossi, Dagomba, Mamprusi) immigrating to the area. The *peo,* commonly known as the administrative chief of one or several villages (canton), rules as a prince whose political power, like that of the *tegatu,* is not secular in nature. Its sacred essence materializes in a hierophane, the *kwara* (usually an ox horn or a ram horn filled with earth from the sacred place of the *peo*'s origin in Mossiland, Dagombaland, or Mamprusiland, and surrounded by a few oxtails and pieces of wood wrapped in skin or cloth), which the *peo* keeps in a specific space within his compound and worships liturgically. The sacredness of his power *qua* power is, however, the very attribute that differentiates it from the *tegatu*'s power. The latter, as has been pointed out, does not carry in itself its own finality, but builds on an external necessity—that of maintaining the spiritual links between humans and the powers of nature.[16]

The distinction between mediation power *(tegatu)* and authority power *(peo)* remains, nonetheless, difficult to establish, since the two aspects of leadership often merge. It is not uncommon to encounter cases where the same man assumes the role of both *tegatu* and *peo* (the chief of the village of Tangassoko in Chapter 8 is an example of such a man). When the two functions coexist separately, they generally do not compete with each other—such, at least, was the case until the intervention of the colonial administration—for the *peo*, who also con-

tributes to the growth and prosperity of a village or canton, fully recognizes the position of the *tegatu* and mainly assumes the responsibilities of a Chief of War. Otherwise, in conference with a number of relatives and elders that form his court, he administers justice on all matters that do not fall within the *tegatu's* competence, such as abductions of women, their desertion of their husbands' homes, or, when he is the *peo* of a canton, the disputes between two village chiefs. "The people belong to me, the land belongs to the *Teńdaná* [*tegatu*]" a *peo* would commonly say.[17] The statement clearly speaks for the different concerns of the two leaders and their mutual dependence. As an immigrant of foreign origin, the *peo* "carefully observed the existing division of the land into Tengani areas," and "appointed relatives, captains, etc., to administer areas whose boundaries coincided with these. At no time up to the

13

arrivals of Europeans," T. E. Hilton asserts in his "Notes on the History of Kusasi," "did the chief [the *peo*] lay claim to ownership of the land, which he, in common with the people under him, regarded as belonging to the Earth God. The powers of a chief derived from the number of his people and not from the extent of the land occupied by them."[18]

The concept of wealth and power deriving from the people rather than from landed property is also found in the social organization of a smaller unit, the compound. (The title "owner" of the land often attributed to the *tegatu* should, naturally, be understood not as "proprietor" but as "trustee," for those who "own" the land and the crops are the ancestors.) In these segmentary Gurunsi societies where a decentralized system of power originally prevails, and, as we shall see, where both collective and individual farming exist, the pattern of set-tlement most widely encountered remains that of dispersed habitations, isolated from one another by large fields under cultivation. In the case studies that follow, the villages of Pouni (Chapter 2), Koena (Chapter 4), and Outoulou (Chapter 6), which are more densely grouped than other Gurunsi villages, present a semi-dispersed type of settlement, while the only example of a nucleated pattern is the older, compact "underground"[19] village that still partly exists in Koumbili (Chapter 7), in addition to more recent, dispersed habitations on the ground.

The notion of house, homestead, or compound in this context conveys not only the idea of space containment, shelter, territorial demarcation, or privacy. It also covers two other realities: one social, the predominantly patrilineal family organization, the other economic, the farming of land granted by the head of the family and cleared collectively by its members. By "compound," the Gurunsi designate the plural entity formed by a number of households (including the ancestors), primarily organized on the basis of agnatic descent, cultivating separately and/or collectively the family farmland, and residing in the same composite habitation. This dwelling and farming group, which also divides into smaller groups or subgroups, is commonly referred to as the joint or extended family—patrilocal and mainly patrilineal (exceptions are the Puguli and Sissala[20])—whose members consist of several close male agnates, their wives and children. Different from the Bwa[21] compound, which constitutes a single farming group exploiting the same, undivided plot of land, the Gurunsi compound shows through its labor division and spatial arrangement a more decentralized system of social organization. Several dwelling and farming combinations are possible within the compound. Among the Nuna, the Eastern Kassena, and the Sissala, for example, besides cultivating for the family, during the rainy season, from 6 A.M. to 3 P.M. or 7 A.M. to 4 P.M., its members also work in their individual fields, either after 3 P.M. or during the weekly rest days. Among the Nankani and the Western Kassena, this type of farming organization coexists with another prevailing type in which each household forms a separate unit of food production and cultivates its plot only for its own consumption, during both seasons, rainy and dry. A third type also encountered in the area is exemplified in the case study of Dakui's compound, in Chapter 6 (Sissala). Here, the family splits into two farming groups, one working for Dakui and the other for his nephew, a division reflected in the design of his compound and in the presence of two gateways.

P.1. Women's collective pounding of millet.

Whatever the form of labor distribution chosen, the compound remains in the traditional setting of a subsistence economy, an autonomous whole which lives in autarchy, ensuring by itself and for itself the production and distribution of almost all products of daily consumption. The cohesion of this whole is maintained through the mediation of the eldest male member of the joint family, known as "head of the compound." When farming is done collectively for the family, the common crops gathered and stored in large granaries are entrusted to the senior man, who, at appointed hours of the day during the rainy season and part of the dry season, distributes to the women of the compound the quantity of millet necessary for each cooking group. For the rest of the dry season, each household uses the products of its individual fields. In cases where farming is done separately, food consumption is independent, but households who have had poor harvests can still count on the assistance of the compound head. Thus, a high degree of cooperation and the concept of interavailability of supplies continue to exist, and the recognition of kinship ties usually involves an obligation to share food in times of shortage.

The senior man also determines the allocation of dwelling spaces for the collectivity, the building of new units, and the destruction of older ones—the compound traditionally grows in accordance with the size of the family or the addition of brides and offspring, as discussed in Chapters 9 and 10. He guards and superintends the entrance of the compound, a role acknowledged by the consistent presence of a daytime shelter that faces this entrance from the outside and provides the senior man with a shaded place to carry out his duty as guardian of the family. Being the "authority" who grants or refuses newcomers permission to incorporate into the compound community, he also undertakes to marry all its members. The young men may choose their wives, but they depend largely on him for the payment of the bride-price. In the religious sphere, he functions as priest of all family shrines, particularly the ancestral shrine, maintaining close communication with the ancestors—the custodians of the laws and customs of the tribe—influencing thereby their intervention, while consulting them on all family affairs. The importance of such a role in strengthening the life of the group cannot be underestimated, for the collaboration of the senior member of the living with the departed constitutes a moral and spiritual force that often serves to regulate the conduct of the group members.

The headship of a compound appears above all as a social and religious responsibility. It is transmitted from senior father to junior father or, when the line of fathers dies out, from father to eldest son. Offering few privileges compared to its heavy responsibilities, this headship is relinquished when the legal successor feels incapable of ensuring the prosperity of the compound. All family responsibilities do not, however, fall solely on the senior man or compound head. They also devolve upon the "head of the court," a term designating the household head who also functions as head of a farming group or subgroup—each household, as we shall see, has its own packed-earth court—and upon the senior woman, who is usually the first wife of the compound head. The most evident example of this decentralized system of organization through spatial distribution is the case study of Buma's compound in Valiou (case study 3). Here, the occupants, numbering 138 (compared to 71 and 12 in case studies 1 and 9), form a relatively important community. The senior man of the compound, on account of his age and, therefore, inability to guarantee the economic or social welfare of the group, has given up the headship to his younger brother, Buma. Buma, in turn, shares this responsibility with the heads of courts, the latter being in charge of their own households, whose dwelling spaces are grouped into separate clusters. The role of the senior woman of a homestead in Gurunsi societies has not yet been the subject of a detailed study and much remains to be done in this area. Generally speaking, she oversees everything that goes on inside the compound, which is considered her domain, and is in charge of all the women within the group.

The foregoing sketch of the social organization among the Gurunsi may perhaps explain the low repute in which they have been held, both by their Mossi neighbors and by the colonial administration. Recently praised for their continuous, fierce rejection of all forms of domination, the Gurunsi were in the past considered "excessively dangerous." They were described as warlike people who lived in constant hostility with their neighbors and prevented communication roads from being built so as to render access to their villages difficult without guides. The deep distrust displayed by outsiders crossing their territories is well known to the people of the region.[22] French writings of the colonial period, on the contrary, repeatedly describe French intervention as the rescue of the oppressed Gurunsi, whose segmentary, thus "anarchic," societies were at the mercy of foreign invaders (the Marka and Zabarima).

Little is known of the history of the Gurunsi people. Their presence was not recorded until the Mossi moved into this zone around 1500, from the northern region of present-day Ghana,

19

to create the various Mossi kingdoms.[23] Diverse accounts relate the numerous incursions by the Mossi into the area to sack the villages and capture slaves for sale. In the sixteenth century, one of the great sovereigns of the kingdom of Ouagadougou, the *mogho-naba* Kumdumye, starting from Tiou, his place of residence near Koudougou at the boundary of the Mossi and Gurunsi territories, undertook an impressive military campaign directed at the Gurunsi land. He reached Boromo, where he died, and never succeeded in subjecting the area between the Red and Black Voltas to Mossi domination. His campaigns there yielded no lasting political result. They seem only to have affected the kingdom of Ouagadougou, whose *mogho-naba* was compelled to grant the chiefs of western districts, such as Tiou, Poa, and Lallé, "constantly at grips with Gurunsi villages rebelling against their authority," a large degree of autonomy.[24]

Farther north, the area of Yako, a kingdom created by the *naba* Konkisse, son of the *naba* Kumdumye, was the site of violent disputes between Mossi and Gurunsi. The chiefs of the Dakola, Batono, and Samba districts launched numerous attacks in Lelaland, but could not manage to annex it to their kingdom (Yako). Lela oral traditions recount a series of Mossi raids on villages such as Pouni (not the Nuna village of case study 2, but the Lela village near Didyr), Goundi, Kordié, Konkouldi, Ninyon, Birou, Doudou, Dassa, Godyr, and Didyr.

Thanks to their fierce resistance, the Gurunsi escaped the domination the *nakomse* ("children of the *naba*," a name reserved in Mossiland to the leading political group and the members of their lineage) imposed on the Ninisi and Nyonyose, also called *têg-bisi* or *tengbisi* ("children of the earth," a name given to the older inhabitants of the area). The Gurunsi

P.2. Kinswomen carrying water back to their compound from a well 2 kilometers away.

territories remained, however, for many years, the theater of unceasing wars, wars of conquest first, which became pillaging operations after the Mossi had forgone their attempts to establish supremacy over Gurunsiland in its entirety.[25] That Mossi infiltration into Lela, Nuna, and Kassena territories occurred over the course of centuries is borne out by the architecture of the zones where they exerted their influence—case studies 2 (Pouni), 3 (Valiou), and 7 (Koumbili). Many villages claim Mossi ancestors who immigrated to the area because of quarrels of chieftainship in their birthplace. It is, therefore, not uncommon to encounter *tegatu* (custodians of the earth) of *nakomse* descent.

Despite the historically strained relations between the Mossi and the Gurunsi, oral traditions among the latter do not retain images of the Mossi as negative as those they remember of the Marka and the Zabarima. More than any other neighboring forces, these two Muslim hegemonies provoked great upheavals in the area toward the end of the nineteenth century. The first was led by El Hadj Mamadou Karantao, a Marka from Djenne who founded a small Muslim state in the surroundings of Boromo, the second by several Zabarima chiefs among whom figured Babatu, a name that remains vivid in the memory of many Gurunsi peoples.

Although comparatively limited, the expansion movement of Karantao and his followers in the loop of the Black Volta fell within the framework of the awakening of Islam, which exerted its influence in the Niger-Sudan countries in the 1880s with the founding of the Sokoto Empire in the east by Ousmame Dan Fodio and his son, Mohamed Bello, and the Dina of Hamdallaye in the west by Sekou Ahmadou. In Upper Volta, the

21

Karantao movement developed subsequent to the spread over the western part of the country (the area of Bobo-Dioulasso) of Sekou Wattara's Muslims from the kingdom of Kong (mid-eighteenth century) and the holy war that ended the Gur-mantche's domination of the Liptako (1810).[26] The beginning of Karantao's incursions into Boromo dates from around 1840. From Boromo, he advanced north toward Massala, conquering a few Ko villages, and was succeeded at his death by his son, Karamoko Moktar Karantao, whose southward expedition met with success in Oronkua and Gueguere but was seriously routed by a Puguli-Dagari coalition in Djindjerma. The only consequences resulting from the Karantaos' holy wars are the religious influences of three Muslim centers: Douroula, where Karantao was born; Safané, where he studied the Qur'án; and Ouahabou, where he settled during the years of conquest. The latter, a Bobo village formerly named M'pheoum and rebaptized "Wa haba illah" ("God has given it to me") by the senior Karantao, was the most important. At the time of the French intervention, it was said to still hold under its authority more than thirty surrounding villages. As for the Gurunsi, the populations mainly affected by the movement were the Ko, whose families were evicted from Boromo (the chiefship of Boromo has remained since then in the hands of Yaya Guira, a Mossi leader appointed by Karantao, and his descendants), and the Puguli, whose hastened dispersion along the Bougouriba River was the movement's probable result.[27] A Sissala chief, Moussa Kadio, was also converted to Islam under Karantao's influence and made his village Sati into a small Muslim center.

The Zabarima originally occupied the area bordering the Niger River southwest of Niamey. They were converted to Islam only in the mid-eighteenth century, following a jihad led by Sokoto. Toward the 1870s, a small group of Muslim Zabarima, whose spiritual chief was Alfa Hano, arrived in Dagombaland. The reason for their arrival has been variously interpreted: either they worked as mercenaries for the king of Dagomba, who owed the Ashanti a significant number of young men and women as annual tribute; or they came as traders to recover the payment for the horses they sold to the Dagomba chiefs; or else they carried out a mission of Muslim proselytism. In any case, from Dagombaland, Alfa Hano's men proceeded northwest to Sissalaland and then to Kassenaland. Stationed in the village of Kasana (Ghana), they launched a series of raids reaching as far north as the Lela territories. At Alfa Hano's death, the Zabarima, led by Alfa Gazare,[28] were defeated by the Dagomba from whom they had separated and withdrew to Sati, among the Sissala, where Moussa Kadio (Karantao's disciple) gave them hospitality. The numerous, wide-reaching expeditions that Gazare organized across Gurunsiland were later carried on by his successor, Babatu Zato, who devastated the area, notwithstanding the vigorous resistance put up against him. Toward 1882, for example, a revolt broke out in Sissalaland around the village of Dolbizan, which resisted for more than a year in spite of the bloody repression carried out in the surrounding area. All villages wishing otherwise to avoid Zabarima raids had to pay heavy tributes in cowries, cattle, and even horses. In 1882–1883, Moussa Kadio decided to break away from Babatu and his men. He erected around Sati a wall 2.5 to 3 meters high, topped by crenels and equipped with loopholes, behind which he stored food and war supplies. According to legend, it took the people "four years and four months" to finish the construction, and the siege which began in 1885 lasted "three years and three days." Out of supplies and hungry, the Sissala surrendered to the Zabarima, who built their own fortified camp a kilometer farther east, the "great robber camp" (G. A. Krause) known as Sansanne Gazari (the former leader's name). Around 1890, the Zabarima returned to Kassena territories. Tiakané, which had by then fortified its compounds with surrounding walls, resisted for seven days, during which the villagers desperately fought back, "their fingers bleeding by dint of shooting with their bows." Numerous other Kassena villages were mercilessly attacked and sacked. A similar fate befell those situated in Lela and Nuna territories; the few that were spared agreed to pay a price of "one million cowries and a hundred slaves."[29]

Neither the Karantao nor the Zabarima movement succeeded in substantially converting the populations under its control to Islam. The latter's activities in Gurunsiland appeared, in fact, less as invasions of Muslim proselytism than as slave-raiding expeditions.[30] These are, indeed, the pictures that emerge from local accounts, missionaries' statements, and writings of several European explorers in the years 1888–1890 (Krause, Binger, Von François). All agree on the ravaging aspect of the Zabarima's incursions and the intensity of their slave trade. Times of cruel starvation during the period of their presence in Gurunsiland are often referred to by oral traditions, a circumstance acknowledged by the French explorer Binger, who traveled through the area in 1888, just after the surrender of Sati. Binger, however, made no distinction between pillager and pillaged; for him, "the Gourounga are plunderers. The chiefs' rapacity is excessive." Throughout the Nuna territories, he encountered numerous ruins, abandoned farmland, half-deserted villages, and grieved over the devastation of the entire area, which had been well populated and prosperous before the Zabarima invasions.[31] These not only caused profound disturbance within Gurunsi society; they were also responsible for considerable dispersion[32] and shifting of local populations.

Rather than evoking Islam, the name Babatu remains nowadays a synonym for cruelty and pillage. It is often associated with that of a Kassena, Hamaria, who has become, in certain people's opinion, a "national hero" of the Gurunsi, the "authentic incarnation of their yearning for independence."[33] Captured at the age of seven, taken thereafter into Alfa Hano's service and converted to Islam, Hamaria first collaborated with the Zabarima, occupying a position of command. He later rose in revolt against the arrogance of their leadership and was enthusiastically supported by the Gurunsi residing in the area of Leo. Those defeated in Sati also joined in, and the fight he led against Babatu toward the end of the century was by far the most important resistance the Zabarima ever met in Gurunsiland.[34]

In the midst of the intense contest between Hamaria and Babatu, two other forces came into play. The Almamy Samory Toure, a Mande leader whose state constituted one of the most important cells of Muslim resistance against European forces during the last twenty years of the nineteenth century, arrived in the southwestern part of the country with thousands of soldiers from his well-trained army and attempted to impose his arbitration. In 1896 the French troops led by Lieutenants Voulet and Chanoine intervened at Hamaria's request and had no difficulty in presenting themselves as liberators of the re-

P.3. The cohesion of a compound is maintained through the mediation of the eldest male member of the family.

gion. Babatu fled southward to the vicinity of Wa (Ghana), and Voulet negotiated a treaty of protectorate with Hamaria, guarding him from both Babatu and Samory. The establishment of a French administration was not, however, accomplished smoothly in this part of the country, where the populations for centuries had rejected all centralized authority. An obstinate resistance against the diverse forms of colonial subjection, more particularly against taxation and recruitment, soon arose on all sides in Gurunsiland and erupted into open hostilities in Lela and Nuna territories around 1915–1916. The repression that followed led to an "era of resignation" during which the Gurunsi realized "they were no match for the colonial machine-guns" (J. Goody).[35]

The historical background of the Gurunsi as outlined here brings into relief two essential attributes: their spirit of inde-

pendence and their capacity for defense. Both are manifested in various domains, particularly in architecture. The first has already been mentioned in relation to the compound structure (division of labor, system of individual courts) and the segmentary system of political organization. This system, in which the absence of a centralized power has conveniently been used to explain the significant number of Gurunsi captives dispersed through the slave trade, has often been disparagingly described as a more primitive form of organization that has "not reached any significant level of political development" or "progressed beyond the family unit" (Delafosse). It was with this point of view that Louis Tauxier tackled the problem of Gurunsi architecture in his study *Le Noir du Soudan* (1912). The quality of this architecture, which he described as "grandiose," astounded him; that it could have been achieved by races he considered

26

socially so inferior to their Mossi neighbors appeared to him inconceivable:

How can these populations, so primitive in many senses—these Nounoumas, Menkiéras, Kassonfras, and the Bobos and Sankouras, as well as the other populations residing around Leo, since they all have this architecture—how can these populations, in which women still dress in leaves and men, not long ago, went naked, without shorts, a single piece of goatskin on their backs, turn out to be so advanced architecturally?

To answer the question, Tauxier traced the architecture in question to the Songhaï, who, he wrote, were believed to have come from Egypt and had dominated the Niger loop for six centuries, until about the tenth century. Arriving in the area only in the twelfth century, and not having benefited from the influence of the northern peoples, the Mossi remain, therefore, architecturally inferior to their Gurunsi neighbors.[36]

Tauxier's hypothesis remains to be verified, for nothing is known of the situation of the Gurunsi with respect to their neighbors through much of the past, and housing can certainly provide one of the most precious opportunities for the historical study of a people. Whatever the issue, Gurunsi architecture is not only elaborate in terms of function and building technology; it also presents, as a reflection of the people and their spirit of independence, a variety of forms and design principles which, when compared to those of Mossi architecture, continue to astonish foreign observers. Writings of European explorers in the past have repeatedly described Gurunsi habitations as "fortresses," "castles," and "citadels." These associations reveal that, in addition to their impressive elaborateness, the habitations are also striking for their highly defensive aspect. Considering the Gurunsi's historical background and social structure, this is hardly suprising. Viewed in the context of a decentralized system that emphasizes the (extended) family unit, the Gurunsi compound stands as a little "kingdom," whose prosperity requires an equal aptitude for defense.

The defensive aspect of Gurunsi architecture is discussed in its many forms throughout the following case studies, not as the only determining factor of the construction, but as a factor in mesh with numerous others. Transitional spaces, passive surveillance (emphasized in case studies 1 [Lela], 2 [Nuna], and 9 [Nankani]), and communal supervision (emphasized in case study 4 [Ko]) are three among others of these related aspects. They may be interpreted as falling within the scope of defense, or they may also be viewed in relation to the inhabitants' social organization. In societies where pyramidal supervision is rejected, the success of community life depends widely on the definition and disposition of space. The architecture is conceived so as to distribute the "power" equally among its members; each individual may, according to his or her situation, alternately play the role of the supervisor and the supervised. When moving into the field of visibility, the person can never be certain when exactly he or she is being observed, but knows that this may occur at any time and assumes responsibility for the constraints of power. The surveillance is, therefore, permanent in its effect, even when absent in its action; "passive," it does not resort to a strong authority or to force for control. In this social-spatial context, emphasis is placed on prevention, not correction. As we shall see, space, one of the factors that has the potential to act upon the conduct of a group member, is often at the same time architectural, functional, hierarchical, social, and spiritual.

Transitions and transitional spaces hold an important place in this study. They should, again, be read in their plurality: at one, very basic level, they are architectural solutions to the problem of connecting elements of space; but they are also precautions, an indirect form of defense, or a means of passive surveillance sustaining communal supervision; alternatively, they can be seen as necessary in-between realms that shape and reflect people's social relations and allow them to drift naturally from one situation to another. Striking examples of this plurality may be found in case studies 7 (Western Kassena), 8 (Eastern Kassena), and 9 (Nankani). Here, transitions expressed through a variety of means—precise definitions of outdoor spaces; changes of light, direction, surface, and level; sequence of doorways; modes of entering; partitioning of areas—contribute to create an intimacy gradient that provides the inhabitants with a choice of spaces with varying degrees of privacy. This gradient, like the codes of a language, is a form of communication; it reflects the subtlety of social interaction among the people. As a means to delay visual and physical access to the more personal areas, transitions also frequently bear a spiritual function: they mark the various stages of life and the passage from one world to another—neutral and sacred; exterior and interior; communal and familial; living and dead.

The deciphering of spatial codes is, like the analysis of form and function, of transition, of defense and surveillance, one attempt among others pursued here to understand the architecture of the people. Its part in this study is limited to the last four case studies, which stress the spiritual significance of the house. These studies will, we feel, suggest the need for further research along these lines. The question of "limit" or boundary remains one of the problems most often encountered during our field survey. In a context where the house is, not theoretically but existentially, a *total* phenomenon, where, indeed, should one define its limit? The case studies presented in the following chapters do not pretend to deal with Gurunsi culture as a whole, nor does the analysis of this group of representative houses attempt to provide an exhaustive picture of the architecture. Much of the information gathered in our visual documentation has not, for example, been exploited in the text for reasons of coherence. These materials may later be woven into the fabric of another text, or serve as the basis for additional research on other aspects of the subject. Here, our presentation, both graphic and verbal, is intended to be selective rather than accumulative. Although closely related, the drawings do not subserviently *illustrate* the text, and the text, having its own logic and unity, does not merely *explain* the drawings. Each constitutes its own line of research and may be apprehended independently.

A similar approach and conception are maintained within the verbal presentation itself. Each case study has its own cohesion and is at the same time self-sufficient and complementary to the others. Generally speaking, the plan followed includes the same basic components: the historical background of the village derived from local sources, the compound's spatial-social organization, the men's and women's units, the building evolution and technology, but the emphasis changes markedly from one case to another, depending on the amount and type of information yielded by each house. Throughout the book, we have used vernacular names rather than attempting to substitute approximations such as living room, bedroom, kitchen, which not only convey the idea of space defined primarily as functional, but also tend to reduce that function to a single activity. The contribution of these vernacular names to our understanding of the people's perception of space emerges most clearly in case studies 7, 8, and 9, where the convergence of other data makes it possible to highlight some of their significance. This, too, is an area that invites further research. Our intention was to avoid a mechanical approach that would have placed this study in the sphere of accumulative knowledge. Again, both drawings and text are selective. In the graphic presentation, however, the selection was made before the drawings were executed. Once the choice for the most representative house, in terms of traditions, was fixed, the drawings were made to carefully record the subject, measuring it down to its smallest details. The same does not, however, apply to the text, since verbal language is, by nature, fictional and the meaning it conveys always tendentious. The selection occurs therefore at the same time as the writing, and the verbal knowledge arrived at is more a truth of reason than a factual truth. The appeal of naïve objectivism is always difficult to resist. We fully acknowledge the subjectivity of our descriptions, and assume, as foreign observers of a culture, the risk implicit in Lévi-Strauss's observation that "the knowledge obtained from the object does not attain its intrinsic properties but is limited to expressing the relative and always shifting position of the subject in relation to that object."[37]

1 LELA

Remote and isolated beyond bogs and swamps during the rainy season, Poa is one of the few Lela villages that still retain their traditional building techniques and offer little evidence of urban influence. Its two quarters, 4 kilometers apart, are Poa and Zyilliwèlè, but Poa is the older of the two and gives its name to the entire village. The compound selected for our study is in Zyilliwèlè, established around 1920 by a man named Bahala Dano, who belonged to the first settlement in Poa. It consists of about ten homesteads or compounds, 150 to 300 meters apart and dispersed over 1 kilometer along a shallow depression.

The compounds, each surrounded by cultivated land, are from 30 to 200 meters from the main path of the village. A transition space is thus created between path and homestead, where visitors may announce their intentions as they approach so the inhabitants may prepare for their coming.

Access to the compound is suggested rather than shown. Off the main path is a track leading to a small shelter (P.4) erected about 15 meters from the blind, undulating wall of the compound. In the example of Ziuma's[1] compound, the shelter is partly enclosed with loosely woven mats that allow anyone inside to see out without being seen. With its light roof of millet stalks (permeable to the rain), it creates a well-ventilated and shaded space where the senior man of the compound takes cover from the sun in the dry season. Receiving his visitors under it, he is aware of both the village life and the main movements of the nearby family members. His presence as an intermediary between the exterior and the interior is indirectly reinforced by the fact that the compound entrance becomes only fully visible when one approaches the shelter.

A heavy wooden door framed by a massive lintel and two

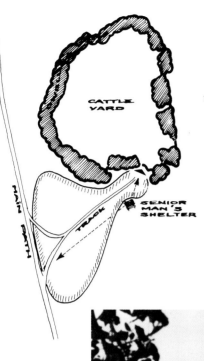

Diagram 1. Access into Ziuma's compound. The distance from the main path and the offset entrance creates a transitional space articulated upon the day shelter of the senior man, whose responsibility as guardian of the compound is to be aware of both the family's comings and goings and the village life.

P.4. On the right, the shelter where the senior man takes cover from the sun. It provides a buffer space in front of the entrance to the homestead, which can be partly seen under the tree on the right.

P.5. Adobe granaries in the *kéléu*. To avoid dampness, the structure is built on logs resting on stones. Millet is stored on the first story and corn on the second, where supporting beams stick out from the 10-centimeter-thick wall. The imprinted V motifs constitute an effective drying device for the water-resistant coating. They are shown here in structurally essential places, such as the top and bottom corners and the doorframes of the granaries.

large pillars on the sides form the gate of Ziuma's compound. Once through the entrance, one's view is absorbed by a maze of large adobe granaries *(bobuin)* (P.5). Their apparently random placement in the large, open interior court (the *kéléu,* encircled by the living units) is equally noticeable in other compounds and can be considered another possible source of visual control. As a visitor crosses the *kéléu,* a multitude of narrow fields of vision, originating from a peripheral ring of small courts *(kono)* (P.5, D.6, D.7), intersects his or her path. There, women carry out most of their activities, weather permitting. The narrowness of the angles of view provided by the layout of the *bobuin* gives the women the advantage of spotting and observing the newcomer without being seen. It is in fact virtually impossible for the visitor moving along the unfamiliar and mingled spaces to tell who is looking, or from where. The density of

Diagram 2. Organization of Ziuma's compound. Independent dwelling units are nested in a circle, each having its own packed-earth court. Erected in the central cattle yard are the granaries and newly built square units that house the senior man and the younger generation of his sons.

Diagram 3. Principle of a passive visual surveillance from the ring of small courts *(kono)* where women work. Visitors penetrating the compound are subjected to a circular field of vision but cannot tell who is looking through the maze of granaries.

D.3. Plan of Ziuma's compound. *Djena:* space for cooking. *Djipu:* locked storage space. *Dina* or *nadji:* storage space. *F:* shrine. *Kéléu:* large internal open court generally reserved for the cattle and men's adobe granaries *(bobuin)*. As space in the *kéléu* runs out, *bobuins* are built on the west, outside of the compound. *Kono:* packed-earth court enclosed by a low wall. *Nachobo:* bathing enclosure. *P:* well. *Tutu:* covered pen for hens and pigs. *Tutuiñi:* space used for household chores and rest. *Voadji:* enclosure for goats. Two secondary accesses in the west lead to the well and to a large tree under which women usually gather to pound the grain before grinding it inside their *tutuiñi*.

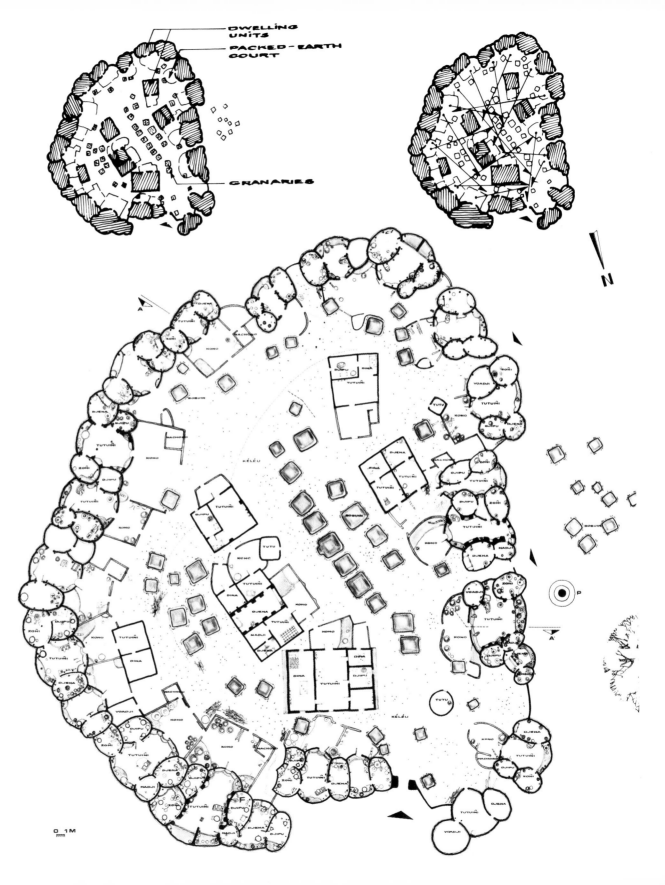

P.6. Partial east view of Ziuma's compound. Besides their possible symbolic value, the white designs also reflect heat and function as an ant repellent, since the paint is made from ashes containing potash. The dark vertical strips of adobe, reinforced with laterite gravel and a locust-bean decoction, are water resistant. They protect the house wall from the water streaming down the terrace roof through the gutter hole.

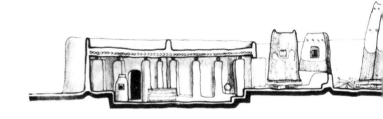

the *bobuin* can vary from compound to compound, especially when no living units are built inside the *kéléu,* but the visitor's subjection to a circular field of vision always remains.

If the *kéléu* can be seen as a link between the exterior of the compound and its interior, the *kono* can be viewed as a link between the outdoors and the indoors. The *kéléu* acts both as a circulation space and as a second in-between realm giving access to the living units, the first being the shelter mentioned earlier. The third, the *kono,* constitutes a locus for social interaction and is the place where daily activities expand from inside the unit. Conversations after dark often take place in the *kono,* and children use it as a playground. This constant activity provides a web of visual and audible communications with the nearby units on both sides. In the hot, dry season, the *kono* becomes an outdoor living area. It provides an open kitchen

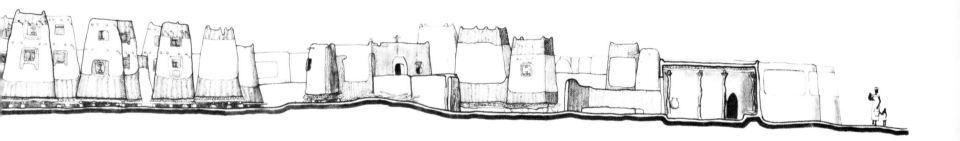

D.4. Section AA' of Ziuma's compound. The mound in the middle of the court is formed by the remnants of the units that were destroyed before the compound's expansion.

0   1M

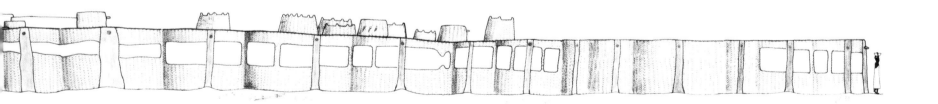

0   1M

D.5. East elevation of Ziuma's compound.

P.7. The enclosed packed-earth courts *(kono)* offer a transition between the *kéléu* and the dwelling units.

and a ventilated place for basket weaving and for sleeping at night. Guinea-corn beer[2] is prepared in the *seḧnokono* (D.7); it requires long simmering, and therefore has to be kept separate from the living space. The bathing enclosure, or *nachobo* (D.3, D.7) must also be placed some distance away, since water might otherwise leach under the floor of the living unit. Both are generally situated at the furthest corners of the *kono*. Since the *kono* floor is often swept, its packed earth acts as a buffer or as an extension of the inside cleanliness, from which dirt or mud brought back from the *kéléu* can be removed.

In the compound plan (D.3), each *kono* has a single entrance door giving access to a cluster of three to seven distinct but connected spaces. Each of these clusters (see D.38 in the Appendix) is inhabited, whether by a monogamous household; a polygamous man, his first wife, and their children (a variant of this custom will be discussed later); a married woman who is not the first wife and her children; two or three sisters married to the same man; or a widow.

The largest interior space, or *tutuiñi,* nearest the *kono* is also used for domestic activities, repose, and sleeping. Some of its furnishings are built in simultaneously with the house structure (P.8, P.14, P.9). The semicircular adobe raised edges along the walls of the *tutuiñi* are carved remnants of the ground level left in place when the first foot of earth was removed to make the tamped roof. Used both as seats and as shelves, these edges also protect the wall and wooden post bases from humidity in case of water seepage. In the rear of the *tutuiñi* are generally located the two entrances to the *zoñi* and the *djena,* each space being used for a distinct type of food preparation. Erected on one side of the *zoñi,* a high clay pot serves as a fish-smoking and

38

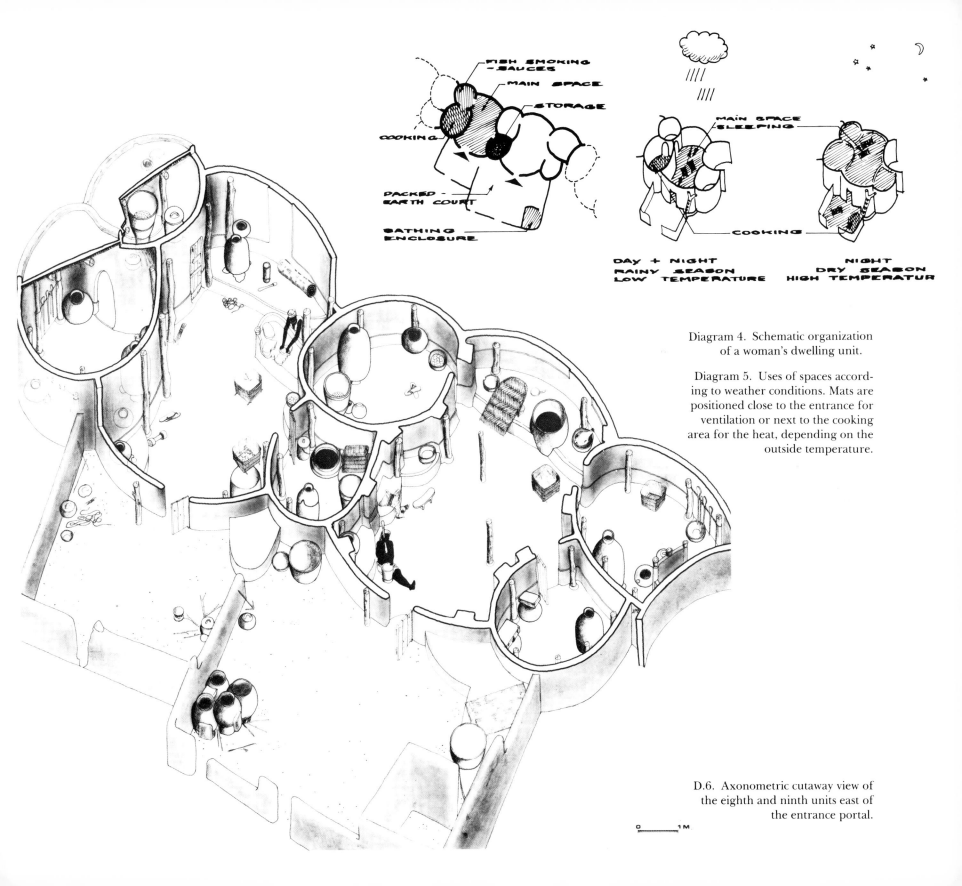

FISH SMOKING
-SAUCES

MAIN SPACE

STORAGE

COOKING

PACKED -
EARTH COURT

BATHING
ENCLOSURE

MAIN SPACE
SLEEPING

COOKING

DAY + NIGHT
RAINY SEASON
LOW TEMPERATURE

NIGHT
DRY SEASON
HIGH TEMPERATUR

Diagram 4. Schematic organization
of a woman's dwelling unit.

Diagram 5. Uses of spaces according to weather conditions. Mats are
positioned close to the entrance for
ventilation or next to the cooking
area for the heat, depending on the
outside temperature.

D.6. Axonometric cutaway view of
the eighth and ninth units east of
the entrance portal.

0   1 M

P.8. The senior wife and her sister's *tutuiñi* (third unit east from the entrance portal) is varnished with a decoction of locust-bean pods. In some older dwelling spaces such as this one, adobe columns support the roof beams instead of the forked tree trunk columns more commonly used nowadays.

shea-nut-heating device (P.11, P.12). The smoke from an adjacent fireplace enters the pot from below. Since the fire has to be kept low, the hearth itself is used solely for cooking the sauces that accompany the millet mush prepared in the *djena*.

Generally wider than the *zoñi*, the *djena* contains another hearth next to a fire wall that insulates the rest of the enclosure from the heat (P.13); it is devoted to food preparation that requires a larger wood fire, such as the cooking of millet. Just like the simultaneous use of heat and smoke in the *zoñi*, all the elements forming the *djena* fireplace are closely interrelated. The cooking pot rests on three points, against the fire wall and on two thick earthen pots that stand on either side of the fire. Each pot has its own precise function: while the millet is cooking over the fire, the water for bathing and the mush left over from the previous meals are warmed separately in the two other pots. The ashes from the fire are stored behind the fire wall for later use in preparing the white paint that decorates the house.

A fourth space, the *djipu*, is often found adjacent to the three preceding ones. Equipped with a door and often with a lock, it contains women's adobe granaries, or *bubuni* (D.7), and clay pots and baskets for storing goods and clothes.

According to Henri Barral,[3] the successive disposition of the dwellings forming a circle reflects a definite order in the organization of the extended Lela family. The rule followed is essentially based on the occupant's family relationship with the senior man, who is in most cases also the "head" of the compound. The unit inhabited by the latter and his first wife always faces the entrance of the homestead; it serves as a starting point for the placement of the other family members. To the right

P.9. Interior of a *tutuiñi* facing its entrance. The height of carved-in shelves and platforms along the wall indicates the previous ground level of the lowered floor. A woman is busy grinding grain on the left.

are built first the units for the family of the brother next to him in age and next those for the family of his eldest son. To the left are the dwellings of his second and third wives and the households of his other younger brothers and sons. This order leads to the conclusion that the right side is reserved for the first of each generation who will replace the senior man in the future. Barral's house plan also shows that the higher the wife's status (according to marriage seniority), the more toward the right her unit is in relation to the co-wives' units.

Neither our research nor the relationships we mapped supported Barral's observations entirely, but both did reveal part of the spatial organization he described (D.38). In Ziuma's compound, the senior wife's unit—the third northeast of the entrance—is undeniably the most important, in terms both of the attention given to it and its maintenance and of the number of

rooms it has. It also contains the family shrine and is closest to the husband's unit in the center of the *kéléu,* but it is next to the compound entrance instead of facing it. If order of seniority is maintained among the senior man's spouses, the first wife still being located on the right of all the co-wives, it seems to be absent in the disposition of his brothers', uncles', and sons' dwellings. In the spatial organization of the compound, it remains to be verified, then, whether emphasis should be laid on the order of the relationships among the men or of those among the women. On the other hand, four of the units located on the west side of Ziuma's compound confirm through their inhabitants that a man *used* to share the same unit with his wife, or his first wife if he was polygamous. The independent units built in the *kéléu* are of recent practice and belong to the "head" of the compound and to his sons and nephew, whose genera-

41

P.10. Pots with their bottoms broken off are stuck into the adobe roof as a smoke exhaust and as a skylight. They are recovered with the severed bottom when it rains. The roof provides a clean area for drying grain and greens.

tion unavoidably comes under the influence of urban imagery. Without exception, these independent units adopt the form of a square or a rectangle and are now more and more often built with concrete blocks and a zinc roof (as in this example of Ziuma's unit).

The appearance of the independent units in the *kéléu* and of the rectangular form is significant. It may be due to urban influences, since the younger generation travels rather more than its parents did; to the advent of compulsory schooling that is largely dependent on European methods and models; or to the examples provided by missionary houses or found in the nearby Muslim Marka architecture. It may also be due to a colonial administration that tended to confuse the senior male's protective role with authority, hence the necessity for a "head" of the family *(chef de famille),* an appellation that reflects the

administration's need to hold *one* person responsible for the entire compound's activities and to *locate* that person without having to hunt for him in his wives' units. Finally, the adoption of the Western iron bed, which does not fit well in a circular construction, probably also encouraged the choice of a rectangular layout. However, to replace the sleeping mat, which can easily be rolled up after use, with the comparatively unmovable bed is to go from a multifunctional to a unifunctional space.

The sequence in which the dwellings were built and their dates of construction are indicated on plan D.38. From them it can be inferred that, as the family expands with a son's marriage, new units are added, if the circle forming the compound is not yet complete. When it is complete, several older units are destroyed and new ones built at their periphery, thus enlarging

D.7. Axonometric cutaway view of the third unit west of the entrance portal. *DJENA* (or *kulëdji*): space intended for prolonged cooking. *Dódo:* pot containing warm water for bathing. *Gulénokono:* Aluminum cooking pot. *Kuabué:* pot for carrying water or guinea-corn beer when leaving the compound. *Kulë:* indicates the whole preparation area, including the fire wall on which the cooking pot rests. *Kulëkuin:* place where ashes are kept. *Kulëyo:* adobe excrescence of the fire wall, adapted to hold an oil lamp or a calabash. *Kulupu:* thick clay pot covered with a heavy lid for warming up or storing food away from insects or animals. *DJIPU* (or *djikoa*): storage space. *Zorchiura:* basket containing calabashes. *IENEDJI:* "end of the unit." *Zo:* jar used for drying shea nuts. *Zobi:* perforated plate. *KÉLÉU:* large open court. *KONO:* packed-earth court; extension of the inside space. *Bobuin:* granary. *Nachobo:* bathing enclosure. *Konobili:* wall surrounding the *kono*. *Konoñi:* entrance to the *kono*, closed with a woven straw mat. *Pino:* sitting or sleeping adobe platform. *Señnokono:* jar in which the guinea-corn beer is prepared. *NADJI* (or *dina*): space where jars are kept and where extra visitors can sleep during feast days. *Bubupu:* granary similar to the *bubuni* (see below). *TUTUIÑI:* space for daily tasks and rest.

Bubuni: adobe granary for millet, peas, beans, and peanuts. *Chiuru:* basket for temporary storage or transport of goods. *Djinibulu:* stair. *Goguin:* niche. *Lunukono:* aluminum cooking pot. *Nankua:* varnished reddish-brown water jar. *Nankuaja:* area where the *nankua* is placed. *Numugorayé:* area where one is not supposed to walk, marked with an indentation on the ground, where the flour falling from the grinding stone is collected. *Numujo:* grinding stone mounted on an adobe base. *Pino:* adobe seat. *Tchizo:* a hen's nest. *Tropio:* adobe column. *Za:* jar in which the guinea-corn beer is kept. *Zar:* broom. *Zi:* basket open on top and bottom, used to catch fish or to keep chickens. *Zoanazena:* calabash.

VOADJI (or *bundjele*): place to guard the goats at night. *Nedji* (or *guinguin*): storage corner. *ZOÑI* (or *zodji*): space for smoking fish, cooking sauces. *Chèrabobuin:* storage containing shea nuts. *Nokuampu:* pot for storing sorrel, grains, peas, and peanuts. *Koloyé:* adobe sphere unit with a handle used to support and chock the cooking pot. *Kuabi:* pot where tobacco is stored.

Señnokono: cracked *za* used to store okra, dry sorrel leaves, and beans. *Topobobuin:* storage for ashes used to filter the water which, mixed with shea-nut residue, is used for making soap. *Zo:* jar generally made out of a cracked *za*. A hollow cylinder supporting it collects the heat and smoke from the adjacent fireplace. *Zobili:* small parapet anchoring the *zo*, behind which ashes are kept.

0 ___ 1 M

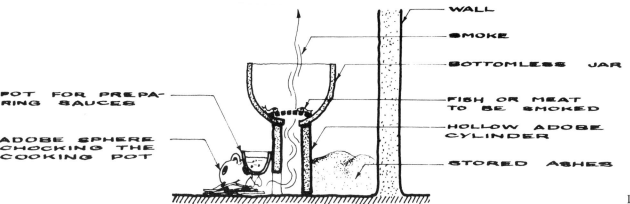

WALL

SMOKE

BOTTOMLESS JAR

POT FOR PREPA-
RING SAUCES

FISH OR MEAT
TO BE SMOKED

HOLLOW ADOBE
CYLINDER

ADOBE SPHERE
CHOCKING THE
COOKING POT

STORED ASHES

Diagram 6. Section of fish-smoking
and nut-drying device in the *zôni*.

P.11. A *zôñi* interior. The tall jar
serves for smoking fish and heating
shea nuts. Ashes stored in the back
are used for making paint.

the circle (the dotted line indicates the interior limit of the first circle). A first change in this practice has been illustrated by the construction of the living units in the *kéléu* and the relocation of the granaries both inside and outside the compound. The ultimate stage of this evolution will consist in erecting a dwelling unit just outside the homestead. The consequences implied when such a change occurs are the disintegration of the compound as a spatial organization of communal life and the appearance of the isolated nuclear family habitat.

Both men and women take part in building a house. Women carry water from the well and participate in the transport of the earth dug in the vicinity of the compound. Men knead the water-softened earth with their feet and prepare clayey balls, which are then piled up and molded together to shape the walls. Since an independent interior post-and-beam structure

P.12. Inside detail of a jar used for smoking fish.

P.13. A *djena* interior showing the
hearth organization adjacent to the
fire wall.

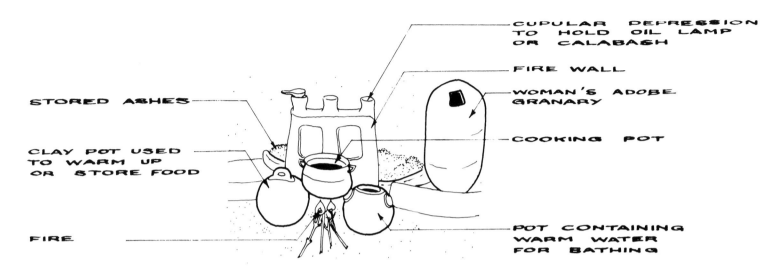

CUPULAR DEPRESSION TO HOLD OIL LAMP OR CALABASH

FIRE WALL

STORED ASHES

WOMAN'S ADOBE GRANARY

CLAY POT USED TO WARM UP OR STORE FOOD

COOKING POT

FIRE

POT CONTAINING WARM WATER FOR BATHING

Diagram 7. Cooking place in the *djena*.

props up the roof, the walls are not load-bearing and can consequently be relatively thin. Their thinness (10 to 15 centimeters) is, however, counterbalanced by their circular design. The intersecting *djipu, djena,* and *zoñi* cylindrical spaces of the women's units are first built back to back. The *tutuiñi* is then formed by erecting curved walls in between those first constructed. Any exterior force applied to one of these spaces is transmitted along its entire perimeter, since it is a continuous surface, and then counteracted by a ring of resisting forces. One can fully appreciate the appropriateness of this form when several cylinders intersect each other: any exterior force applied is naturally distributed to the whole honeycomb structure and therefore diluted. No similar resistance and economy of materials can be obtained with the newly adopted rectangular form, since a flat wall of the same thickness is not backed by a

chain of resisting elements. The older method not only is economical of materials, since less adobe has to be transported, prepared, and set up, but also permits a stable roof structure that is independent of the walls, which can then easily be pierced by arched openings without the use of lintels (D.6, D.7).

To ensure the general waterproofing of the house, several other responsibilities are also carried out by women. A final coating of small laterite gravel is first tamped on the adobe floor and roof and generously sprinkled with a decoction of locust-bean pods *(Parkia biglobosa)* that dries into a glossy, waterproof, varnish-like finish (P.8). The outsides of the walls are then covered with a thin layer of adobe mixed with cow dung, on which nested-V motifs are imprinted by repeatedly pressing two segments of corn cobs to form regular vertical patterns (P.5, P.6). These impressions are also found in Nuna architecture and,

47

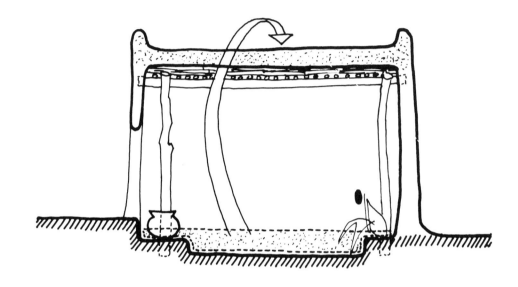

Diagram 8. Section of a dwelling space. The foot of earth removed from the lowered floor is used to tamp the roof. Carved remnants left in place serve as shelves and seats. The average inside temperature at noon on a hot day is about 4° to 6° C. below the outside temperature. The further sunken the dwelling, the lesser heat gain and heat loss.

with varied techniques and patterns, among the Kassena and the Nankani of southern Upper Volta. Besides being decorative, they function as a device to break up the flow of rain into smaller streamlets, thus preventing a localized erosion of the walls. They also provide better ventilation for the coating, which then dries more effectively and resists longer the deterioration caused by humidity.

The intertwinement of structure, form, and function reflects the intimately interrelated life of the inhabitants among themselves and with their environment. The unity between dwelling and dweller is even more graphically displayed in drawing D.4, which shows two interlocked units belonging to two sisters. Each unit comprises the same number of spaces: a *tutuiñi,* a zoñi, a *djena,* and a *djipu.* Only one sister, however, is equipped with a *seħnokono* for the preparation of guinea-corn beer, while

the other has a *numujo* for grinding grain. Access between the two units is facilitated by the presence of a small adobe platform that interrupts part of the wall dividing their *nuwo.* Thus, the architecture reveals at the same time the inhabitants' close dependence and self-sufficiency.

P.14. Engaged columns, raised adobe
edges, and carved-in seats along the
inner wall of a *tutuiñi*.

2 NUNA

A Semi-dispersed Settlement

Are the Nuna the descendants of the Lela, whose land extends beyond their northern border? If such is the opinion of the administrative chief of the village of Pouni, several elders nonetheless trace the origin of the Nuna people to the inhabitants of "Navarongo, near Tamale in Ghana," who, one may assume, are the Kasem-speaking peoples of the actual Navrongo district of northern Ghana. As for us, bonds between the Lela and the Nuna can be perceived both through their language—it is not difficult for a Nuna to follow a conversation in Lyele, although the reverse does not hold true for a Lela—and through some elements of their architecture, as revealed further in the case study from Valiou (Chapter 3).

According to local accounts, the village was founded by a Lela man who came from a northern village also called Pouni, close to Didyr. This man first settled down in Vili. One day, he got into a serious argument about the ownership of a well with one of his neighbors. Unable to prove that the well belonged to him, he lost his case and was given, as compensation, the land where he subsequently founded the present village of Pouni.

Situated along the eastern limit of the Nuna land, Pouni suffered repeated aggressions from the neighboring Mossi. This constant threat was certainly an important motivation in the grouping of the houses. The village organization seems to be a blend of two main patterns of planning typical of this area of Upper Volta: the nucleated type of Nuna village found in the northwest of the Nuna land, with narrow passageways between the dwellings; and the dispersed type of compound settlement located in the center and the south, extending to the Ghana border. Each of the compounds—about 50 to 100 meters apart—houses an extended family and constitutes in

P.15. The market.

P.16. Upper-story room of the senior man. The circular hole in the wall (another can be found on the opposite wall) provides a means for visual control of the surroundings. The shea-nut grindstones are located underneath the tallest tree, in the large open space (visible in the background) around which the compounds are built. On the right, in the foreground, stands the men's and elders' daytime shelter.

itself one of the seven quarters of the village. The entire built area of the village forms a general circle whose diameter does not exceed 500 meters. Directly south of it are scattered a two-classroom school, a maternity, a dispensary, and an administrative building; on its west side, about 100 meters away from the nearest compound and close to a few mango trees, is the site where the market meets at seven-day intervals (P.15).

The immediate periphery of each homestead is cultivated; only in the dry season, when the crops have been harvested, does a large central open space around which the houses are loosely built become fully exposed (P.16). Here most of the village activities take place, and the space serves as an arena for social interaction. On one side, underneath the deep shade of large trees, the men and elders gather around an open shelter roofed with millet stalks, while the women, when it is time to

P.17. Mask dance in Pouni.

P.18. Mask dance in Pouni.

make shea butter, meet and work around eight grindstones grouped some 30 meters away. Each grindstone is mounted on a high clay pot and is used mostly for grinding shea nuts; their circular disposition mirrors the close interchange among women of different quarters. The rest of this central space accommodates larger festive activities, such as the triennial parade of the masks (P.17, P.18), which, besides providing the disguised men with means of asserting their authority over their women,[1] also maintains feelings of ethnic adherence and solidarity.

Originally, Badu's Compound stood alone (D.8). His brothers' homesteads were later added to his own on the south and west sides. The structure of the house shows two planning principles that reveal the evolution of the architecture. In the north, the more recent units are built around a relatively large

Diagram 9. Layout principle of Badu's compound. Juxtaposed L-shaped women's dwelling units define a narrow passageway in the southern part and a large court in the northern part.

D.8. Plan of Badu's compound built in 1939. His brothers' compounds, not drawn in this plan, are erected on the west, south, and southeast sides, beyond the heaviest dotted lines. *A:* outside cooking area to prepare the guinea-corn beer. *B:* exterior covered cooking area. *Bandiè:* bathing enclosure. *Bobuin:* storage space for small adobe granaries and other personal belongings; it also contains a cooking area in some houses. *Buré:* earth-filled well. *C:* storage for various heavy tools, wood, and bicycles. *D:* pigpen. *Dibi:* a man's dwelling space. Badu's *dibi* rests above the central part of his three-space storage area (F). *Diè:* a woman's dwelling space. *E:* covered hen house. *F:* Badu's reserve and storage area. (We have not been granted access to this place. Only Badu knows its contents and has the key to its door.) *Flu:* rest room. *G:* granaries in adobe or matting supported by a wooden structure. *Kowa:* open court for storage and for occasional sleeping during warm nights. *Nemudiè:* area where grindstones are built in. *Nuwo:* courtyard. *Pon:* open space covered with matting where Badu rests, receives visitors, or chats with neighbors.

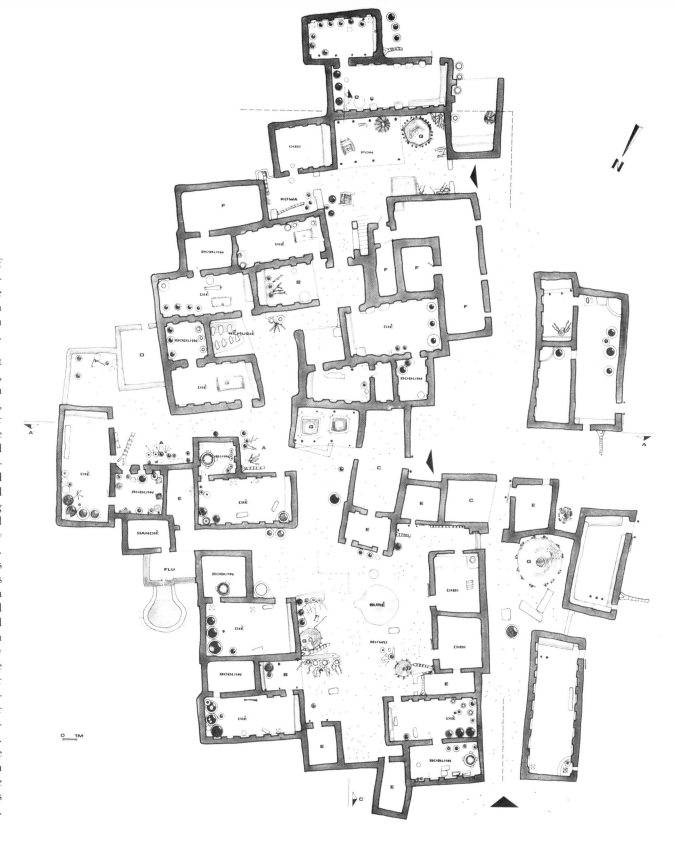

D.9. AA′ and CC′ section of Badu's
compound.

court, while in the southeast, the older units are assembled
along a narrow, meandering passageway.

This passageway is actually larger when one is in it than the
plan can show, since it expands visually on both sides into covered open spaces. Well ventilated, these spaces serve many purposes and provide an adequate means for climate control. They
facilitate the performance of daily tasks, which may then be
carried out at any time, under a heavy rain or a scorching sun.
Ventilation can, indeed, be particularly important for activities
that induce perspiration, such as the grinding of the grains in
the *nemudiè* (where several grindstones are grouped), or the
diverse preparations that make use of the outside cooking
fireplace (B).

The covered open spaces serve otherwise as a place to rest
and sleep at night *(kowa)* or to welcome visitors and carry on

discussions *(pon)*. Of great interest is the location of the senior
man's wicker chair in the *pon;* as with the shelter outside the
Lela compound, the position of the seat allows the sitter to
remain in visual contact, through the entrance and through a
section of the passageway, with the comings and goings of both
family members and visiting outsiders. The covered spaces are
set out perpendicularly, so that two open sides never face each
other, providing thereby a relative visual independence. Their
very juxtaposition shapes the passageway that alternately turns
right and left at right angles.

Such a design, frequently found in Muslim architecture,
grants the inhabitants a relative privacy and moreover reduces
the transfer of heat into the wall during the day; the greater the
number of offset spaces, the larger the amount of shadow pro-
jected on the adjacent walls. The roof covering each semi-open

P.19. Passageway turning alternately right and left at right angles between the *diè*. The upper-story room is the senior man's *dibi*. Leaning against the wall on the left is a woven millet-stalk frame on which the mat behind it can be laid for sleeping.

0 1M

space plays, furthermore, the role of a horizontal *brise-soleil* that constantly shades the adjacent enclosed spaces. Of equal importance is the compact juxtaposition of the living units, which limits the sun-heated area to the roof and part of the exterior walls, thereby keeping the inside temperature during the hot season an average of 5° to 8° C lower than outside. The thick adobe walls that are exposed to the sun, on the other hand, soak up the day's heat and delay the peak heat flow into the interior until far into the cool nights, so as to keep the inhabitants warm until the next morning. On warmer nights, this advantage becomes a drawback that is then offset by leaving the access door of the sleeping room open. These principles for climate control, also present in the Ko and Sissala architecture, allow more continual use of interior spaces during the hot season. The occupants among the groups mentioned, for example, hardly ever use the roof area for sleeping at night, a practice that remains current in the less compact habitats of the Nankani and the Kassena.[2]

The construction in the northern part of the compound follows a different planning principle. Here, the dwellings are loosely assembled around a wide, open court (nuwo), and the means for climatic adaptation to the sun's heat found in the older section of the house are lost. The principle focuses, however, on the role of the court as an arena for distribution and reception. The long, meandering passageway gives the observer a sense of gradual discovery; in it, one experiences space as a dialectic of secret and offered realms, or as a succession of fragments of drawers, whose contents are not fully shown (such spaces can be woven into variable patterns by the human eye) and have the potential to surprise. The court, on the other hand, exposes its contents to full view. Its openness is an invitation, an incitement to participation; it favors communal activities and acts as a center of attraction.

The shift of emphasis from the passageway to the court denotes two different concerns: the first lays emphasis on defense—it constitutes a means of passive control—while the second stresses social interaction. Such an observation may also be reinforced by the fact that Badu, the "owner" and senior male of the compound, is a veteran of the French Army. The question arises, then, of the antiquity of the southern section of the house and its relation to the Nuna's traditional way of building. Although this section was erected in 1939, about twenty years before the northern section, one still wonders, however distant the comparison, whether the passageway principle reflects the influence of the defensive military zigzag trenches.

56

P.20. Inside a *diè*. A small adobe granary and a number of clay pots, in which guinea-corn kernels germinate and water, goods, or beer are stored, are aligned on one side of the wall; a cooking place is often installed in the back of the room.

The use of the *nuwo* in Badu's compound, on the other hand, speaks for the shift of concern. Several uncovered cooking areas (A) have been set up in this open space; they are not clearly defined by walls (as in B), but simply suggested through a zone of packed earth. With their series of large clay pots, they serve mainly for the preparation of guinea-corn beer, the sale of which constitutes one of the women's sources of modest cash income (others are the sale of dead wood and millet mush). In Badu's compound, several women are brewers and live in the northern section. They prepare, sell, and serve their product in the open spaces right in front of or next to their living units *(diè)*. The *nuwo* is the place where groups of people meet, sit, and drink together. The three women whose dwelling units partly define the *nuwo* (D.8, D.39) each receive their own customers in this court. The purchasers regularly buy from the same woman; they are her kin or neighbors, but the gatherings we attended were exclusively composed of male members.

The overall compound is formed by the nesting of the women's L-shaped units, the men's individual square units *(dibi)* being scant and unoccupied. Each L shape is created in its turn by the juxtaposition of two connected spaces, the *diè* and the *bobuin,* the volume of the latter being half the size of the former.

A unique entrance, located at one end on the longer side of the *diè,* connects the outside to the inside. Light brought in by this opening defines a first small area where "semi-public" activities take place. Here, on a raised adobe edge along the shortest wall immediately adjacent to the door (P.22; P.29), people sit and talk, rest while waiting for the rain to stop, welcome and offer water to visitors. Taking advantage of this source of light,

P.21. Interior decorations can often be found, as in this case in the *diè* where visitors are welcomed and invited to sit.

women would often spread a mat close by to take care of their babies and do some basket weaving or cotton spinning. The farther one moves away from the light, the deeper one penetrates into the intimate realms of the dwelling. The dimmer part of the *diè* gives more privacy and is the section where people sleep, positioning their mats closer to the entrance or to the fireplace at the other end of the room, depending on the outside temperature. Goods are·stored along the walls, as well as large clay pots in which millet and guinea-corn kernels germinate (P.20, P.26). Cooking takes place close to the *bobuin*, in the furthest corner of the *diè* opposite the entrance-sitting area, or in the *bobuin* itself, so as to make use of the smoke that acts as an insect repellent and protects the nearby granary.

Having the door on the long side of the *diè* provides the inhabitants relative privacy. The door can be kept open all day

P.22. Entrance into the *diè* with an adjacent raised adobe edge serving as bench or shelf.

P.23. Nuna woman.

long and the interior still remains visually out of reach of the exterior, the only portion within the passerby's sight being the entrance area. The same principle applies to the entry of the *bobuin*. Located at the opposite end of the *dié* from the entrance door, its position indicates that access is reserved, since it requires an indiscreet outsider to cross the whole length of the room in order to reach it and peep in. The contents of the *bobuin*, such as the women's adobe granary, jars, suitcases, clothes, and other personal belongings, remain thereby safe from unwanted looks when its door, equipped with a bolt, stays open.

It is common practice for the heads of the compounds in the village to erect their unit a story higher than the rest of their house. Badu's *dibi* stands, for example, on the roofs of his three-space storage area. Such a principle was probably neces-

sary in the past for supervising a territory frequently threatened by the Mossi's aggressions, since sight control from the ground level is impeded by the neighboring compounds. The clear position of each senior male's room also created a web of visual connections, strengthening communications among the members of the village community. It denoted a sense of defense and stood out as evidence of their solidarity. (P.24).

Nowadays, this second-floor unit remains an indicator of the senior man's presence and location (P.16). Generally built close to the visitors' entrance, it allows him to keep track of all approaching comers and gives him the privilege of welcoming them. The explicit location of the senior man still provides the family, although in a more indirect manner, a certain degree of security. The members know that all strangers coming from

P.24. Brick patterns on a senior man's dwelling unit. Visual contact with the neighboring senior man is facilitated by the location of his sleeping room on the second floor.

outside will first be met by the elder man; they rely on him for public affairs. Furthermore, this upper-story room can be seen as a means for passive surveillance. Whether the elder man is in his room, on the surrounding terrace roof, or away, he is potentially always present for the outsider. This helps to discourage possible unwanted intrusions.

Besides its location, two features characterize the senior man's upper-story room. The first is a low parapet that crowns its roof as well as the edges of the terrace roof surrounding it. The tapered adobe merlons of the parapet were probably adopted from the Muslim Marka and the Zabarima, who, when raiding the region toward the end of the nineteenth century, built numerous mosques and fortified houses with a similar design. If, in the latter case, the merlons performed a defensive function, one may assume that they also served as a protective device for the essential parts of the structure. Corners, for example, deteriorate more rapidly than any other upper part of the walls. With the above design, the rain would degrade the adobe merlons first, before getting to the structural parts of the wall. The tapering end helps to speed up the flow of the water, preventing it from infiltrating these areas. For similar reasons, merlons are generally built over places where the wooden beam is anchored into the bearing wall. This keeps the beam from rotting through humidity.

The second feature is the vertical indentations that ornament the parapets and walls of both the upper story and the ground-level storage rooms. These indentations are achieved through varying brick patterns. Here, in Badu's unit, they are brought about by changing the course of one of the two rows of bricks that form the walls. Instead of following the overall juxtaposed

61

P.25. Façade of an L-shaped woman's unit and its small adjacent court where daily activities expand from the inside. Embedded jars along the wall contain guinea-corn beer. The woven mat functions as a sliding door.

stretcher course, the exterior row temporarily adopts the vertical alignment of the soldier course with intervals of 10 centimeters between each brick. Numerous other patterns can be seen in the village, such as bricks laid horizontally on their shorter side (rolok course) or in chevron. In some cases, they form a clerestory parapet that might once have functioned as a device for passive surveillance and/or active defense (P.24).

The walls of the compound are made entirely out of sun-dried adobe bricks. Although one might think the use of bricks is a recent practice, we found no clues to support this hypothesis. One may recall here that "evidence of construction in sun-dried mud bricks, formed by hand like loaves of bread," found in Jericho, dated back to the eighth millennium B.C.[3] The Egyptians erected their first pyramids in adobe bricks; if we give credit to Cheikh Anta Diop's thesis tracing the origin of African blacks to the Egyptians,[4] we may assume that brick construction has been used for centuries among various African ethnic groups.

The bricks here are composed of adobe mixed with fine laterite gravel to reinforce it. Each is compacted in a wooden mold that is then removed while it is left in place to dry. Walls are erected on the ground without foundations; once they are built, women coat them with a mixture of earth taken from the paddy field, water, and a decoction of locust-bean pods. The coatings must be renewed once every two years or less, depending on the yearly amount of rain. Where the water table is low, as in Pouni, water is kept for drinking and none can be used for maintaining the house. This may account for the overall run-down aspect of the compounds in the village, since the deteriorated walls remain unpatched and expose the underlying bricks

P.26. Sunlight entering from the roof openings of the *diè*.

to view. Another important factor at work is the growing tendency of the village to resort to a mason's services for the building of a house.[5] The search for an income has driven the educated young men to the urban areas and left those who remain with insufficient labor assistance. To compensate for such a loss, these young men generally bear the cost of construction, and their wages in turn serve for the hiring of another laborer. The monetary system has substituted material participation for human participation. "We used to build our own house," says Badu, "but nowadays people call more and more upon the mason's services." The house is no longer an outgrowth of the people's seasonal activities, but rather a consumed product, whose defects can be imputed to and must be repaired by the "specialist."

3 NUNA

A Dispersed Settlement

Situated about 4 kilometers west of Pouni, Valiou was founded many years ago by a Mossi educated in Ouagadougou, whose utmost desire was to return to his native land, in the vicinity of Sabou, where his parents lived. Taking his cattle out to graze, he discovered the present village site, which owed its fertility to the proximity of a shallow depression, 5 kilometers long, filled with water during the rainy season. He decided to erect his dwelling at the limit of the humidified arable area, and named the site Valiou, or "top of the low ground" in Nuni. Several other Nuna families then settled next to him along the depression and formed the present village spreading over 3.5 kilometers.

In contrast with the tightly nucleated pattern of Pouni, Valiou represents one of the most scattered groupings of dwellings that may be found in the Nuna land and Upper Volta. The village plan is thus very difficult to perceive from the ground; only an aerial view shows its setting of six quarters along the southern side of the depression. Each quarter, about 200 to 500 meters apart, is composed of five to fifteen compounds situated 50 to 150 meters away from each other (P. 27). Easy access to the tillable zone determines the choice of location of these houses and accounts for the linear development of the village. A cart track runs through the elongated layout of these six quarters, linking the community to the eastern and western villages nearby and functioning as a backbone from which flows a network of pedestrian paths connecting the compounds. Vestiges of the former French colonial administration can still be seen in a section of this track where large, mature trees are aligned on both sides. Their deep shade creates, as intended, a determinable locus for social activities. They presently shelter a

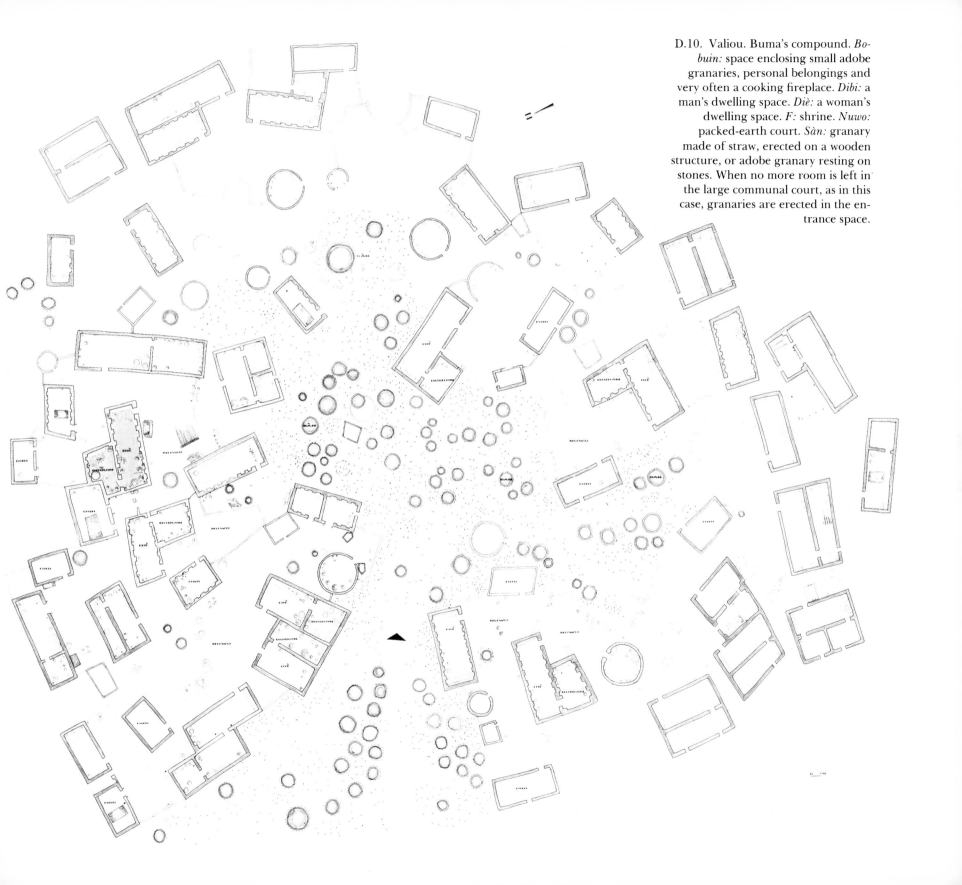

D.10. Valiou. Buma's compound. *Bo-buin:* space enclosing small adobe granaries, personal belongings and very often a cooking fireplace. *Dibi:* a man's dwelling space. *Diè:* a woman's dwelling space. *F:* shrine. *Nuwo:* packed-earth court. *Sàn:* granary made of straw, erected on a wooden structure, or adobe granary resting on stones. When no more room is left in the large communal court, as in this case, granaries are erected in the entrance space.

one-classroom school for rural training and a marketplace, physically defined by light wooden structures roofed with millet stalks, where people gather once a week to exchange or sell goods.

Buma's compound seems at first sight to reflect in smaller scale the random dispersion of the village settlement. No order stands out as obvious from its maze of fifty-four dwellings, and a newcomer strolling inside without preliminary guidance cannot help but be at a loss. The open internal court, which is, in most cases, clearly demarcated by a peripheral ring of dwellings and serves as a reference space, has no well-defined shape here. The labyrinth of granaries fragmentizes and delays our perception of its totality, while the protruding, irregular arrangement of the living units unmakes and alters its outline. Composite as it is, however, the court keeps its distributive role; it still pro-

vides an intermediate ground related to the exterior by a triangular entrance space (west on D.9) that points the way back to the circular inner realm of the compound. Thriving mainly on agriculture nowadays, the inhabitants of Valiou do not emphasize cattle raising. This is reflected in the significant number of granaries *(sàn)* that fill the large internal court of their homesteads and leave no room for animals (as compared to Ziuma's house in Poa, for example). Granaries grow with the size of the family; when they can no longer be added inside the court, they are built, as in this case, on the entranceway, whose function as an extension of the interior becomes even more evident.

As our understanding of the spaces and their interrelationship grows, so does our awareness of an overall principle of organization. With closer observation, the setting conveys, in place of the first feeling of disorientation, a sense of precise

P.27. Nestled in the L-shaped woman's unit is a small packed-earth space adjacent to the door, where items that support activities closely associated with the inside realm are located: a grindstone, a bench, and a notched forked trunk giving access to the terrace. The remaining part of the court *(nuwo)* is surrounded by a low wall. Adobe granaries are protected from the rain with a woven thatch mat. The pointed roofs of those erected in the compound entrance can be seen protruding over the unit. In the background is a compound of the nearby quarter.

order within a natural growth. The compound spreads according to a cluster plan of development. Its overall circular layout evolves from the large internal court, whose neutral presence serves to decentralize spatial organization. The same holds true for the layout of the clusters, which contains in itself all the elements that constitute the general compound plan.

Each cluster is defined by a smaller court *(nuwo)*. Often enclosed by a low wall, this court in turn leads to a limited number of living units that belong to a single or several households. In the latter case, the householders who share the same *nuwo* are either brothers (D40, taking the compound entrance as a point of reference, first cluster to the left), co-wives (second cluster to the right), co-wife and stepsons (one of the four women married to a brother of Buma and this brother's first wife's sons, third cluster to the right), or father and sons (fourth cluster to

the right, behind the third just mentioned). Except for one household and an old woman who recently came to live in the northeast, the 138 dwellers of the entire compound are four generations of descendants of the same male ancestor. The picture of a village within a wider village, the complex setting of the homestead justly reflects the genealogical breadth of the family. The gatherings of such a community require a compound planning scheme that fosters both spatial bonds and spatial independence. Here, dwelling units are loosely assembled, as compared to the tightly knit pattern of Badu's house in Pouni; they are, however, linked together by connecting walls that fill the gaps between them, thus closing both the external boundary of the compound and the periphery of the clusters. All openings are, moreover, oriented toward the interior, looking out on a definite *nuwo*. Their disposition indi-

P.28. The opening situated on one end of the longer sides of the *diè* brings in indirect lighting, allowing a transition from bright to dark toward the deeper inside realm of the room. Here, the intimacy of the *diè* is proportional to the amount of light: "semi-public" activities take place near the door-bench area, while storing goods, preparing food, and sleeping occur in the dimmer part of the *diè*.

cates the cluster to which the dwelling belongs. (A slight change occurs in the southwest section of the compound, where units recently built on the periphery have windows that open onto the exterior.) Access to the *nuwo,* just like access to the large court, is then limited to a single entrance.

Visual participation and control over the household's comings and goings within each cluster is further facilitated by the positioning of the men's units *(dibi)* in relation to their wives' and children's units. Of particular notice are the household heads' *dibi,* located on the right half of the compound entrance (D.40). They belong to four brothers, three of whom are polygamous, and all have their openings oriented so as to maintain visual contact with their wives. Thus, the senior man's[1] protective role, as observed in the case studies of Poa and Pouni, equally devolves upon the other elder males of the compound,

each of them being immediately responsible for the activities of their cluster. Another possible clue to this decentralized organization is the fact that Buma's *dibi,* although situated in a cluster that directly faces the compound entrance, does not visually control either the clusters around him or the communal inside court, where the erection of granaries manifestly impedes his field of vision.

Men's *dibi* can be identified by the single space they contain and by their bare walls. Women's units are, on the other hand, often decorated and composed of two spaces, the *diè* and *bobuin.* Their juxtaposition forms, as in Pouni, an L shape. Change detected in Buma's compound shows, however, the evolution of this L shape into a long rectangle or a large square in which the *diè* and *bobuin* are built successively next to each other on the long or short side. The principle of having the

69

door on one end of the longer side, as seen in Pouni, is consistently used throughout Buma's compound, with exceptions found only in some of these evolved rectangular or square units. Another detail that disappears with the newer dwellings is the protruding columns along the inside walls, peculiar to both Nuna and Lela interiors.

Surface decorations of women's dwellings among the Nuna recall in many instances those found among the Lela. The white painted patterns, the nested V impressions on the exterior walls (P.6, P.7, P.27, D.4, D.11), and the adobe reinforced door openings are noticeable examples. Upon entering a woman's dwelling unit, besides the engaged columns along the walls (P.8, P.14, P.34, D.7, D.11) one also notes other parallel features such as the location of the red varnished water pot in a corner of the room that faces or is next to the door (P.8, P.29, D.11) and the presence of a fire wall in the cooking area (D.7, D.11, P.13). This fire wall often bears depressed figures on the side that faces the cooking fire. Among the Lela, they form two rectangles or squares similar to the white motifs on the exterior walls of the compound; among the Nuna, they are either two rounded squares or a round and a squarish shape that widens out toward the top. One also notices these rounded and splayed square figures on the side of grindstones, on small raised adobe edges that define the hearth, and on flat interior walls (which all constitute women's intimate realms, P.29, P.33).

The above coupled figures can clearly be seen in the axonometric cutaway of a woman's unit in Buma's compound (D.11). As possible symbols, they recall the woven basket with a square base and circular opening (set on top of a clay pot in D.11) that is widely used in Africa to carry, among other things,

D.11. A woman's unit (slightly dark-
ened on the plan in D.10). The red
varnished pot, (P.29) which contains
drinking water, faces the door. Adobe
raised edges along the walls are
carved remnants of the ground level
left in place when a foot of earth was
removed to make the tamped roof.
Carved wooden sticks are stuck into
the upper part of each niche defined
by two columns. Hanging from these
sticks are, from right to left: a wood
head-carrier for women; an hourglass
drum; a braided string-bag for storing calabashes; an oil lamp; two water
gourds; and two calabashes—over the
door—containing grain and food.
The large pots stored on the raised
edge of the side contain the
humidified guinea-corn grains which,
once germinated, will serve for the
preparation of the local fermented
drink. At the bottom of this first space
(diè) is a door—equipped with a
lock—that opens onto the *bobuin*,
where the cooking area is situated and
the woman's small adobe granaries
and storage pots are kept. The organization around the fire wall is similar here to the one encountered in the
Lela architecture. The outside nested-
V patterns also serve to break the flow
of rain on the walls as previously described for the Lela compound. Part
of the roof is represented here in the
lower middle part of the drawing. A
man's granary, filled from the top, is
built outside the house. Its structure is
made of woven thatch matting coated
with adobe. During the rainy season,
it is entirely covered by another
thatch mat. The seat, carved from a
single piece of wood and reserved for
men, allows him to sit in a reclining
position.

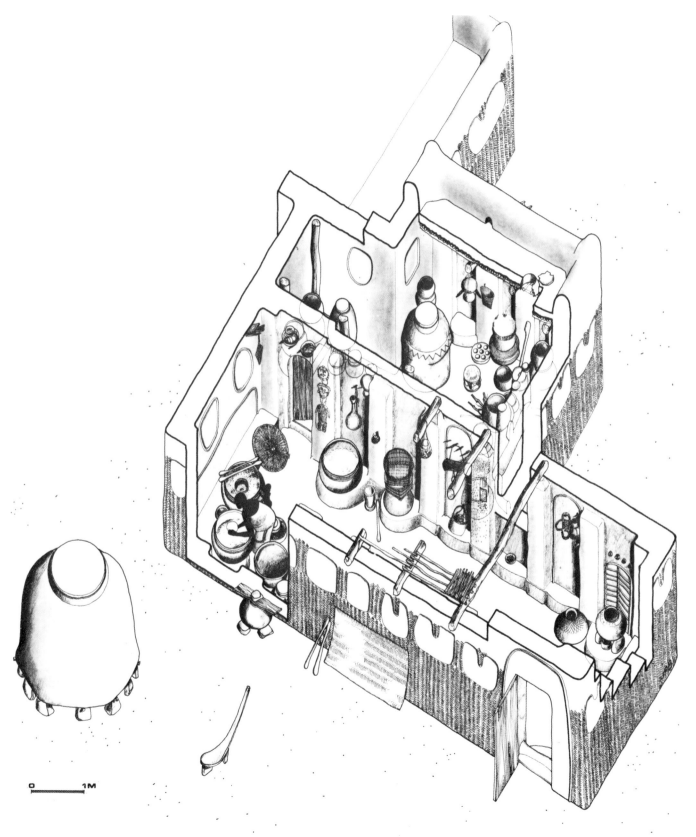

0   1M

P.29.   Buma's compound. Varnished
pot that contains drinking water and
faces the entrance to the *diè*.

P.30. The drinking water pot is often associated, as in this photograph, with a bas-relief representing furrow patterns and the breasts, womb, and feet of a woman.

earth and puddled clay necessary for the construction of houses. In Dogon (Mali) cosmogony, this basket upside down symbolizes the world system in which the circular foundation represents the sun, the square roof the sky, and the circle in the center of this roof the moon.[2] In the Fali (Cameroon) theory of the origin of the universe, these figures take on equally complex symbolic value. The terrestrial space, according to Fali myth, has been formed by two square earths revolving in opposite directions. It came into being when an attempt to organize the world was carried out by the turtle, which ordered the two earths to draw nearer to each other. The earths yielded to the order while continuing to turn in opposite directions and collided, causing their angles to become thereby gradually rounded. The welding of these two different-sized elements gave the united earth a shape that recalls a peanut hull. The

P.31. The lower part of a grindstone is covered with adobe mixed with laterite gravel. It is then generously sprinkled with a locust-bean pod *(Parkia biglobosa)* decoction and tamped with a wooden mallet.

P.32. Basket ornamented with leatherwork.

square or rectangle represents the stage when they remained separated, and is attributed to the male principle, whereas the circle symbolizes the stage after their unification and corresponds to the female principle. Thus, the shapes of openings in Fali houses determine, for example, whether a space belongs to a man or a woman.[3]

The same does not apply to Nuna openings, and the interpretation given concerning the rounded square needs further research. It is, however, interesting to note that the Nuna trace the origin of man and woman to the creation of a number of human-shaped statues. These statues were made of clay and were given life by god's (Wè or Yĩ) breathing into their ears. They came to the earth down a gigantic ladder and formed the Nuna's first ancestors.[4] Strikingly, the elements contained in such an explanation—clay, breath, ear, ladder—are the very

elements that lay the foundation for Dogon cosmogony. (The Dogon live only 150 kilometers away from the Nuna.) The essence of man's and woman's creation may be summed up as: *water,* the divine seed, indispensable to the molding of clay, and the *spoken word,* or fertilizing word, whose passage through a woman's body (coming in from a bisexual aperture, the ear, and going directly to the female sexual parts, where it encircles the womb as the copper spiral encircles the sun) maintains the moisture necessary for procreation.[5] The "water-word" theme is equally essential to Fali cosmogony. Here, the fecund water, represented by the crocodile and the monitor lizard, is also either divine (Fay's first rain) or male, whereas the earth, symbolized by the turtle and the toad, is female. The union of these four animals, or of water and earth, gave birth to four of the eight twin ancestors of man and woman.

75

P.33. Interior of a woman's *diè* with
its row of engaged columns. The light
coming from the roof openings shows
a splayed square and a circular motif
on the wall. These coupled figures
may also be seen on the side of grinding platforms and on the edge of
hearths.

Further features in Lela and Nuna architecture have the same symbolic value as those found in Fali and Dogon cosmogonies. The axonometric cutaway of a woman's unit in Buma's compound (D.11) shows, for example, white rounded square (or rectangular) patterns on the exterior walls. Some of the patterns are whole squares; others are partly split on the top so as to give the image of two unequal welded shapes. (Patterns on Lela exterior walls may be seen as a variation of these split shapes.) The first motifs come in series of fours, as is frequently seen on the walls of other Nuna women's units. Here, they are combined with the second kind of motifs, which stand in threes.[6] The result is the sum of femininity, 4, and masculinity, 3, that constitutes the number 7, considered by the Dogon to be the symbol of perfect union between male and female. Noteworthily, the woman who lives in the unit is said to have had twins of different sexes (which, in Dogon mythical thinking, refers to the perfect pair of genies called Nommo, and in Fali belief to the first pair of humans born from an androgynous papaya.[7] In Lyele, the term *nékili*, used to designate twins, is equally the name of an elf who, in Lela myth, is the genie of fire and fecundity[8]). One of the clay pots seen in her *diè* carries two human shapes in bas-relief; it symbolically encloses food for the twins. A further anthropomorphic bas-relief, often associated with the red varnished pot that contains drinking water and faces the entrance of the *diè* (P.29, P.30, D.11), represents furrow patterns and the breasts, womb, and feet of a woman. Although the number 4 is female, in other women's *diè* the protuberances that portray the breasts come in twos. Does the double of 2 relate, then, to the twins' birth? The possibility of a positive answer is high, since the association

77

P.34. A woman's *diè*, her grindstone and water jar facing the entrance.

male-female-water-earth-mother-fecundity-life (carrying, preserving, and offering water are women's responsibilities) speaks for the symbol itself.

Buma's compound reveals Mossi influence in some of its other details. The round constructions or remnants of constructions dispersed within its boundaries recall the founder's kinship with the Mossi people, whose compound architecture consists of single circular dwelling units connected to each other by curved surrounding walls so as to enclose a large communal space or courtyard.[9] The round units in Buma's compound are the oldest constructions (the order in which they were built is indicated on D.40) and most are uninhabited. Their location shows the former limit of the homestead and its evolution. Dwellings decrease in density toward the periphery, and connecting walls become less and less curved, as compared

to those that trace the limits of the senior man's (Buma) cluster or the one right next to his. Although the components differ, Buma's compound, like Badu's in Pouni, is a blend of two planning principles: the Mossi's principle of individual units and connecting walls, and the Lela's principle of clusters and secondary courts. Such a combination offers an adequate means of solving a problem faced by a large growing community, since the compound keeps enlarging its circle without having to destroy its older units, as in the case of the Lela.

P.35. Entrance to a *nuwo* that leads to
a woman's L-shaped dwelling unit
and to a man's *dibi* on the left.

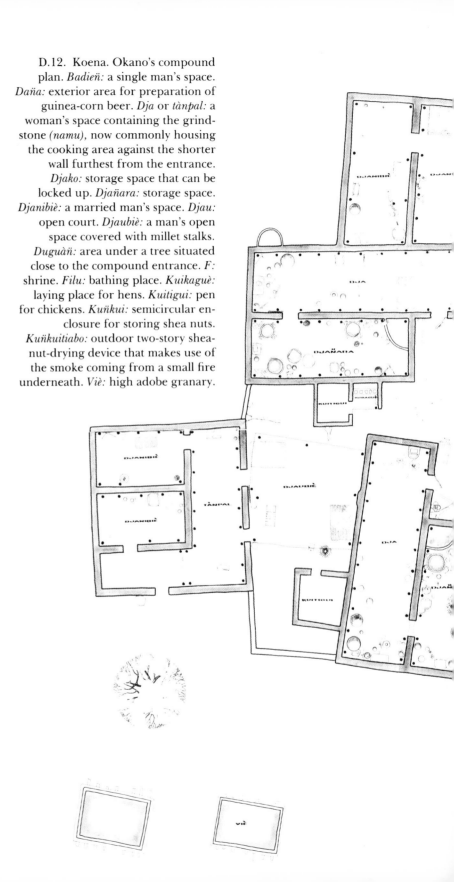

D.12. Koena. Okano's compound plan. *Badieñ:* a single man's space. *Daña:* exterior area for preparation of guinea-corn beer. *Dja* or *tànpal:* a woman's space containing the grind-stone *(namu)*, now commonly housing the cooking area against the shorter wall furthest from the entrance. *Djako:* storage space that can be locked up. *Djañara:* storage space. *Djanibiè:* a married man's space. *Djau:* open court. *Djaubiè:* a man's open space covered with millet stalks. *Duguàñ:* area under a tree situated close to the compound entrance. *F:* shrine. *Filu:* bathing place. *Kuikaguè:* laying place for hens. *Kuitigui:* pen for chickens. *Kuñkui:* semicircular enclosure for storing shea nuts. *Kuñkuitiabo:* outdoor two-story shea-nut-drying device that makes use of the smoke coming from a small fire underneath. *Viè:* high adobe granary.

4 KO

A village with over 300 inhabitants, Koena is, according to the elders, one of the places where the Ko first settled during the eighteenth century, before they spread out into a dozen surrounding villages. Originally composed of two quarters gathered on top of a hill, Koena gradually increased in size and presently includes five more quarters. These quarters, each formed by one or two compounds, extend to the northern slope and base of the hill and are 500 meters away from a perennial pond. No definite outdoor communal space can be seen, except for an open wooden post structure covered with millet stalks, close to the village administrative chief's compound on the hill, which provides the men with a meeting place. Further down, on the side of the hill, a small Catholic church stands as a standard model of concrete-block construction with a corrugated-metal roof.

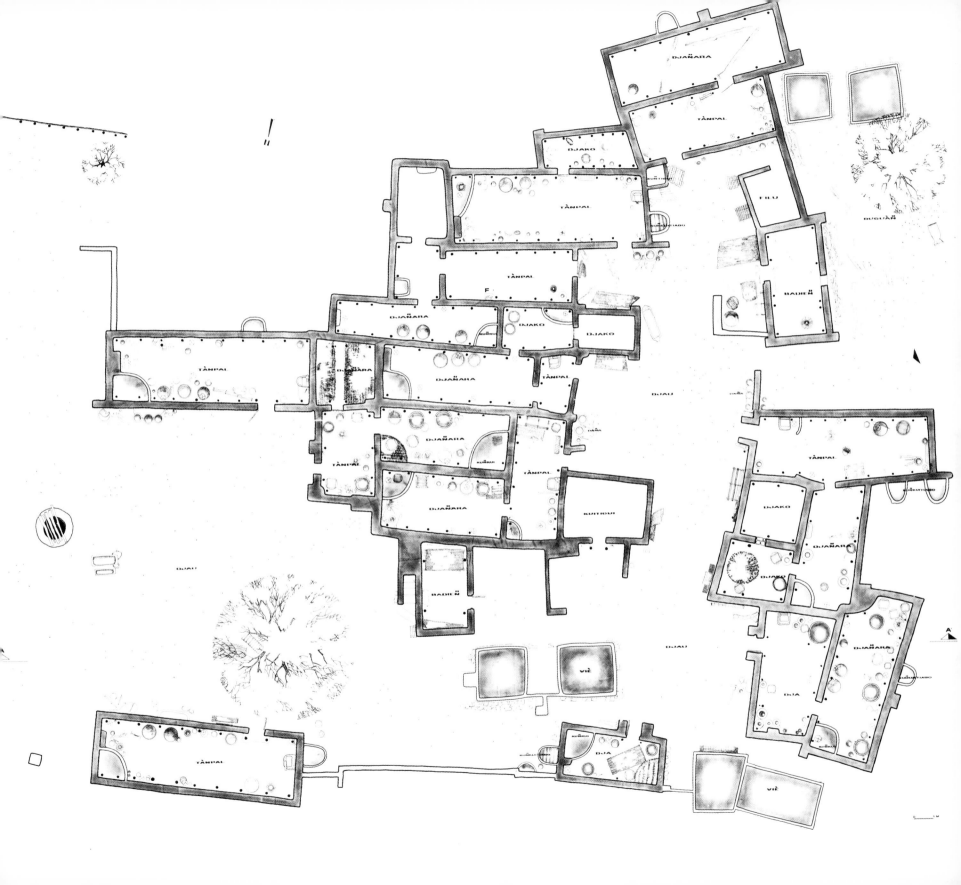

D.13. Axonometric cutaway of the northwestern part of Okano's compound. *DJAU:* court. *Biñi:* covered entrance space protecting from rain and wind as well as from exterior side views. *Biñi bogo:* wooden door. *Dañau:* hearth. *Tinté:* jar supporting the cooking pot and containing water. *Viè:* large men's adobe granary containing millet corn and occasionally peanuts. *DJAKO:* storage space which usually contains women's granaries *(suñ).* *Tugu:* fire wall. *DJAÑARA:* space used for storage; it usually also contains a cooking fireplace and a *kuñkui* or enclosure for storing shea nuts. *Dugu:* wall. *Sompuébiè* and *sompué:* small calabashes for carrying water when leaving the compound. *TÀNPAL* or *DJA:* space used for reception, sleeping, and carrying out daily activities. *Bana:* basket. *Dañapuru:* jar filled with stones serving as a support for the *totolo* or cooking pot. *Dassi:* wooden mortar. *Dayapul:* stone to support the *totolo.* *Fóo:* calabash. *Hué:* large jar for water storage. *Kakao:* basket to keep chicks or a hen sitting on eggs. *Kuñkuitiabo:* shea-nut-drying device. *Namu:* grindstone. *Sóñon:* wooden head-carrier for women.

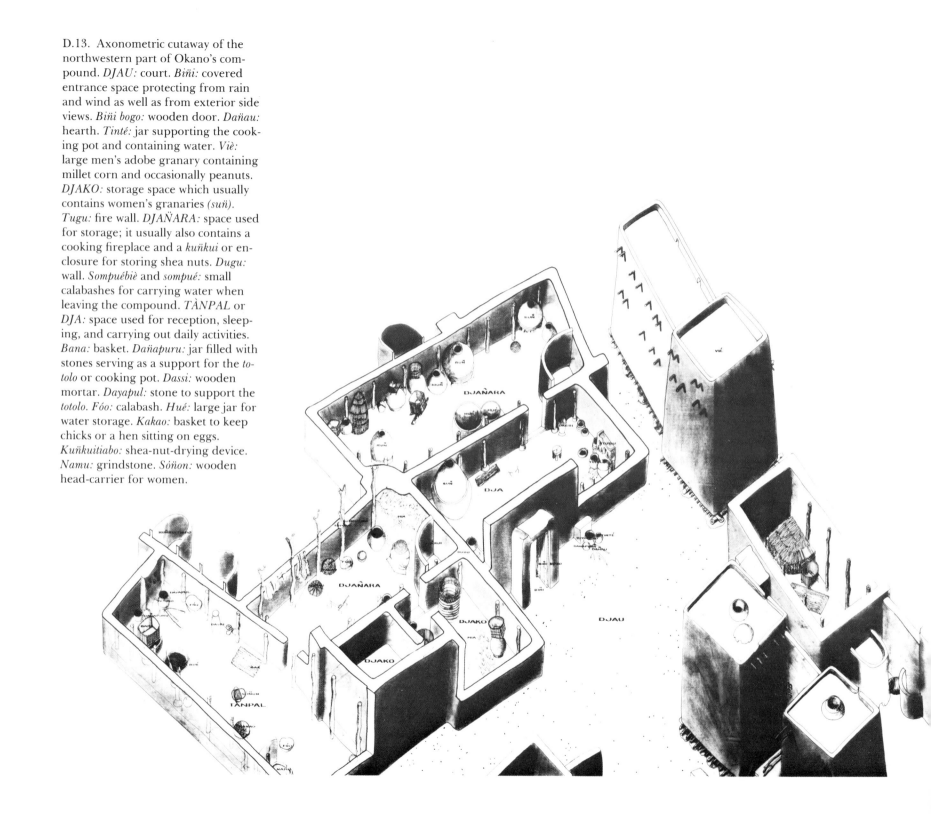

Okano's compound plan (D.12) offers a clear view of the interactions between social and architectural evolution. The west side constitutes the oldest part of the compound. It is characterized by a compact pattern that contrasts with the loose fabric of exposed, newly built units in the east. A comparison of the two parts reveals changing architectural elements that plainly speak for the transition from a strong to a more detached communal life.

Several accesses lead to the interior of the compound. Upon entering the west entrance, one sees a common feature of Ko habitations, which is the long, narrow open court or *djau* (P.36, D.12) shaped by adjacent sets of tightly knit rectangular spaces. Most of these sets do not open directly onto the *djau* but to outdoor intermediary realms created either by the limits of protruding constructions (such as the *djako* and *kuitigui*), a con-cept often encountered among the Ko, or by partly enclosed walls. Playing a role similar to that of the secondary courts found in Lela and Nuna compounds, these realms act as buffers, delaying access to the intimate insides of the dwellings. They constitute the necessary link in the chain of open spaces that progressively lead the way from exterior to interior, or vice versa. Privacy is thus conveyed through a sense of gradual penetration, and smaller spaces are conceived so as to offer a view out into larger ones. Here, the transitional realms open onto the *djau*, while in the exterior of the compound the *dungàh*, an area defined by the shade of the tree near the entrance, looks out toward the compound vicinity.

The layout of the older part of the compound favors communication among units alongside the *djau*, which all stand within sight and hearing distance of each other. The same does

83

P.36. View from the southwest over the *djau*, or long, narrow court defined by adjacent sets of tightly knit rectangular spaces. The exterior spaces nestled between the two protruding constructions (the *djako* and the *kuitigui*) on the right serve as an intermediary realm and are usually not covered. One can catch sight of the second large *djau* behind Okano's upper-storied room, where the tree is situated.

not, however, hold true for the eastern part. Here, the units belong to couples of a generation younger than Okano's (D.41); they are added so as to enclose a second large open court and expand the compound farther. Instead of erecting another compound or freestanding individual houses, fathers and sons stay together by attempting to form new buildings as continuations of older ones. However, very few of the design principles that govern the older units are carried out in the younger constructions. Distance is the first element that sets the sons' households apart. Compared to the west *djau,* the east *djau* is too spread out and loosely shaped to maintain the same degree of interaction among dwelling spaces. Thus, visual and auditory contacts lessen not only with the rest of the family but also among these younger households whose dwellings do not have openings that relate to each other as in the older part.

Of equal importance is the degree of enclosure necessary to the creation of transitional realms. Except for the *djaubiè*, which is only used for repose and friendly gatherings by the man living in the unit next to it, no well-defined space acts as buffer between exterior and interior in the eastern part of the compound. The *djau* spills out into the corners of the units and leads abruptly to their interiors. This lack of progression from communal to private accounts for the decrease in women's outdoor activities—which are then transferred indoors—and above all for the advent of the wooden door equipped with locks. Wooden or metal doors (instead of woven thatch mats, for example), like rectilinear and two-story buildings, may often be adopted simply for the image of urbanity, progress, and prestige that they convey. In this case, however, the preference for doors raises significant questions. The compound plan

P.37. *Tànpal* housing the family shrine with its two male and female statuettes and a calabash containing water in between them. The hand motifs on the walls remind one of those found on numerous rock paintings of the Sahara and in the region of Bamako in Mali.

(D.12) indicates their consistent and almost exclusive use in new dwellings of the east side. None of the older ones in the west resort to such a means for protection; their openings are, instead, simply emphasized by an adobe frame (*biḥi,* see D.13) 50 cm. thick that projects beyond the outer wall so as to obstruct side views into the interior. Although varying widely in form and size, such frames are commonly found in African houses. These frames are not only functional—they divert rain and prevent it from leaking through the entrances—they also subtly announce the boundary between familial and external worlds and are part of the intimacy gradient mentioned earlier.

The lack of in-between realms and of progression in space is equally noticeable in the interior design of dwelling units. One can further understand the necessity for wooden doors and metal locks when one studies the evolution of spatial arrange-

ment within the women's units. As shown in the plan (D.12), the latter are originally composed of two or three spaces: the *dja* or *tànpal*, which provides a place for reception, repose, sleeping, or performance of domestic activities, and always contains a grindstone (*namu*, P.38) near the door area; the *djaḥara,* which is consistently furnished with a *kuḥkui* or shea-nut enclosure and is used for storage, cooking, and preparing guinea-corn beer, as well as sleeping during cold nights; and the small *djako,* usually the most remote space from the *tànpal* entrance, which also serves for storage and is the place where granaries are kept. Of these three spaces, the *djako* is the first to be dispensed with in the newer units; the *djaḥara* comes next. The result is a large single-room unit that absorbs all functions into the *tànpal* (see units 7 and 8 in D.41). This simplification of space presents some advantages as far as economy of building

85

P.38. Grindstone (*namu*) near the
tànpal entrance.

materials and labor is concerned, but it also entails the remodeling of a way of life and perception of space. The unidirectional single-room unit that opens straight onto the external world impoverishes the kinesthetic experience of space and reduces the range of intimate realms where the inhabitant can retreat, should the need to withdraw arise. The door offsets this inconvenience and allows the dweller to preserve her/his intimacy.

The existence of locks raises a different but closely related problem. As units shrink in number of spaces, they also tend to stand independently. Instead of forming an interlocked, compact whole with shared walls leaning against each other for support and economy of materials, they are erected as isolated structures (units 7, 8, and 11 in D.41), often with unused space around them. Attempts to relate and define space by connecting walls do not yield the same result as in the case study of

P.39. View inside a *tànpal*. The *kuñkui* with its circular wall in the bottom left of the space encloses shea nuts while the heat generated by the adjacent hearth on the right keeps insects away from them. The woman is taking water out of the large jar where millet germinates.

Valiou, where the compound has a circular layout and is composed of clusters of dwellings with openings that relate to each other. Thus, in this example, too great exposure of the buildings not only presents temperature inconveniences, as discussed in the case study of Pouni, but also gives rise to a certain feeling of insecurity. Added to earlier observations on the eastern part of Okano's compound (the width of the *djau* and the unrelated orientation of dwellings), this tendency toward isolation implies an obvious weakening of communal supervision. As a possible consequence, locks come into use, denoting a sense of individual defense and, also, of material possession. Privacy in such a context seems closer to the notion of privacy as conceived in Western cultures.

Progress toward individualization can be further detected in Okano's present and future living units. In Ko habitations, men used to live either with their wives under the same roof or have their dwellings—*djanibiè* for marrieds and *badieñ* for singles—built on ground level and adjacent to the women's. Okano's *djanibiè* is, however, erected on a story higher than the rest of the compound (D.14; located on top of the space where he is indicated in the plan D.41). Although commonly found among the Gurunsi, such as the Nuna, Puguli, and Western Kassena, and other peoples in western Upper Volta, such as the Bobo and the Bolon, such a practice is scarce among the Ko. Okano's eldest son has also introduced change by building an elaborate, freestanding dwelling unit with two *djanibiè* and a *tànpal* at the furthest east end of the compound. At the time this study was carried out, Okano was having a modern individual house (not included in the plan) built about 15 meters south of the compound. Erected with concrete blocks, corrugated-metal roofs,

87

P.40. Against the fire wall *(tugu)* in the bottom of a *tànpal*, a woman prepares the millet mush. Triangular niches serve for storing hot pepper, salt, and other condiments.

metal doors and locks, it was to become Okano's dwelling, where his male grandchildren may join him once they reach the age of fifteen.

Long bricks (generally 65 by 20 by 8 centimeters) are, in older buildings, the basic module for wall construction. Made of a mixture of adobe and laterite gravel, they are shaped by hand and erected first on a small foundation trench 15 centimeters deep. The thickness of the adobe mortar in between each layer varies from 2 to 6 centimeters. Once the wall is erected, the external surface is coated with clayey silts from the nearby pond mixed with cow dung and a viscous decoction of crushed roots. The interior coating does not make use of the last two components, whose only purpose is to ensure water resistance.

Penetration of wooden beams into adobe walls in dwelling interiors reveals a composite structure that employs both the bearing-wall and post-and-beam systems. The relative instability of the ground may have prompted the need for such a structure. Both the wall and the wooden post sustain the roof. Thus, when one of them settles, the roof weight can still lie on the other. One also notices the thickness of the walls erected with a double row of bricks. Standing by themselves, rectilinear walls would not resist compression as successfully as the Lela's thinner, circular walls would. They must therefore be reinforced in thickness or follow, as in the western part of Okano's compound, a system in which a single or a series of parallel spaces are wind-braced by being juxtaposed perpendicularly to other transverse strain-bearing spaces (see oldest units 1, 2, 3, 4, and 5 in D.41).

Beams are spaced approximately a meter apart. The gap

D.14. AA' section on Okano's compound. Okano's *djanibiè* can be partly seen behind the tree.

between every two beams is bridged with a series of wooden sticks slightly over a meter long. On top of these sticks and in an opposite direction, smaller pieces of dead wood are then laid by an experienced man before they are covered with earth. This earth, dug up from a nearby area outside the compound, is mixed with water and molded into clods by vigorous young men who then pass them on by throwing them to the elders stationed on the roof. Once the layer of earth is spread to a thickness of 10 cm., women cover it with laterite gravel and a locust-bean pod *(Parkia biglobosa)* decoction before they tamp it to obtain a smooth varnish-like surface. The same coating process is applied to the inside floor of the dwelling, which may then last over five years without repair. The roof, however, needs maintenance every two or three years, depending on the degree of erosion from rain.

5 PUGULI

According to the administrative chief of the village of Nyiémé, the Puguli, who also call themselves Pwa, trace their ancestry to a man named Sankiolo and his spouse Sankulini. The couple would have been natives of the village of Usa (Ghana) and "would bear resemblances to the Sissala"[1] established on both sides of the border between Upper Volta and what is now Ghana. Beaten off by the Dagari and at war with their neighbors the Bobo, the Puguli first settled down in Dano. Upon the first chief's death, and probably under pressure from the Marka led by Karantao, the inhabitants dispersed to create a dozen other villages, among them Nyiémé. The village was founded by a man named Bènata; the inhabitants' resistance to Bobo and Dagari aggression has inspired its present name, Nyiémé, which means "we shall remain here by force."

Situated along an affluent of the Black Volta River, which is about 5 kilometers away, the village comprises ten dispersed compounds that are divided into two distinct quarters. Both of these quarters function under the mediation of the administrative village chief. Their common point of reference is a large, mature tree, near the chief's compound, whose deep shade provides the men with a refreshing meeting place. The village thrives on agriculture; its other subsistence activities include fishing and hunting. Most women of the community make pottery that they barter nowadays with their Dagari neighbors for millet. Only three blacksmiths are counted among the men, who pursue, in addition to their other responsibilities, cattle, goat, or horse breeding.

Zingè is one of the three blacksmiths, while his wife and her kin are skilled potters. Upon approaching his homestead, the outside observer is immediately struck by its conspicuously

P.41. Bouni. Puguli house surrounded with white and red sorghum during the rainy season. Corn is dried and spread along the edge of the roof.

D.15. Nyiémé. Partial axonometric of
Zingè's homestead. The courts
(dawolo) on the left indicated in D.16
and D.18 are not covered.

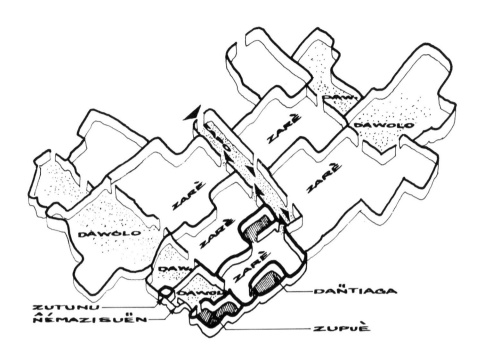

Diagram 10. Spatial organization in Zingè's homestead. The central distributive corridor (*zapo*) gives access to five independent dwelling units. Each unit, composed of a main living area (*zarè*) and a cooking space (*dañtiaga*), opens into a packed-earth court (*dawolo*) that leads to the man's space (*zupuè*), the chicken pen (*zutunu*), and the bathing enclosure (*ñémazisueñ*).

DAWOLO

ZARÈ

ZARÈ

ZARÈ

ZARÈ

ZARÈ

ZAPO

DAWOLO

DAW

DAW

ZUTUNU
ñ ÉMAZISUËN

DAWOLO

DAÑTIAGA

ZUPUÈ

fortified aspect. Like other Puguli habitations, it acutely reflects the historical determination of its occupants to resist their neighbors' aggression. Visitors seeing this type of construction consistently describe it as "castle-like." The same term may be used, however, to portray the exterior aspects of many other Gurunsi compounds, such as the Lela's; what makes Puguli habitations seem more fortified, then, is perhaps the bulky appearance of the walls and the compact, roofed-in spaces that form the core of the houses.

Originally conceived with a single entrance, Zingè's homestead presently opens out through two additional entrances that lead only to its two outer units. Access to the five other households' units is gained, as in traditional Puguli habitations, through a long distributive corridor, or *zapo* (D.15, D.16, D.42). Stepping into the *zapo* is like starting a blind walk into an underground world. The total absence of light offers such an unexpected introduction to the compound, and the transition from the public exterior to the private interior is so sudden, that the outside observer cannot help feeling slightly like a trapped intruder. All senses alerted, one can only grope one's way forward as directed by the longitudinal orientation of the space. The *zapo* used to shelter cattle; it is easy to imagine, then, intruders breaking in among these animals: by the time they made their way through these obstacles in opaque darkness, the occupants would all have taken their stand, ready to fight back.

Nowadays, Zingè's *zapo* contains only a communal grindstone (*nazé*) and is devoid of obstacles. Goat pens have been added north of the homestead to keep the animals well separated from the dwellings (see O on D.16; note the unique opening leading out of and not into the compound). Dispensing with its

93

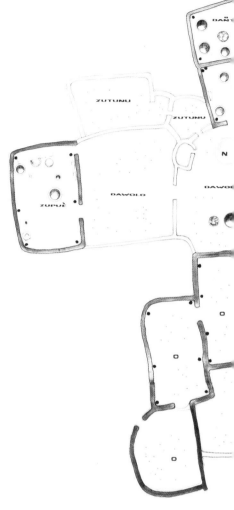

original defensive function, the *zapo* stands now as an empty but nonetheless necessary circulation space that links and distributes sets of other spaces along its sides. The progress into darkness leads indeed to a series of labyrinth-like realms whose arrangement prolongs the *zapo* principle of distribution. Thus, each series or dwelling unit comprises a large, long space, or *zarè*, that expands on both sides into smaller subspaces, such as the *agora* (for storage of women's small adobe granaries), the *samè zikiè* (for storage of large guinea-corn-beer or water jars), and the *viubéla* (voluminous family adobe granary). Adjacent to the *zarè* is a separate space, the *daħtiaga*, which houses each woman's inside cooking area.

The construction of two *daħtiaga* in a unit denotes the presence of two adult women, usually an old widow and a younger woman with her children, who live together but prepare their meals separately. This is the case in the two units situated northeast and southeast of the compound, each of which contains an impressively large *viubéla* (units 2, 3, 4 and 6, 7 in D.42). Here, however, instead of having her cooking fireplace in the *daħtiaga*, one of the two women in each unit places hers directly in front of the *viubéla* (D.15, D.18). Such a change is in fact a common feature in Puguli dwellings and is meant to be a preventive device: the smoke from the cooking fire surrounds the *viubéla*, where it gets imprisoned in the space between the walls and the granary and forms an envelope protecting the latter against insects, before it spreads out along the rest of the *zarè*. Outsiders visiting African houses have wondered about the suffocating mass of smoke found in interiors and the inadequate ventilation through openings in the roof. The black soot, however, allows the wooden sections of the roof structure to

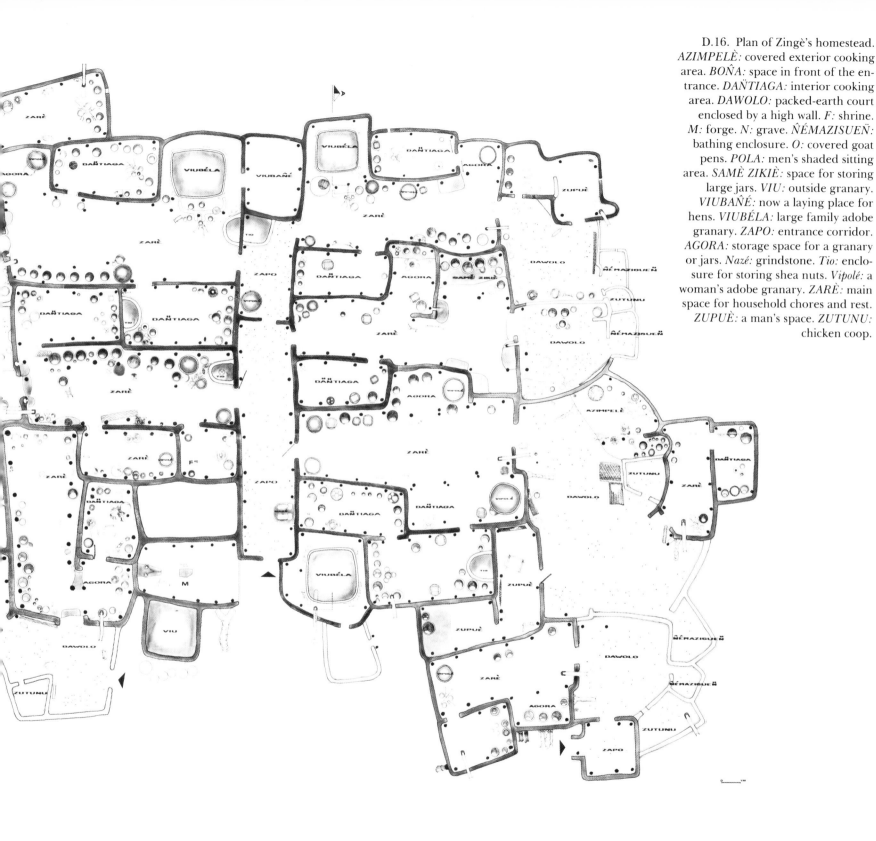

D.16. Plan of Zingè's homestead. *AZIMPELÈ:* covered exterior cooking area. *BOÑA:* space in front of the entrance. *DAÑTIAGA:* interior cooking area. *DAWOLO:* packed-earth court enclosed by a high wall. *F:* shrine. *M:* forge. *N:* grave. *ÑÉMAZISUEÑ:* bathing enclosure. *O:* covered goat pens. *POLA:* men's shaded sitting area. *SAMÈ ZIKIÈ:* space for storing large jars. *VIU:* outside granary. *VIUBAÑÉ:* now a laying place for hens. *VIUBÉLA:* large family adobe granary. *ZAPO:* entrance corridor. *AGORA:* storage space for a granary or jars. *Nazé:* grindstone. *Tio:* enclosure for storing shea nuts. *Vipolé:* a woman's adobe granary. *ZARÈ:* main space for household chores and rest. *ZUPUÈ:* a man's space. *ZUTUNU:* chicken coop.

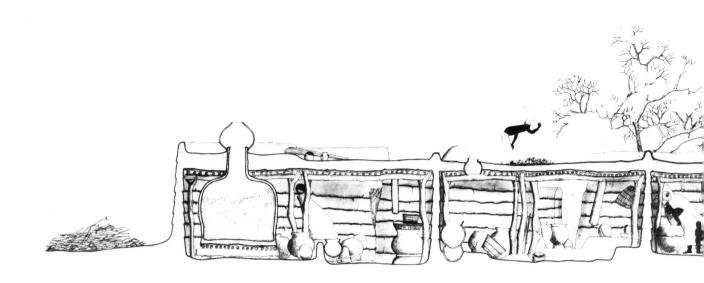

resist termites (P.47), hence the intentional positioning of inside fireplaces away from door openings. The hearth is also generally kept in the deepest part of each dwelling unit, since it is considered a woman's intimate realm. Both technical and cultural arguments given here may be accounted for in the two above examples of Zingè's compound. Each of these units has two doorways: one that leads to the *zapo* and may be closed off by mats hung outside it, and another that looks out onto a small private court, the *dawolo*. The coupled *viubéla* and fireplace are, in both cases, placed near the *zarè* entrance and away from the access to the *dawolo*. Such a choice reveals that light is one of the main factors determining the degrees of intimacy of a space (since the area near the *zapo* is still the darkest part of the *zarè*); it also enables the smoke to spread and travel through the entire space before escaping into the *dawolo*.

Subspaces forming the *agora* and, less frequently, the *samè zikiè* and *daħtiaga* (units 8 and 10 in D.42) may once have been created to serve a defensive purpose. Besides their function as storage or cooking areas, they contribute to the succession of protective devices consistently developed in this type of architecture. When moving to these niche-like realms, the inhabitants put themselves visually out of reach of the *zarè* entrance; they may, in case of danger, then station themselves so as to use them as bulwarks. On the other hand, subspaces break the single rhythm established by the longitudinal orientation of the *zarè*, while maintaining its fluidity of movement. With undulating walls that do not square off at angles but curve smoothly in and out, these spaces and especially those found in the older units (D.18 and units 6, 7, 8, 9 in D.42) flow continuously and interpenetrate each other in their movement. The result is an

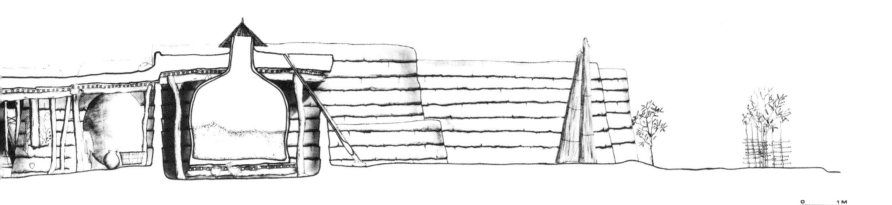

D.17. AA′ section of Zingè's homestead. Both family granaries *(viubéla)* on the right and left are built with their cylindrical openings projecting above the roof surface and are covered with conical grass lids. An example of the gargoyle drainage system can be seen on the right of the larger *viubéla*.

aggregation of nonfinite shapes that cannot easily be apprehended by newcomers and a continuity of spatial interaction that constitutes the very vitality of this architecture.

Such a dynamic perception of space is not only visual. It also often involves the other senses, such as touch. As we have seen in previous studies, wall and ground-floor textures play an important role in people's shaping of space. Transitional realms leading to the inside of a dwelling are usually felt: the finished, packed earth becomes smoother once the entrance is crossed. Here, in Zingè's homestead, the *zapo* used for animals in older times does not have a ground texture different from that of the exterior. The boundary of each dwelling unit is announced not only by a doorway and the smooth surface of the tamped earth, but in addition by a depressed ground-floor level. This breaking off of the horizontal plane is achieved through the same

technique as that found among the Lela, Nuna, Kassena, and Nankani. The height of carved-in earth furniture, such as small knoll-like seats with wooden posts as their backs (P.47) and sleeping platforms, indicates the previous ground level of the inside spaces, which was the same as the *zapo* and *dawolo* ground level. Besides its functional aspect, the lowered floor thus marks the differences between private and communal, and indoor and outdoor. One goes up when one steps out of the *zarè* into the small open court, or *dawolo*.

The presence of the *dawolo* raises a number of questions. Previous case studies show that the small open court has consistently served as an introduction to the dwelling inside. Never has it played, as in this instance, the role of an impasse. The issue is not whether a court as a transitory realm begins or ends a set of habitable spaces, but why it closes off instead of opening

97

out. The wall surrounding the compound is, indeed, high, and the *dawolo* has neither an opening nor a view out to the exterior. One may, at first, assume that such an arrangement serves a preventive purpose. When comparing it, however, to the other careful defensive features of this architecture, one cannot refrain from asking: how does the presence of the *dawolo* relate to the tight defensive layout of the compound? The most tangible reasons for sheltering all animals and granaries—including the voluminous *viubéla*—within the compound interiors were the necessity to keep them out of reach of enemies from the outside and the need to maintain self-sufficiency in case of a siege. Why, then, bother roofing them in and having such a defensively unique compound entrance as the *zapo* if access from the roof or the walls into the *dawolo* is possible?

Looking at other Puguli compound plans and those of their neighbors the Dagari, Birifor, LoWiili, Dyan, and Lobi, who have a similar type of architecture (although the interior spatial organization does vary), one notices that the *dawolo* is not always present.[2] Zingè's compound evolution (D.42) shows that the constructions numbered 1 to 20, or the entire roofed-in part of the homestead, were indeed built together in 1950. Three years later, Zingè's dwelling unit and his three *viubéla* were erected (units 21 to 24), followed in 1957 by the unit of his younger brother's household and their granary, or *viu* (units 25 to 28). All constructions that close off and define the limits of the eight *dawolo* on the periphery—north, northwest, south, southwest—were built later. This immediately prompts the following question: has the *dawolo,* in general, always existed in Puguli architecture, or is it a recently adopted feature?

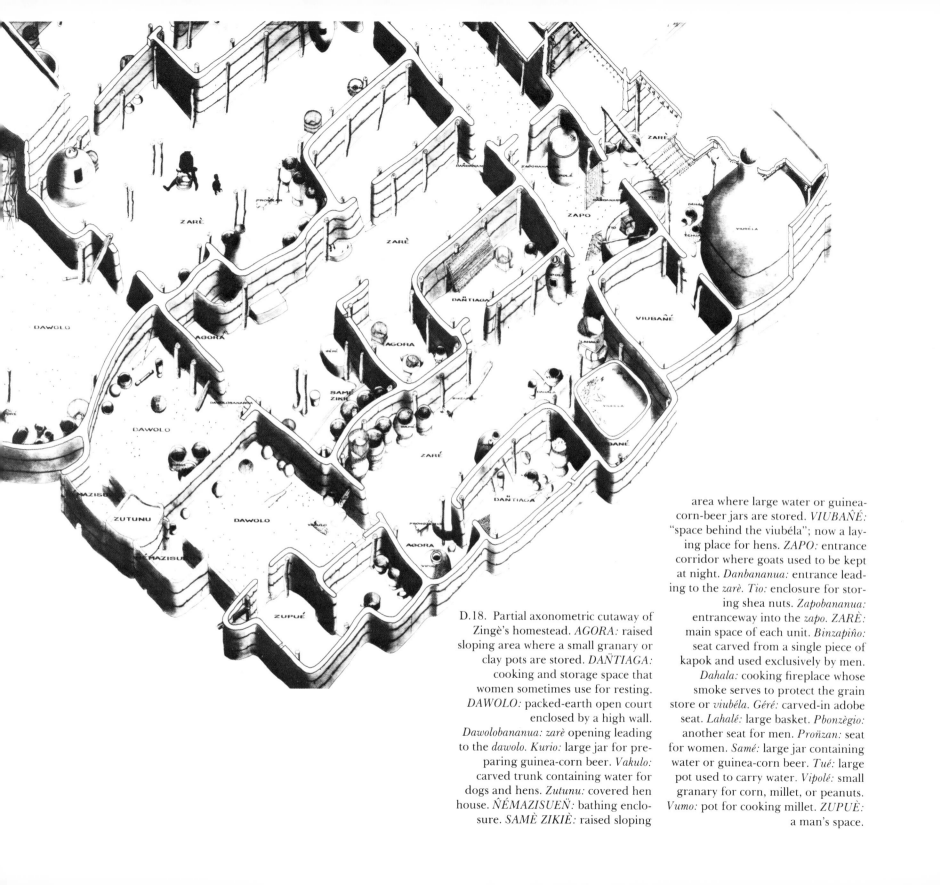

D.18. Partial axonometric cutaway of Zingè's homestead. *AGORA:* raised sloping area where a small granary or clay pots are stored. *DAÑTIAGA:* cooking and storage space that women sometimes use for resting. *DAWOLO:* packed-earth open court enclosed by a high wall. *Dawolobananua:* zarè opening leading to the *dawolo. Kurio:* large jar for preparing guinea-corn beer. *Vakulo:* carved trunk containing water for dogs and hens. *Zutunu:* covered hen house. *ÑÉMAZISUEÑ:* bathing enclosure. *SAMÈ ZIKIÈ:* raised sloping area where large water or guinea-corn-beer jars are stored. *VIUBAÑÉ:* "space behind the viubéla"; now a laying place for hens. *ZAPO:* entrance corridor where goats used to be kept at night. *Danbananua:* entrance leading to the *zarè. Tio:* enclosure for storing shea nuts. *Zapobananua:* entranceway into the *zapo. ZARÈ:* main space of each unit. *Binzapiño:* seat carved from a single piece of kapok and used exclusively by men.

Dahala: cooking fireplace whose smoke serves to protect the grain store or *viubéla. Géré:* carved-in adobe seat. *Lahalé:* large basket. *Pbonzègio:* another seat for men. *Proñzan:* seat for women. *Samé:* large jar containing water or guinea-corn beer. *Tué:* large pot used to carry water. *Vipolé:* small granary for corn, millet, or peanuts. *Vumo:* pot for cooking millet. *ZUPUÈ:* a man's space.

As an extension of the inside, the *dawolo* usually contains an open or covered cooking area *(azimpelè)*. It leads to other newly created spaces such as the bathing enclosure *(ñémazisueh)*, the chicken coop *(zutunu)*, the goat pens, sometimes the man's room *(zupuè)*, or another recently established household's dwelling unit. It is through this same *dawolo* that the inhabitants gain access to the terrace roofs by means of notched poles leaning against the wall. Each household has its own terrace, whose surface corresponds to the surface of its dwelling unit and is delimited by low parapets that are a continuation of the perimeter walls of the spaces below. Commonly used among the Gurunsi, this method of building walls to a level higher than the roof surface is particularly striking in the Puguli's and their neighbors' (Lobi, Dagari, Birifor) architecture; its emphasis may derive from the fact that life on the terrace used to be highly animated. Observers have often attributed the presence of parapets to a form of individualism that forbids a woman to infringe upon her fellow women's property, or else to the necessity for a clear territorial demarcation that avoids all conflicts when the time for drying crops arrives.[3] However, in such a tight compound community where boundaries do not need to be physical and strongly manifested to be respected, it seems more likely that parapets simply meet the minimum degree of enclosure that a person requires of a space in order to feel comfortable or protected from too great exposure.

The need for certain visual protection from other family members and from outsiders is yet more convincing when one realizes how prominent a part the terrace used to play in the inhabitants' daily lives. In many compounds, and especially in those where small open courts are absent or scarce, the terrace

P.42. School in Bouni.

provides a circulation and meeting place that overlooks the distant landscape and is used extensively at night for sleeping[4]—the parapets function therefore as a defensive device in case of an alarm. In fact, the terrace substitutes for the court, with the additional advantage of being at the same time a strategic point. This gives validity to the question raised earlier concerning the presence of open courts in this particular type of architecture. The extensive use of the roof seems to fill in the gap created by the absence of communally oriented spaces so necessary to the vitality of a community. It also explains why in some compounds people still prefer to gain access to their rooms from the exterior via the terrace through a narrow roof opening[5] (just large enough to let one person through), instead of walking around the compound and entering by the *zapo*.

No such roof opening exists in Zingè's compound or in neighboring compounds of Nyiémé, which are all equipped with either *dawolo* or secondary doorways that lead directly to the exterior without having to pass by the *zapo*. The terrace is used nowadays mainly for drying grains, diverse condiments, and clothes. For gatherings and daily communal activities, the inhabitants prefer the *boña*, or outdoor space that spreads from the front of the compound entrance to well beyond the shade of the large tree nearby (D.16). The men have, underneath this same tree, their own sitting area *(pola)*, defined by a raised wooden structure. In Zingè's compound, people sleep on the roof or in their *dawolo* on hot nights, while in other compounds where courts are absent, they lie scattered on the outside of the compound, positioning their mats next to their doorways.

The use of outdoor space has become more popular as outside aggression has ceased and a feeling of security has settled

101

P.43. Nyiémé. Family adobe granary
(*viubéla*).

in among the inhabitants. Family granaries (*viubéla*), which used to be kept inside the dwellings, may now also be built outside the compound. In Zingè's example, two of them can be seen close to the *zapo* entrance (D.19, D.15). The *viubéla* on its right shows a first stage of evolution: enclosed in a roofed space adjacent to a peripheral unit, the granary stands by itself and occupies a room of its own. A low wall (1.5 meters high), which partly exposes it to view, is erected to complete the corridor space around it. The resulting unusual (to the observer) visual effect is that of a container within another container. The *viu* situated in front of the forge on the left side of the *zapo* entrance was built four years after the three *viubéla*, at the same time that the dwelling unit of Zingè's younger brother and his family was annexed to the compound. The *viu* retains little of the *viubéla:* its location outdoors entails a change in both the

P.44. Bouni. Granaries can easily be located through the protrusion of their openings above the roofs.

design and the working material. Traditionally, the *viubéla* is erected on log trestles and molded into the shape of a wide-bottomed bottle (D.15, D.17) using a special clay mixed with a substantial amount of straw. It is completed before the compound (or dwelling unit in which it is located) is roofed, leaving the neck of the bottle, or its opening, projecting 30 to 40 centimeters above the roof surface (P.44). From the exterior its presence can thus be easily detected through its protruding conical grass lid, which protects the grain from insects and is taken off when access to the grain store is necessary. The *viu*, on the other hand, is built up in courses with the same technique and material (puddled mud) as the compound walls. Although still standing on log trestles, it is simply conceived of as another room of the compound—a solid parallelepiped that takes upon itself the role of container and flattens out the intriguing image

of an envelope within an envelope offered in the previous setting of the *viubéla*.

The *zupuè*, or men's individual rooms, also represent recent adaptations. Most of them were built after 1950, the date when the compound was first erected (D.42). Added onto the outside of the women's units, they are usually located on the peripheral zone of the homestead and can be reached only through the *dawolo*. To a certain extent, this arrangement reveals the men's position in the family. Although an upper-story unit (built on top of spaces 13, 14, and a filled space that serves as its support,[6] D.42) overlooking the *zapo* entrance still indicates the male's protective role, this role seems to be reduced to a minimum. The upper story belongs, in fact, to the previous head of the family, but it remains uninhabited and has been left to rain erosion since the senior man's death. Zingè, who is the present

103

P.45. Nyiémé. A woman working in her *zarè*. The craft of pottery may be compared to the mode of wall construction used by the inhabitants; the coiling of layers shaping the jar recalls the superimposition of courses that form the walls of a compound.

head, prefers to stay in his *zupuè* rather than build another upper-story unit next to the older one. It is worth noting, then, that in a society where both matrilineal and patrilineal descent are recognized,[7] the relationship between men and women shows through the evolution of spatial adjustments. Different from other architectural instances among the Gurunsi[8] where men's visual control over their family circulation space can easily be felt and recognized through the siting and/or orientation of their rooms, Zingè's compound reveals that men's spatial supervision is of little importance. Since the homestead is roofed in, the upper-story room offers a view of the distant landscape and the immediate entrance area preceding the *zapo* underneath, but it does not really look over any of the women's *dawolo*. Access to the men's *zupuè*, on the other hand, is possible only through the *dawolo* and, most of the time, after the women's *zarè* has been crossed. Furthermore, these *zupuè* never face the *zarè* openings (except for *zupuè* 34 in D.42, whose distance and separation from the corresponding *zarè* by the construction of a second *dawolo* do not allow efficient supervision). They merely stand on one side of the women's units and are, sometimes, even hidden from view from the *zarè* entrance.

The entire family participates in the construction of a compound. Other villagers known for their knowledge of building techniques also join in when requested by the family head. Men carry wood and clay, they build the walls, frame up the roofs, and set the gutters. Women supply the work site with the necessary water and plaster the inner walls with special adobe dug from a swamp; they tamp floors and roofs and apply a coating of cow dung and laterite on their surfaces. Finally, they are responsible for the entire interior arrangements and furnish-

P.46. Once prepared, the millet mush is poured into bowls to make flat cakes.

105

Diagram 11. System of rain drainage
with gargoyles in a Puguli dwelling.

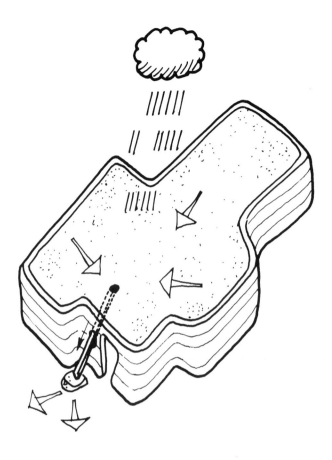

ings, such as the carved-in seats and platforms, the grindstones, the small granaries, the hearth, and the fireplace.

Before building a compound, the plan is outlined on the ground. Walls are then erected through the superimposition of courses of adobe embedded into each other with a technique similar to that used by women when modeling pottery (P.45). The first course, slightly thicker and higher than the succeeding ones, is put up on a shallow foundation trench 10 centimeters deep. Clods of puddled mud are flattened out into a continuous band 50 centimeters high and 25 centimeters thick that tapers off at the top to a thickness of about 15 centimeters. While building this first course, the men smooth both the outer and inner surfaces with their hands, then form small adobe cones at 40–60-centimeter intervals on its top so as to anchor the following layer. Starting with the *zapo,* the men proceed next to a *dahtiaga,* then to a *zarè,* continuing in the same order until all the first courses defining the boundaries of the homestead and its interior spaces are completed. The second course cannot, however, be added on top until the first had dried and hardened. This technique thus requires that construction work be interrupted for two days between courses. Depending on the number of participants and the size of the homestead, the completion of the walls may take anywhere from forty to sixty days.

The wall construction usually stops with the sixth course, whose outer and inner faces are each set back 5 centimeters further in at mid-height to allow the wooden frame and adobe terrace to overlap the wall and make it more watertight. Once the masonry work is accomplished, the men pass on to the carpentry. They dig holes in the ground every meter or more along the walls and drive in forked trunks that will sustain the

P.47. View from a *zarè* out to the
dawolo. The *agora* can be seen on the left.

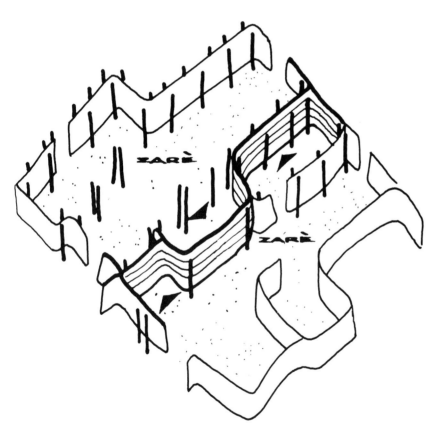

Diagram 12. Wall design in a Puguli dwelling. Post-and-beam system allows non-load-bearing partitions to be erected with a minimum of material and to undulate in crenellated patterns. These patterns not only brace the walls; they also create semi-enclosed subspaces that serve diverse purposes.

beams. The procedure for the roof structure and terrace is the same as in other Gurunsi architecture (described in Chapter 4) except for the gutter system, which consists of having gargoyles drain the rainwater off the roof (D.17, D.15, D.16). Made of hollowed logs, these gargoyles run diagonally through the *zarè* of each dwelling unit, with one end leaning against the edge of a hole in the roof and the other coming out to the *dawolo* from a hole pierced in the wall. Instead of streaming down the walls through gutter holes in the terrace periphery, as in other architectural cases (see Chapter 1, P.6), the water is collected in the gargoyle through a hole in the terrace itself (a meter from its edges) and is led out of the house into the *dawolo*. Moreover, to prevent it from spilling out and eroding the bottom of the immediate wall, a large stone is always placed underneath the gargoyle to break the flow of the water coming out.

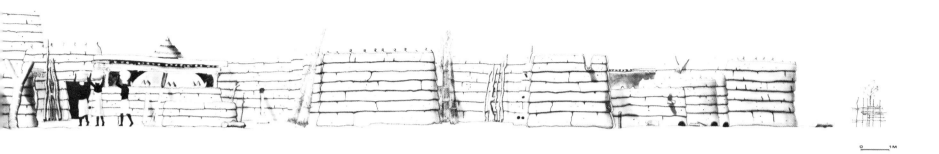

D.19. West elevation of Zingè's compound. The women in the drawing are walking toward the *zapo* entrance. The two family granaries, *viubéla* and *viu,* can be seen on its right and left sides. The notched forked trunk gives access to an upper-story unit that belongs to the previous head of the family. At night when the inhabitants sleep on the terrace roofs, they use the small adobe balls placed around the edge of the roofs to scare away hyenas or other approaching animals.

The same preoccupation is shown in the constructional courses of the walls, which taper off so that the external surface of each course projects slightly beyond the surface of the layer below. Besides interrupting the rain flow and delaying its erosive action, such a structure also visually increases the weight of the walls and contributes to their defensive aspect. It has the same function as the nested-V imprints on the walls of Lela and Nuna compounds, but does not look harmlessly decorative. This impression, however, is mainly visual, since these walls, no more resistant than those found in other types of architecture, must even slope slightly in order to maintain their stability. Their incline has given all the openings of the homestead a noticeably splayed shape (D.15, D.18, D.19).

For further stability, the walls do not generally progress in straight lines but undulate freely throughout the compound.

Instead of the Lela type of honeycomb structure, the Nuna's tight nesting of L-shaped units, or the Ko's skilled insertion of transverse strain-bearing spaces, Puguli habitations are braced by the crenellated patterns of their internal partitions. The post-and-beam system has partly freed the walls from their load-bearing function, allowing them thereby a greater flexibility of movement. The independence of walls and roofs presents further advantages. It takes into consideration the potential of a building to expand or shrink, since roofs and walls may be repaired and modified separately, and corresponds to a way of perceiving space as a dynamic element.

P.48. Sorkon. A homestead and its
environment during the dry season.

P.49. This small basket (20 centimeters wide) is used as a container for cowries, some of which are sewn in eights and fours on the outside. Cowries function as a means of expression and a medium of exchange. The numbers 8 and 4 may symbolize, as in Dogon cosmogony, the Word of the ancestors and the four cardinal points, referring thereby to the mobility of the cowries and their potential to multiply. "To have cowries," says Ogotemmêli, "is to have words."[9] This basket is also frequently seen in the Nuna area.

6 SISSALA

The Sissala land has traditionally been an area of low population density. The Centre Voltaïque de la Recherche Scientifique map[1] indicates fewer than 5 inhabitants per square kilometer, as compared to 10 to 20 or 50 to 75 in neighboring Dagari areas. This low population is thought to result from two factors: ecological pressures and historical invasions by foreign troops. Sissala villages have, in the past, been subjected to severe outbreaks of trypanosomiasis (sleeping sickness), onchocerciasis (river blindness), cerebrospinal meningitis, and influenza, endemic both to their thickly vegetated environment in the valleys of the Kulpawn, Sisili, and Kanyanbian rivers and to their compact, nucleated pattern of settlement.[2] In addition, they were devastated by the Zabarima wars during the latter part of the nineteenth century more than other Gurunsi villages. Besides death in warfare, the Zabarima conquest under Babatu's leadership (1880s), followed by the raids of the Almamy Samory Toure (a Mande leader), caused constant migration into, out of, and within the Sissala land. The results can still be seen in its segmented, heterogeneous communities, which present a wide cultural and linguistic diversity.[3]

The village of Outoulou lies east of the Kulpawn River, about 4 kilometers from the borders of what is now Ghana. Unlike other neighboring villages, which often contain two or more different ethnic groups, it is an exclusively Sissala community. Its inhabitants trace their common ancestry to a man named Manda, who immigrated three generations ago (starting from the eldest of the village) from Ouado, a village that no longer exists but that once stood between Boara and Boura. Evoking Manda's wanderings in search of a new territory, the name of the chosen site is Outoulou, which means "to move about."

D.20. Dakui's compound plan. *A:* exterior cooking area. *B:* small open court prolonging a roofed kitchen-storage space. *F:* storage space. *FE:* shrine. *G:* granaries. *H:* sleeping space. *I:* reception and resting space where women carry out their daily activities. *J:* interior cooking space. *L:* storage and sleeping space. *O:* bathing enclosure. *P:* grindstones.

0   1M

The Outoulou landscape is no more thickly vegetated than the rest of the Gurunsi environment. The abundant surface deposits of iron ore in the village vicinity may have influenced the choice of the site, since twelve blacksmithing hearths can be counted in a total of twelve compounds. Breaking away from the tight, nucleated pattern of settlement often attributed to the Sissala's need for defense and to Islamic influence,[4] these compounds are erected on the slopes of a wide depression and dispersed in a radius of 450 meters. In the bed of the depression, the villagers have sunk a well that serves the entire community but fails, during the dry season, to supply them with the amount of water needed. Thus, depending on the volume of its content, the well acts as a locus for friendly or hostile interaction among the women. Water shortage often compels them to walk several kilometers from the village each day to fill their jars. It also accounts for the generally run-down aspect of the dwellings, whose exterior wall coatings lack maintenance.

Dakui's compound is among the four oldest compounds of the village, which stand only about 50 meters away from each other and define through their limits a communal meeting area populated with large, mature trees (P.51). Upon approaching the homestead, the observer is first met by two low adobe shelters. Equipped with flat roofs supported by wooden posts and beams, and entirely open on one side, these dark shelters serve several purposes. They are used as goat pens at night, but their lighted entrance areas also provide the men with a shaded place to rest and receive their visitors during the day.

Once past the two shelters, the observer walks up a passageway that leads to two entrances, one on each side. Each entrance gives access to a separate part of the compound, defined

P.50. Outoulou. A compound interior court.

by low demarcating walls. The east part, which comprises most of the dwelling units, is occupied by several male agnates, including Dakui, and their wives and children. The west part lodges only the household of Dakui's nephew (D.43). The splitting of the compound does not, however, reflect a dissension within the joint family, but only a division of labor. The residents of each part form different farming groups which store their grain apart but readily share it among all members of the compound in time of shortage.

Progressing into the compound, the observer notices at first sight two features that seem peculiar to Sissala buildings. The long court defined by the dwelling units looks like those encountered elsewhere. It does not meander as in the case of Pouni, nor is it interrupted in its movement by the irregular protrusion of covered spaces as in the Ko's habitations. It fol-

lows, rather, a relatively straight course, hence its resemblance to a wide alley or village street (P.50, P.51).[5] Often, while walking along the court, the observer has a fleeting impression of being outside the compound. This feeling is further enhanced by the presence of walls whose vertical relief gives them the aspect of tall fortifications erected to shield the inhabitants of a town or city from external attacks.

The row of buttressing columns by which walls deviate from a flat front is indeed one of the features that catches the eye most in Sissala compounds. Broadest at the bottom, these engaged columns taper toward the top, favoring thereby an upward reading of their movement. The vertical rise has the effect of making the walls look higher than they really are. To prolong this emphasis on the upright further still, the columns do not always end at the same height as the walls (P.50), but

115

P.51. The shade of the large trees standing in between the four oldest compounds of the village provides a ground for social interaction.

often terminate in pinnacles that extend well above (over 50 centimeters) the roof parapet (P.54, P.50). Besides fortifying the buttresses, the pinnacles also serve the defensive purpose of a battlement. The walls thus crenellated are reminiscent of the fortifications that surrounded the Sissala villages Yoro (c. 1875) and Sati (c. 1880–1885) during the Zabarima wars. Erected under the leadership of two Sissala chiefs, Issaka and Moussa Kadio, for prohibitive and defensive purposes,[6] these adobe brick walls measure around 3 meters high. They start at the bottom with a thickness of 1.5 meters and taper to 60 centimeters on the top.

Besides the need for fortifications, the presence of the columns raises a few additional questions. Used to reinforce load-bearing walls, these columns as buttresses may have resulted from the problem of horizontal thrust introduced by flat roofs.

They are indeed, as in Dakui's example, evenly distributed and located consistently at structurally important places like corners and wall junctions.[7] This technique, not necessary in round-house constructions or those built with a post-and-beam system, cannot, however, satisfactorily account for the choice of buttressing columns. Dwelling units built at a more recent date have done away with this feature by simply increasing the thickness of their walls, while some older units resort to both the post-and-beam and buttress systems (southeast on D.20). Function thus relates to form but cannot fully determine it.

Looking at the more recent empty walls that will undoubtedly supplant the older column style in Sissala compounds, one becomes strongly aware of the psychological and spiritual meanings shapes convey. A blank wall whose surface is devoid of depth, movement, and direction appears strangely ordinary,

116

inoffensive, and insubstantial. It does not wish to stand out and lacks perceptual forces to establish its solidity. In a way, it fails to fully assume its role as an obstacle and shield. Such a role is naturally no longer required, since the buttressing columns as a defensive feature answered only the inhabitant's need for protection in the past. As a contribution to the dynamics of a wall, however, they still express the collectivity's perception of shape and space.

The long vista of tapering columns, created by the alignment of several dwelling units in a court (P.50), evokes the image of a procession and may respond, through its theme of vertical rising, to the inhabitants' spiritual aspirations. The motif of vertical and horizontal crenellation immediately recalls Muslim Dyula architecture,[8] or what is widely known as the Sudanese style that characterizes the ancient mosques of West Africa and

P.52. Adobe granary in Dakui's compound.

117

P.53. The administrative chief of the village.

pervades, for example, the familiar Djenné and Mopti (Mali) house façades. Pinnacles and engaged buttresses, which form the substance of this style, are said to have found their origins in the conical earthen pillars commonly found in the Voltaic and Upper Niger basins of West Africa. Standing singly, in pairs, or clustered in great numbers, the pillars possess a wide range of symbolic values—such as patrilineal continuity or family viability—and often serve to spiritually protect a consecrated site.[9]

In the evolution of the building, the southwest part is the oldest of Dakui's compound. Here, the constructions still resort to the system of buttresses and load-bearing walls (the few wooden posts have been added at a most recent date), although little remains of the deteriorated pinnacles. The dwelling interiors are better preserved and have conspicuous rows of en-

P.54. Southeast of Dakui's compound. A partly enclosed veranda on the right leads to an open court defined by a wall raised above eye level.

P.55. A veranda-like space whose wall is punctured with a series of four doorways. The sitting area is lighted while the grindstone remains in the dimmer end of the room.

gaged columns similar to those used by the Lela and Nuna to establish the inner wall rhythms. The woman's unit has a layout theme that often recurs in Sissala compounds. It is composed of three main spaces: a veranda-like reception area (I in D.20) preceding both a sleeping-storage (L or H) and a kitchen-storage room (B or J).

The veranda-like space is a feature frequently found in villages that have undergone strong Islamic influence. The covered open spaces in the Nuna case study of Pouni, for example, may be seen as a variation of the same feature. It is used in Dakui's compound as a sitting and resting area. Partially open on one side or equipped with two doorways (see I in D.20), it also provides women with a well-ventilated and semi-private place to perform their daily work. It is worth noting here that veranda façades punctured with a series of three or four door-

ways are not uncommon (P.55). This alternation of solid supporting columns with empty openings constitutes another attempt to relieve walls of flatness and inertness. It denotes above all the significance given, in this architecture, to columns and their expressive potential.

Several other features present similarities with Nuna architecture, and more particularly with the Islamized architecture of Pouni. One of them is the small, narrow open court (B southwest in D.20) that prolongs one end of the kitchen-storage room. It somewhat recalls the *dawolo* among the Puguli but is barely large enough to serve as a bathing place and to accommodate an open cooking area. Marked off from the rest of the room by a small adobe edge that prevents water from running onto the inside floor, it can be reached only by crossing this room. The other features are the communal grindstones built

120

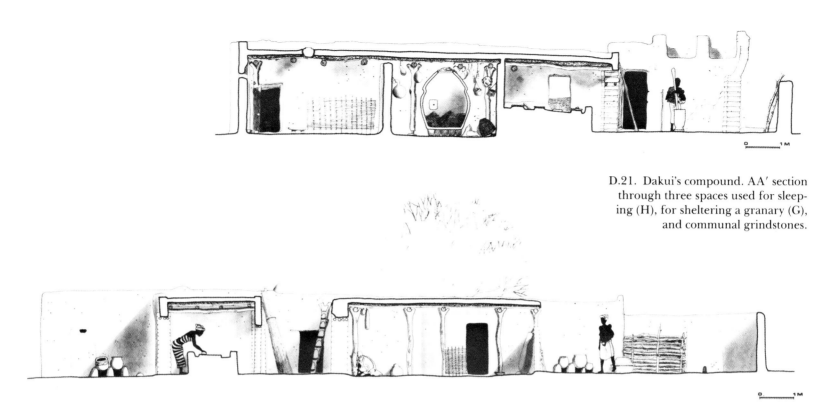

D.21. Dakui's compound. AA' section through three spaces used for sleeping (H), for sheltering a granary (G), and communal grindstones.

D.22. Dakui's compound. BB' section through the grindstones' shelter and a veranda-like space (I) where women carry out their daily activities.

in a roofed, partly enclosed area (southeast in D.20; *nemudiè* in D.8) and the granaries.

Three main types of granary exist in Sissala compounds, besides the women's small individual type. The first, kept outdoors, is made of woven thatch with an inner adobe coating like that of the Nuna and erected on a wooden structure (west in D.19, P.15). The second, located in a roofed storage space (P.52, D.21, G in D.20), is molded in adobe and resembles the type encountered in a Nuna *bobuin* (D.9, D.8), although the conception of a self-contained space made to shelter a grain store recalls Puguli design. The third is peculiarly built into the wall with adobe bricks. It stands out like a large square-bottomed pillar that tapers to a rounded top and is covered by a conical grass lid.

Except for the two young households in the northwest, all the men in Dakui's compound live apart from their wives (D.43). Their dwelling units are composed of either a single room or two separate spaces for sleeping and storage (H and F in D.20). The newer the units, the straighter their walls and the less intricate their layout. The difference between the southern and northern parts of the compound is drastic (D.20). Instead of weaving into each other in a tight, meandering pattern like those in the south, the newer units of the north form three independent square and rectangular blocks related to each other only by low connecting walls. The three units belonging to Dakui's three sons and their families, in the northwest section, further detach themselves from the rest of the compound by orienting their doorways so as to look out onto a common court and create a cluster apart.

Some villagers of Outoulou affirm that the Sissala used to

121

P.56. Sissala woman and child.

P.57. Locust-bean pods *(Parkia biglob-osa)* (on the left), whose decoction serves to waterproof and reinforce the roof and floor surfaces. Their yellow pulp may be eaten naturally or mixed with water once it is pounded into flour. Their black seeds (in the calabash) are used as condiments *(sumbara)* in the preparation of sauces.

build their houses like the Dagari, with the puddled-mud technique. Nowadays, the adobe courses have been replaced by rows of bricks. Obtained, as in Pouni, from a mixture of puddled mud and laterite gravel, and molded in wooden frames, these sun-dried bricks are usually erected on a foundation trench about 40 centimeters deep. The use of bricks presents a drawback, however, when compared to the technique of superimposing hand-shaped adobe layers. A careful look at the dwellings in the village will not fail to discover the numerous cracks developing in their walls, some of them already splitting along the entire height. Such a defect comes from the fact that when the brick construction settles, the wall does not form a uniform whole and minor cracks will gradually extend along the vertical joints of the bricks. Furthermore, the heterogeneity of the wall surface (made up of two distinct elements, brick and

adobe mortar) is not conducive to a strong adhesion of the final coating as is the wet clayey soil. Both these factors account for the easy infiltration of rainwater, the rapid loosening of the coating, and, finally, the active erosion of the wall.

7 WESTERN KASSENA

On Semi-sunken Dwellings

The Kassena are thought to have formed a single people with the Nuna. A famine in the remote past would account for the split in the group and the creation of the Kassena faction. This faction would have separated itself from the Nuna to settle down further east.[1] Among them one distinguishes the Kassena of the west, also called the Fra, Kassuna-Fra, or Kassonfra, from the Kassena of the east, also known as the Kasm, Kassuna-Bura, or Kassonbura. Both speak dialects of the same language but differ significantly in their social organization.[2]

Situated at the boundary of the Nuna and the Kassena lands, Koumbili[3] was one of the rare Gurunsi villages to be spared during the Zabarima conquest, thanks to the *mogho-naba*'s intervention in its favor. Such a generous gesture from the *mogho-naba,* or supreme chief of the Mossi, resulted from the fact that the founder of Koumbili was a Mossi. According to local ac-

counts, this man, named Asanga, came from Ouagadougou on horseback, accompanied by another man from Tiébélé (one of the six districts presently occupied by the Kassena in Upper Volta, the others being Kampala, Koumbili, Guiara, Pô, and Sia). He first stopped in Bassan, 6 kilometers from the present site of Koumbili, where he stayed as the only Mossi among Gurunsi villagers. Water scarcity in the area compelled him to lead his horse to a caiman pond every morning, near which he finally decided to settle down. He was later followed by a few Kassena who admired his bravery and thus was founded the village of Koumbili.

Another version relates the founding of Koumbili to a Mossi who came from Loumbila with his two brothers, hence the term Koumbili, which is possibly a distortion of the name of the original village. The first brother established his home in Kassougou, among the Nuna, the second in Koumbili, among the Kassonfra, and the third in Tiébélé, among the Kassonbura.[4]

The name Koumbili can, however, be traced to yet another source. Luru, the present chief of the village of Kolo (an example of a Kassena house presented in the next chapter was selected in this village), relates that Kolo originally stood where Tiébélé is now and bore the name of its founding ancestor, Koumbouli, which means "to have grown from the earth." Coming from Loumbila or Lombila (northeast of Ouagadougou), a man named Patũengomi and his wife Poko had asked Koumbouli for lodging and protection in the past. Later on, surpassing Koumbouli in number of offspring, Patũengomi moved out and erected his own compound. During a Kassena annual feast, a fight broke out between Koumbouli and Patũengomi, who had decided to lead the dance

(mwanu) on the grounds that his family was larger and thus more important. The contest for superiority grew worse and became an open war in which Koumbouli was killed after three years of battle aided by his brother's men, or the village of Panda. Patũengomi, who was supported by Mossi troops, took over the chieftainship of the village and forced Koumbouli's eldest sons, Kolforo and Akolo, to settle down further north.

It did not, however, take Patũengomi long to realize that "the land of the tribe never belonged to the Chief."[5] He then sought cooperation from Akolo, whose knowledge of rituals and influence in religious matters were indispensable to the well-being of his (Patũengomi's) village. The foreign territorial ruler thus recognized the ritual leadership of the autochthonous inhabitants whose manners and customs he had adopted. Akolo's son, Katoni, was nominated chief of Kolo after his father's death; he was the ancestor, nine generations ago, of the present ruling family. The inhabitants of Kolo continue nowadays to assume their priestly functions as custodians of the earth *(tegatu)*, of both Kolo and Tiébélé.[6]

This historical account of Kolo cannot fully explain the origin of the name Koumbili. It does, however, confirm the strong ties between these villages and shed light on the duality of an organization that often sets "invaders"—who hold political power—against "natives"—who retain religious power, but also makes their mutual cooperation indispensable. This satisfactory blend of the old and the new[7] may ultimately provide a more comprehensible explanation of the possible naming of a Mossi-founded village after an autochthonous ancient ancestor.

Formerly compact and surrounded by a high wall, Koumbili is now divided into four quarters and composed of a total of

fifteen compounds dispersed in a radius of 250 meters. As in other villages, the shade of a large, mature tree situated 20 meters from the administrative chief's compound serves as the men's meeting place and a locus of communal interaction.

Spreading over a length of 60 meters and a width of 20 meters, the administrative chief's compound (P.58) presents a striking example of a cultural blend. A historic building, it was described by Binger in his travel notes of 1888.[8] The 4-meter wall encompassing the compound that Binger mentioned no longer exists, but the overall structure remains very much the same. It consists of an agglomeration of dwelling units whose typical composition is presented here through the case study of Atiga's independent homestead (D.23). Each unit comprises several flat-roof constructions topped by one or two cylindrical spaces with conical thatched roofs. Characteristic of these flat-

P.58. Koumbili. The administrative chief's compound. The entrance to the women's semi-sunken dwelling units may be seen on the left with two earthen pillars on top of its terrace roof.

roof constructions is their location halfway below the ground. They are indeed built with floors 50 to 80 centimeters below ground level, and their occupants communicate with each other throughout the compound, either by an underground system of intricately meandering corridors or by means of terrace roofs.

These dwellings stand as rare examples of semi-sunken housing still inhabited in this area nowadays. The lowering of the inside floor level is, as we have mentioned, common practice among the Gurunsi, and more particularly among the Lela, Nuna, Puguli, Kassena, and Nankani. The case of Koumbili appears, however, far more emphatic, since the floor depression is deep enough so that the flat-roof constructions are almost halfway below ground level. This type of semi-sunken habitation has been interpreted as a transition between the semi-underground dwelling (entirely sunk into the ground and visible only through its flat wooden roof coated with adobe and punctured with a narrow opening that gives access to the inside) and the dwelling built on the ground.[9]

According to the village elders, the sunken floor serves a practical defensive purpose. From the exterior, walls of houses throughout the village bear, indeed, knee-high loopholes (15 centimeters wide) that enable a person inside to look out and shoot while making it almost impossible for the invader to send an arrow back and hit the target from a standing position. Furthermore, the dimness of the interiors and their labyrinthine spaces give the inhabitants an advantage over their adversaries, who, unfamiliar with the place and unable to see when rushing in from the outside, cannot pursue them without taking high risks. Abrupt transition of light and nonlinearity of space as defensive principles appear frequently in Gurunsi architecture, especially in Puguli homesteads, which, according to our analysis, seem closest to semi-sunken inhabitations.

Semi-sunken habitations form an elaborate system of defense which, in the past, ran through the entirety of a compact village. Binger, visiting the village of Diabéré or Zabéré in 1888, described it as being composed of "an ordinary village and an underground village." Access to this underground village, he wrote, was gained through the only visible opening, near the chief's dwelling, the other openings being so well disguised that one might live on the first floor without realizing their existence. Subterranean communication throughout the village was feasible. While speculating on the difficulty of laying siege to such a village, Binger mentioned the possibility of openings that led out to the country. In another village, Ladio, Binger was received by the chief in a large basement room which was so dim that it was a long while before he became aware of the presence of others around him. Even after ten minutes, during which he felt ill at ease, he could discern nothing of the chief but his silhouette.[10] Semi-underground habitations among the Tyefo (living in the circle of Banfora, southwest of Upper Volta) have also been said to serve an effectively defensive purpose: all who took refuge in them during Samory's raid escaped the massacre.[11]

In all villages where semi-underground and/or semi-sunken dwellings still exist along with constructions on the ground, the former types consistently appear to be the older styles of housing. The semi-underground type has been recorded in villages occupied by the Tyefo (Tanga) and the Nyonyose (in the circle of Ziniare, northeast of Ouagadougou),[12] while both the semi-

P.59. The administrative chief's compound.

underground and semi-sunken types exist among the Bobo-Fing (in Bobo-Dioulasso, Koroma, Kotédougou, Koumi, Bambalawakoro, Silenkoro)[13] and the Gurunsi (among the Nuna in Diabéré and Ladio, and among the Mossi's "Gurunsi slaves" in Bussansi and the Ouagadougou area).[14] It is worth noting that the above peoples are the older inhabitants of the region, those whom the Mossi classify among the *tengbisi*, "children of the earth" or "autochthons," hence the hypothesis of the antiquity of flat-roof constructions and the newness of conical thatch-roof dwellings (which, in the case of Koumbili, probably derive from Mossi influence). Some outsiders, like Binger, go as far as comparing semi-underground habitations with caves and suggesting that the inhabitants' ancestors were cave dwellers. Although describing these dwellings as "nothing more than caves," Binger was nonetheless aware of the improb-

ability of this loose supposition. He then preferred to conclude that "all these peoples must have dug holes to dwell in before they built huts," since the Mande, who were cave dwellers, had only one verb, *élé*, in their language to express "open, lift up, climb, or rise," and called a door, a hole or orifice, *da*, which also meant "mouth."[15]

Semi-underground dwellings are unlikely to be descended from caves, for besides lack of proof concerning their inhabitants' troglodyte past, they represent an original style of construction. Technical knowledge required to build this type of habitation is, indeed, as significant as that needed for thatch-roof cylindrical constructions on the ground. There is a more revealing interpretation of this older mode of housing. G. Le Moal notices, for example, that while semi-underground dwellings are uninhabited nowadays (in some villages they are only

131

used during the day by basket makers, who work better in their cool and humid interiors), most semi-sunken constructions still standing turn out to be either the first dwelling of the village-founding ancestor (the *wasa* of Tirico among the Bobo-Fing) or temples (in the Lobi area, among the Koulango-Loron).[16] As the following myths will show, this observation confirms the prominent part that religious and mythical values play in the location and shaping of habitations.

The earth as the spirit of fecundity for both the family and the land is a widely known, recurring theme in African mythologies; it is often referred to as a living thing whose presence pervades every single aspect of daily life. The earth is, thus, not just a piece of land to live on, but a being to live with or a sacred mother's womb to live in. The rituals and mythology of the Bobo (the Gurunsi's western neighbors) abound with references to the close relationship between man, woman, and the earth. In order to obtain peace and health for his family and plentiful crops, for example, a farmer speaks to Nyiulé (the earth or the bush) and makes sacrifices, thanking Her (or Him) for what She has already given and promising Her other sacrifices for what She will offer in the future. Another powerful deity in Bobo myths is Kani. Kani, to whom women owe their fecundity and men their abundant grain, lives in a hole dug in the ground. The villagers' offspring are said to have come out of Kani's dwelling, and no hunter or farmer is allowed to enter "Kani's holes" to kill porcupines, nor can he smoke burrows to drive out game for fear that one of them might be Kani's.[17]

A Bobo story which is said to have been eyewitnessed relates how a hunter named Dindiko discovered and became friends with the inhabitants of a termite hill by trying to smoke a hole in it. These inhabitants, who seemed to be family members of a certain man, were described as very ordinary people. They offered Dindiko hot millet cakes and kept him in their dwelling for three days, beneath the termite hill. In return for their hospitality, Dindiko occasionally shared the game he shot and kept their relationship secret. The orifice of the hole was closed again by the man living in it after each visit from Dindiko. Dindiko's son, who later learned of the secret and betrayed it to the villagers, died three days after he let the words leak out. As it unfolds, the story reveals the termite-hill inhabitants' acute knowledge of spiritual and religious matters and refers to the man living there as the "old priest."[18]

The above accounts are only two examples among many that bring out the sacredness of dwellings in the earth and the wis-dom attributed to its inhabitants. The mythical ancestor of the *tengbisi* ("children of the earth") is, for example, named Tenghin-Pusumdé. This appellation, which contains the verb *pusi,* "to pierce and emerge to the surface," indicates that the ancestor came out from an opening in the earth. The Nyonyose also have several myths of origin in which their ancestors, who descended from the sky, are known to have sunk into the earth afterward. This is the case for the Guisga-Pandé pair, ancestors of the Nyonyose of Boinsa, and for Suti, an ancestor of the Ouagadougou area, whose name is believed to derive from the term *sudi,* meaning "to sink into the ground."[19]

These myths present obvious analogies with the Dogon myth of creation. One may briefly recall here that the Nommo Pair, God's creation and essence, were conceived in the womb of the earth, their mother, and taken back to Heaven, where they

133

D.23. Koumbili. First- and second-floor plan of Atiga's homestead. *Buntugu:* goat pen. *Chietugu:* chicken coop. *Digapóro:* storage and sleeping space where a woman receives her husband and close female friends. *Digayugu:* storage and cooking space, the "head of the house" and most intimate realm of a woman. *Duwaga:* outdoor unroofed cooking area. *Duwogo:* packed-earth court. *Gëri:* grindstone. *Kara:* semi-public sphere that surrounds the homestead and is delimited by the outside granaries *(pulu)*. *Napóro:* interior space for daily work and reception. *Nayugu:* terrace. *Pisildiga:* a thatch-roofed room, here used for drying and smoking fish. *Pisili:* a man's space. *Poñ:* millet-stalk-roofed shelter used by the senior man or head of the family to rest and receive visitors. *Püna:* bathing enclosure. *Tchapoè:* nesting holes for hens. *Zira:* covered entrance to the homestead.

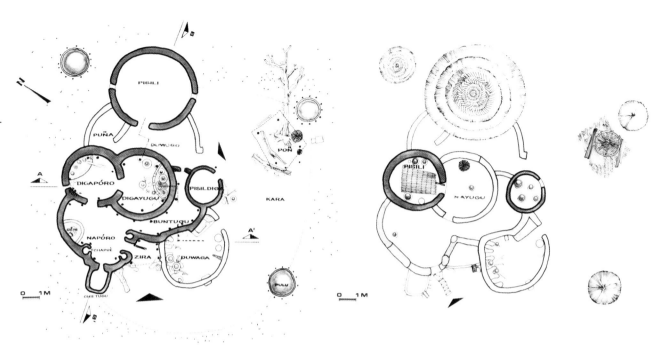

received their father's instructions. In order to improve human conditions, the Pair came down to earth and entered the anthill (their mother's sexual organ), where, taking the places of the male and female elements ("her womb became part of the womb of the earth"), they proceeded to the work of regeneration. Men, at that time, had no knowledge of death, and the eight ancestors born from the first human couple lived on indefinitely, until the eldest decided to liberate himself from his earthly condition, and after putting his feet into the opening of the anthill, slowly sank into the earth's womb. There

the ancestor was taken in charge by the regenerating Pair. The male Nommo led him into the depths of the earth, where, in the waters of the womb of his partner, he curled himself up like a foetus and shrank to germinal form, and acquired the quality of water, the seed of God and the essence of the two Spirits . . . Thus perfected by water and words, the new Spirit was expelled and went up to Heaven.[20]

"Men . . . lived in holes dug in the level of soil like the lairs of animals" until the time of the ancestor's descent into the anthill, the shape of which they then noticed and took as a model in the transformation of their underground dwellings.[21]

To descend into the earth is to be regenerated. The dwelling in the ground is, therefore, the place which allows the inhabitants to come into contact with spiritual forces and renew themselves. It expresses the dynamics of retreat and is a simple, concrete form of the widespread womb symbolism attached to houses. From this life-giving home, one cannot break away without knowing that sooner or later one is bound to come back. Thus, among the Nuna, a dead person is said to "have returned." The Gurunsi family vault, for example, is a form of underground dwelling, the place where family members withdraw after death and live in communion with the mother earth

Diagram 13. Principle of access in a semi-sunken dwelling.

spirit. It is sunk in the form of a cylindrical shaft (sometimes this vertical cylinder, 4 meters high, intersects at mid-height with a horizontal transverse gallery, less than a meter long on each side) that widens into a conical space where the dead lies.[22]

Retaining little of the highly defensive character often attributed to semi-underground dwellings, the inhabited semi-sunken constructions, which stand half—or two thirds, as in some other villages—below ground level, present, above all, formal evidence of the cultural ideology of built form. The lowering of the interior floor reflects the inhabitants' conception of the house and may be interpreted as a residual desire to remain in intimate contact with mother earth's spirits. Nowadays, these basement spaces are occupied by women, upon whom the guardianship of traditions most often devolves. In Koumbili and in other nearby villages (Guiaro, for example)

where such architecture still exists, the men erect their rooms on the first floor, above the sleeping rooms of their wives.

Although representative of what is, in larger compounds, a dwelling unit, Atiga's homestead presents a slight change. Since the death of Atiga's father, the basement spaces which belonged to Atiga's mother are occupied by his wife and daughter, while the elder woman moves to her husband's *pisili,* or sleeping room, on the first floor. As for Atiga, he has constructed, on the ground and behind his parents' dwelling, his own *pisili,* which he shares with his son (D.44). The evolution of the homestead goes, thus, through a shift of occupancy and a change of modes of access into interior spaces. Instead of climbing up (with a notched tree trunk) or stepping down into a room, one just walks into Atiga's *pisili,* a construction which appears strangely rootless next to the older building.

135

D.24. AA′ section, southwest elevation, and BB′ section of Atiga's homestead.

0   1M

0   1M

0   1M

The man's first-floor *pisili* (meaning "grass roof") is usually a circular space covered with a conical thatched roof and built on top of his wife's *digapóro* as a prolongation of her space. The *pisili* opens onto the *nayugu* (*na:* "water"; *yugu:* "head"), or terrace area, delimited by low parapets that are a continuation of the perimeter walls of the *digayugu* below. Access to the lower floor, from the *pisili,* is gained from the exterior by means of a notched tree trunk which is always placed next to the *zira* (D.23, D.24, P.61). Preceding the interior space that forms a woman's dwelling unit, the *zira* serves as a small transitional realm. Its terrace roof prevents rainwater from running into the dwelling, while its floor slopes slightly toward the *napóro* doorway to allow a smooth descent into the interior. In order to reach it from the outside, a person must bend forward to pass underneath the roof, a requirement that emphasizes the act of entering through a change of body position. This bent position is kept while one progresses inside the *zira,* so that one does not stand up until one goes through the *napóro* doorway and walks down a steep entrance slope.

In Atiga's homestead (D.23), the *napóro* doorway is framed on each side by an earthen pillar. These two pillars (discussed in the case study of Outoulou), frequently encountered in Kassena and Nankani compounds, either on the *zira* roof (P.58), on the sides of *napóro* entrances (P.62), or in internal open courts, are each pierced with a hole, thereby serving also as a laying place for hens (D.24, Section BB′). The *napóro* is the space where a woman carries out her daily work and where the family shrine often stands. It usually contains a grindstone *(gëri)* and communicates with both the goat pen *(buntugu)* and the chicken coop *(chietugu).* Visitors coming by for a short while to chat or to

P.60. A cooking area in a *digayugu*.
Pots are always stored in piles on
carved-in adobe shelves, each pile lying on an earthen vessel as seen on
the right.

wait for the rain to stop are received in this *napóro*, which is also
the place a woman chooses to deliver her child. Functioning
somewhat as an "antechamber," the *napóro* leads to two cleanly
swept and more personal spaces: the *digapóro* and the *digayugu*.
A woman sleeps, stores her belongings, and receives her husband or close female friends in the *digapóro*. She keeps her daily
pots and prepares the meals in the *digayugu*, where her cooking
fireplace is installed. *Digayugu* means "head of the house" (*diga:*
"house" or "dwelling space"; *yugu:* "head"—hence the image of
the head receiving rainwater in the word *nayugu*, or terrace
above the *digayugu*). The space is thus named because, like all
interior kitchens of Gurunsi homesteads, it constitutes the
heart of the dwelling and the starting point for the building of a
home.[23] Considered to be a woman's most intimate realm (this is

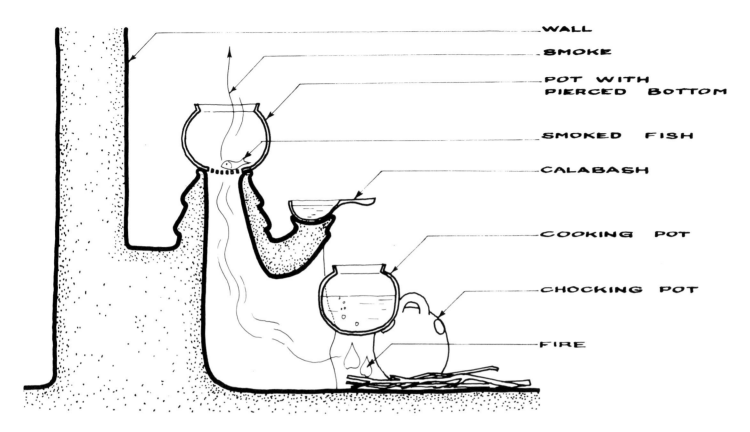

WALL

SMOKE

POT WITH
PIERCED BOTTOM

SMOKED FISH

CALABASH

COOKING POT

CHOCKING POT

FIRE

Diagram 14. Section of fish-smoking
device in the *digayugu*.

made even more manifest in P.60, where the cooking area contains a relief molded in the shape of a female sexual organ, serving as support for the cooking pot), the *digayugu* is the place where she would retreat for two days after childbirth.

Adjacent to these three main spaces, the *napóro, digapóro,* and *digayugu,* are the *duwaga* and the *pisildiga,* accessible only from the exterior in Atiga's homestead (D.23). This arrangement appears awkward at first, since the openings of both spaces are oriented away from the *zira,* and Atiga's wife has to pass around these spaces to reach them. Careful observation reveals, however, that the homestead stands next to a village path running south-north on its west side. An opening of the *duwaga,* or walled exterior cooking area, to the west or south would thus mean too much exposure to the passerby's view. Since his father's death, Atiga has also transferred the older man's *poh,*

or reception shelter, from in front of the west entrance (or about 5 meters away from the *zira* entrance) to in front of the southeast access that leads to his own *pisili.* It seems comprehensible, then, that Atiga would prefer to have his wife's *duwaga* and *pisildiga,* a thatch-roofed, high-ceilinged room used for drying and smoking fish, look out onto his *poh.*

The *poh* (D.23) is a light, millet-stalk-roofed structure similar to that found among the Lela, Nuna *(pon),* Nankani *(pohga),* and Kusasi *(paa).* Its shade provides, as mentioned, the men, or more particularly the senior man, with a well-ventilated place to rest, to oversee both his family members' main activities and the homestead's environment, and to receive his visitors. Thus, when the chief of the village wishes to talk to a man, for example, he will send word to the man saying he will come and sit in the man's *poh.* The *poh* is always situated so as to maintain visual

139

P.61. Atiga's homestead and its entrance to the *zira*.

contact with the homestead entrance, and within the limits of the *kara*.

The *kara* (pl.: *kare,*), meaning "farm," "field of the bush," or "to walk," may be interpreted as the semi-public sphere that surrounds each homestead (dotted lines in D.23). Although not physically expressed by fences, walls, or stones, for example, its boundaries may be detected through several observances by the inhabitants. Outside granaries *(pulu)* should, for example, be placed around the *kara*, while new dwellings erected by a senior man's sons, when they get married and form households apart, may be located both inside and around it. The earth needed for house construction and maintenance should also be taken from outside the boundary of the *kara*. What stand as constants inside it, finally, are the *poħ*, the tree(s) (thus, trees and granaries often serve to identify the *kara* of a compound), and a fairly

clean zone around the homestead where visitors will sit when they are not closely related to the family and come in great numbers, such as for a funeral.

Atiga's homestead is a striking example of architecture in which space is designed so as to materialize the conventional formulas of social etiquette. Thus, the emphasis does not lie only in the definite use of a space—as a kitchen, a bedroom, or a living room—but also in its potential to define or act upon people's relationships. The inhabitants' acute sense of space and distance and, through this sense, the subtlety of their social interaction are reflected in the intimacy gradient that permeates the layout of their homesteads. A sequence establishing the different degrees of privateness is thus: (1) the social realms—the *kara* and the *poħ;* (2) the transitional realms—the *zira*, the *nayugu,* or terrace area above the *digayugu*, and the

duwogo, or small court, in front of Atiga's *pisili;* and (3) the personal realms—the *pisili* for men, or the *napóro* ("antechamber"), the *digapóro* (personal realm), and the *digayugu* (intimate realm) for women. With such a sequence, a villager stopping by to visit the family knows exactly where he or she will be received and how far into the homestead he or she may penetrate.

Walls in the past were built up in courses, with a method similar to that of the Puguli. They are now erected with rows of bricks whose resistance to rain erosion is increased by adding to the usual mixture of earth and fine gravel a viscous liquid obtained from the maceration of okra stems. Other useful steps are taken to further reinforce the construction. The outer wall is plastered with a blend of sand, fresh cow dung, and water collected from shea-nut-butter preparations after the butter has solidified. Then another coating of ashes mixed with this

same water is applied on top to whiten the wall, so as to reflect heat and repell ants at the same time. The inner wall, on the other hand, is covered with a mixture of sand and a fine black earth taken from a nearby pond. Once it has dried, the coating is sprinkled and sealed with a decoction of *Faidherbia* bark, a treatment which is repeated three times at one-day intervals. The roofs and floors are smeared with a thick paste of fine gravel and cow dung, then tamped smooth and finished with a decoction of locust-bean pods *(Parkia biglobosa),* which is renewed for four consecutive days to give the surfaces a luster as well as greater water resistance.

141

8 EASTERN KASSENA

The village of Tangassoko was founded by a Kassena named Nugatéré, who came from Tiébélé. Puatega, who presently fulfills the role of chief of the village and at the same time custodian of the earth, is a sixth-generation descendant of Nugatéré. His ancestors (or Nugatéré's parents), he recalls, immigrated from Mossiland, but he does not say whether they were Mossi or originally Kassena, as their descendants have remained up to the present. Tangassoko was a field that belonged to Nugatéré's father, whose large, expanding family experienced a land shortage in Tiébélé. Nugatéré came first to settle down on the site; he was joined afterward by three Kassena householders, Burura, Vorobié, and Vepiébié, whom he sheltered in his compound. The latter's growing families soon compelled them to move out and build their homesteads elsewhere, forming thereby the first quarters of Tangassoko.

Around 1890, shortly after it was founded, the village was attacked and sacked by the Zabarima, whose raids began during Nugatéré's time and ended only with French intervention during the chieftainship of Kwarsé, Nugatéré's grandson and second successor. Puatega relates further that Tangassoko was known for its strong resistance not only against the Zabarima but also against the French, who "succeeded in stopping tribal wars but wanted to impose their order in land matters." "They have only won," he concludes, "because of the strong arms they possessed."

The compounds in Tangassoko are dispersed over a length of 5 kilometers and width of 2 kilometers. The irregular intervals between the compounds, 50 to 400 meters apart, make it very difficult to perceive the layout of the village from the ground. Only an aerial view can confirm its loose grouping into

142

Diagram 15. Fields of vision from the peripheral courts *(kuñkolo)* and from inside the dwellings. Door entrances of women's dwellings can only be perceived by visitors once they have penetrated far enough into the compound to be subjected to a circular field of vision.

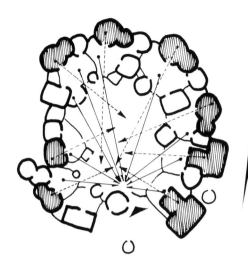

D.25. Tangassoko. Plan of Tanga's compound. *DIBU:* a man's storage space. *DIGA:* a woman's space. *DJUNA SONGO:* the spirits' home, usually preceding the compound entrance. *Djan:* ancestral shrine. *Mintchiopo:* access to the compound facing west. *DIYU:* interior cooking space. *DRA:* a man's sleeping space. *KALGUNGU:* outdoor cooking space covered with millet stalks. *KUÑKOLO:* packed-earth court enclosed by a wall. *Luguri:* built-in nesting boxes for domestic fowl. *NABA:* large internal court serving also as cattle kraal. *Tula:* outdoor adobe granaries. *NAÑKONGO:* space where the cattle keeper sleeps at night. *NAPÓRO:* roofed space open on one side, used for the preparation of guinea-corn beer or functioning as an "antechamber" that precedes the *diga. POÑ:* shelter where the senior man rests and receives his visitors during the day. *TUGU:* covered goat pens. *VRADIGA:* guest room.

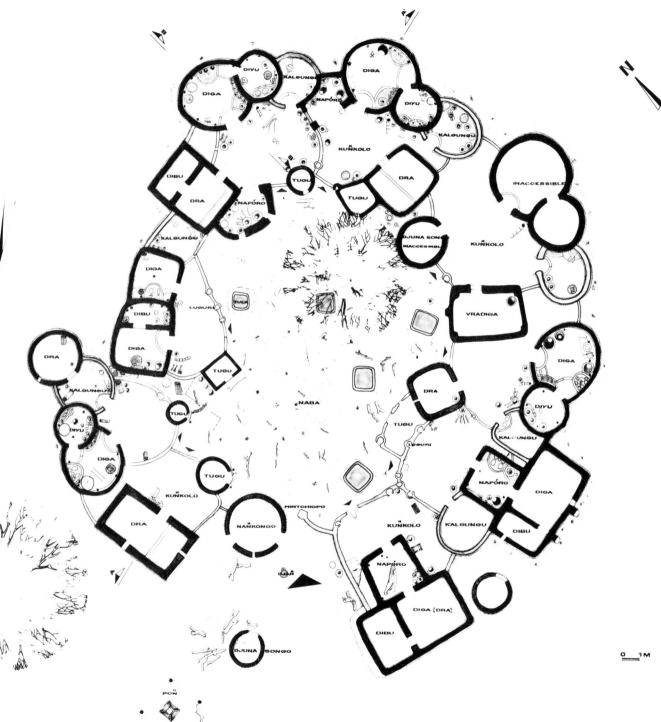

eleven quarters, each composed of ten to thirty-five homesteads that are named after the first men who settled down in the different parts of the locality. Several wells are spread along a depression that runs the length of the village. The low variation of the water-table level accounts for the continuous maintenance of the buildings and the tending of small enclosed gardens during the dry season. Due to the fertility of the soil and the abundance of water, the village does not suffer from rural depopulation as almost all other villages do. Most young men who emigrate to Ghana usually come back after two years to establish their home here indefinitely.

The general layout of Tanga's compound (D.25) resembles Lela architecture in many respects. Access into the homestead is gained through a unique entrance, or *mintchiopo,* which is preceded by: first, the *poh,* or the senior man's reception shel-

ter; second, the *djuna songo,* or the spirits' home (see also the *zongo* among the Nankani), a circular construction oriented so as to look toward the inside of the compound; third, a *djan,* or male ancestral shrine; and fourth, the *nahkongo,* or room pierced by two doorways on opposite sides, in which the cattle keeper sleeps at night. The path leading to the entrance lies thus under several guardianships, and a person wishing to penetrate inside goes through these successive steps, acknowledging each guardian's (dead or living) presence before being admitted in.

Once through the entrance, one steps into a wide, open court which, as in the Lela compound, is surrounded by a peripheral ring of dwelling units. Serving as a cattle kraal (*naba*) and a circulation space, the court is also populated with large adobe granaries (*tula*) whose peculiar shapes appear as if modeled after the ancestral pillars so often encountered at the entrances or on the roofs of dwellings. Square at the base with curved sides that taper up to a rounded top, they are erected on log trestles and protected by conical grass lids. At the periphery of the *naba* stands a first irregular row of low circular and square flat-roof constructions that serve as goat pens *(tugu)* and open only into the *naba* itself. These protruding constructions, added to the scenery of dispersed voluminous granaries, offer an interplay of volumes that impedes the sight and fragmentizes one's perception of space, making it difficult for a newcomer to apprehend the compound in its totality. This principle, applied with differing degrees of intensity among the Lela and Nuna, seems most efficient as a means to delay visual access into the dwelling units.

The concern for protection from too great exposure is further expressed in the erection of walls a meter high that connect the goat pens to the dwelling units and define their private courts, or *kuħkolo*. Access to each *kuħkolo* is gained through a dip in the wall *(manchoħoni,* D.26) over which one strides, aided by a large stone that functions as a step. All animals remain thus in the *naba*, except for domestic fowl, whose nesting boxes *(luguri)* are built in the inner wall of the *kuħkolo*. As a transitional realm and a locus of interaction, the *kuħkolo* (P.67) is used for a large array of activities, from daily household chores and basketry or mat weaving to funeral dances and social gatherings. Bearing, on a smaller scale, the same distributive function as the *naba*, it also constitutes a necessary link to the various spaces that form the totality of each dwelling unit. From the *kuħkolo* one may therefore reach the terrace roof, the man's *dra,* and the woman's *napóro, kalgungu,* and *diga.*

145

D.26. BB′ section of Tanga's compound. The features that characterize a woman's *diga* are shown here, from left to right: the woman's adobe grain bin, or *zuin;* the grinding platform above which are hung a few calabashes; the low wall facing the entrance to the adjacent cooking space, the *diyu;* the *chira yuga,* or serrated "sideboard" on which pottery is piled; the *bimbim,* or sitting platform where a ground-nut bin is usually kept. Next to the *diga* is the *kalgungu,* or outdoor kitchen, with its arched doorway.

In Tanga's compound, the men's spaces, or *dra,* show three stages of evolution. Looking at the three oldest units situated opposite the compound entrance (units 1, 2, and 3 in D.45), and progressing in order of age, one notices that, from Tanga's unit to the one furthest left, the *dra* successively take on the shape of a circle, a square, and a rectangle. The circular *dra,* the first to be built, stands now as a *djuna songo,* or ancestral sacred home. The square *dra* has curved angles and a low inner partition wall (50 centimeters) that divides the space into a sleeping and a storage area. In the next stage, the partition becomes the wall of a new storage room, the *dibu,* built adjacent to the *dra,* with straight, square angles.

A woman's dwelling unit is mainly composed of a *kalgungu,* a *diga,* and a *diyu.* The *napóro* does not appear as a constant feature. In older units of Tanga's compound, it serves as a covered area for the preparation of guinea-corn beer and either fills in the interval between two circular sets of spaces (unit 2 in D.45) or is added in the *naba* on a side of the *kuhkolo* (unit 3 in D.45). The installation of the *napóro* as "antechamber," so often encountered among the Kassena of the west (Koumbili), whose architecture traditionally makes no use of open courts, is found only in the two more recently built units on the right of the compound entrance (units 7 and 8 in D.45). Here, the house planner (the man who lives with Tanga and is the head of these two households, D.45) has done away with the older style of construction and has designed the women's spaces like the men's room pattern, except for the addition of a *napóro* to compensate for the absence of an intimacy gradient in the new design. The *napóro* becomes then multipurpose, serving to establish degrees of privacy in spaces.

146

P.63. Tangassoko. Southeast view of Tanga's compound. The outdoor cooking spaces *(kalgungu)* may be recognized by the millet stalks that protrude beyond their walls.

P.64. Exterior façade of a Kassena compound. The curved outer wall of a *diyu-diga* is divided into horizontal registers and painted with two widely used design patterns—the double serration (upper register) and the "broken calabashes" (lower registers). One may compare here the quality of the older black pigment with the newer dripping asphalt applied on the side of a man's rectangular *dra* on the right.

P.65. View of a Kassena compound during the rainy season. On the right, the decorated façade of a man's dwelling unit.

The woman's older style of dwelling establishes its sequence of intimacy through two means: the variety of spaces accessible from the *kuħkolo* and the entry system of each space. Upon striding over the *manchoħoni* of this private court, a male visitor, for example, knows exactly where he may be allowed in. Being neither the husband of the woman living there nor a close female friend, he will either make his way to the *dra* to speak to the man (men) of the family, to the *napóro*, which is entirely open on one side, if he belongs to this woman's group of regular beer purchasers, or stay in the *kuħkolo* and talk to her from the outside while she works in the *kalgungu*, a dry-season cooking space covered with millet stalks. No visitor would enter a woman's personal and intimate realms, the *diga* and *diyu*, without her consent. The choice of space defines the degree of social interaction between guest and host; it is a form of lan-

P.66. Decorated façade of the man's dwelling unit seen on the right above.

149

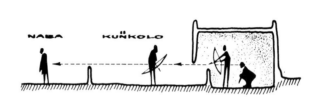

D.27. AA' section of Tanga's compound. Note the entry system on the right, which requires that a person stoop down and, immediately upon entering, stand up halfway to stride over a small, semicircular wall.

Diagram 16. The entrance lock protects the interior from rain and wind as well as from wild animals. In the past, it served a necessary defensive purpose, allowing the inhabitants squatting inside to have a direct view into their *kuňkolo* (small individual courts) and the *naba* (cattle yard); thus they could see without being seen.

guage often used to express the guest's accurate feeling for the dweller(s) and position toward her family, and vice versa.[1]

Direct access into the woman's private spaces, the *kalgungu, diga,* and *diyu,* is made even more difficult by a peculiar system of entry, also found among the Nankani. The arched doorway (*digani,* P.67, P.68, P.71), framed by a ridge that projects (5 to 10 centimeters) beyond the outer wall of the rooms, strikes one above all by its lowness. Measuring less than a meter high, it requires that one stoop down, head for the dark in this position, then, immediately upon entering, stand up halfway to stride over a small semicircular wall, or *galséga* (D.26, D.27, D.28, D.29). The three steps or body movements necessitated in the act of entering correspond, in fact, to the three zones of each entrance that bear definite names and progress in the following order: the *digani,* the *diyuma cuňo,* then the *galséga*

(D.28). The doorway thus created is bound to slow down access into the interior and discourage all intrusions.

The *galséga* varies in height. Low and easy to step over in the outdoor cooking space, or *kalgungu,* it is high enough in the sleeping-storage room, or *diga,* to suggest that the act of "entering" becomes that of "climbing in" (D.28; compare *galséga* of AA' and BB' sections). The height of the *galséga* corresponds to the degree of privacy of the interior space; it remains, however, always lower than the entrance arch apex to allow a person squatting inside to look outside without being visible. A woman cooking in the *kalgungu* can easily see into the *kuňkolo,* her private court, and a portion of the *naba,* the cattle kraal. From the *diga,* the *galséga* serves even more explicitly as a vantage point, since it is always aligned with the *manchoňoni* (access into the *kuňkolo*) and allows thereby a wider and deeper field of

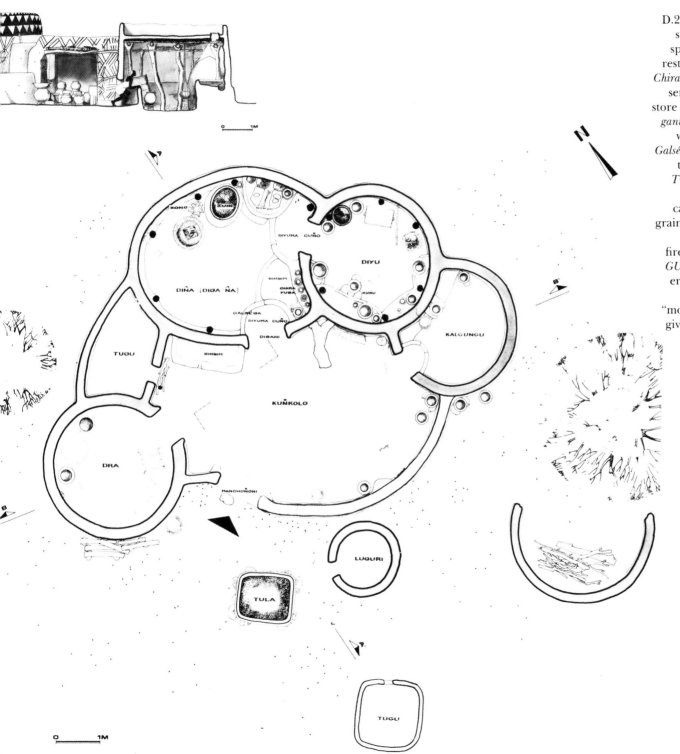

D.28. Kolo. Plan of Waonté's home-stead. DIŇA (diga ña): a woman's space. *Bimbim:* platform for sitting, resting, or storing a ground-nut bin. *Chira yuga:* "the face of the deceased," serrated adobe "sideboard" used to store or display pottery collections. *Digani:* "mouth of the house," or door-way. *Diyuma cuño:* entrance space. *Galséga:* small semicircular wall facing the entrance. *Nongo:* grindstones. *Tutogo:* large basket. *Zono:* braided string construction for storing calabashes. *Zuin:* a woman's adobe grain bin. *DIYU:* "head of the house," interior cooking space. *Kuru:* fireplace. *DRA:* a man's space. *KAL-GUNGU:* exterior cooking area cov-ered with millet stalks. *KUŇKOLO:* packed-earth court. *Manchoñoni:* "mouth of the court," dip in the wall giving access to the court. *LUGURI:* chicken coop. *TUGU:* goat pen. *TULA:* outdoor adobe granary.

P.67. A woman working in the *kuṅkolo* in front of her *diga*. The serrated pattern on the upper register of the wall and around the doorway is named "neck of the dove." The incised series of lozenges filled with cross-hatchings also decorate the interior wall and built-in furnishing of the *diga;* it is one of the most widely shared patterns in the area.

vision. In Tanga's compound, all doorways of dwellings are placed beyond sight of the compound entrance (*mintchiopo,* D.25). Newcomers who first step into the *naba* cannot perceive them—hidden by the goat pens, the men's *dra,* and the *kuṅkolo* enclosing walls—until they proceed further inside, about 5 meters from the *mintchiopo.* There they will be able to see into the dips, or *manchohoni,* of the *kuṅkolo* walls and become aware of their being subjected to a circular field of vision, originating from the dark openings of the women's *diga* and *kalgungu.*

The design of a doorway is, as we have seen, highly indicative of the degree of privacy of a space. The smaller and lower the opening, the more intimate the interior realm. Of related interest, naturally, are the shapes of the rooms. Among the Nuna, for example, privacy in a longitudinal space is obtained by placing the door at one end on the longer side (see Chapter 2). The

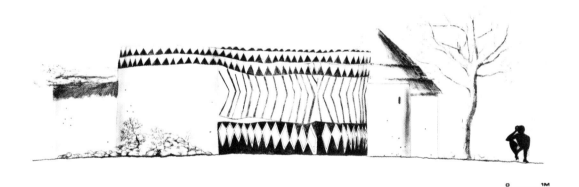

D.29. Kolo. AA′ section, northeast
elevation, and BB′ section of
Waonté's homestead.

P.68. Entrance to a *diga*.

P.69. Exterior of a Kassena compound surrounded by millet during the rainy season.

P.70. Interior of compound.

degrees of intimacy thus rely on lighting and distance from the entrance area. Among the Kassena and the Nankani, emphasis is shifted to the doorway itself, which becomes then the focusing point of a space. This apparent concern for doorways may be due to the fact that Kassena and Nankani dwellings, more than other Gurunsi houses, are conceived of as human beings. The fetal forms of the coupled *diga-diyu* (all oriented clockwise, with the *diyu* coming first in Kassena compounds, D.23, D.25, D.28) are constant reminders of the womb image of the house. As in many African habitations, names given to spaces do not refer to a specific function such as cooking, sleeping, or reception, but to the different parts of the human body.

The *diyu*, a variant of the *digayugu* among the Kassena of the west, stands as "head of the house"; it is the woman's intimate realm and interior cooking area. The *diga*, also called *diña*

155

P.71. Façade of a *diga* looking onto the *kuñkolo*. The series of lozenges, representing the braided string construction that is used to store a woman's collection of calabashes, is here bordered with a semicircular motif figuring either the calabash itself, a pot, or the handle of a cane.

(D.28), which means "the woman's dwelling space"—the term *ña* is used to designate a woman who has borne a child—contains six features that always stand together and define the woman's personal realm (D.26). Connected to a side of the *galséga*, or small wall, of the *diga* entrance is a high, curved platform (*bimbim*, P.73) which provides the woman with a place to rest or to keep a large sealed pot storing ground nuts. The location of the *bimbim* enables the woman lying on it to look out into the court just by rising up on her elbows. Above this *bimbim* is a semicircular serrated adobe edge whose rounded crenels, or depressions, hold piles of finely crafted clay pots (P.72, P.73). Looking like a crown partly embedded in the wall, this "sideboard" stands out as one of the most striking features of Kassena and Nankani interior design, and is referred to by the inhabitants as *chira yuga*, or "the face of the deceased." Im-

P.72. The *chira yuga,* or "the face of the deceased," is the name given to this serrated "sideboard" that holds a woman's pottery collection. Mats are rolled and stored on rafters suspended from the ceiling beams.

mediately following the *bimbim* is a small wall facing the low doorway that leads to the adjacent room, the *diyu,* or cooking space. The partition, usually of easier access than the *galséga* of the *diga* entrance, forms the curve of the *diyuma cuħo* (D.28, P.73; see earlier description of the *diga* entrance), an area which functions as a transition between either the sleeping and the cooking spaces or the *chira yuga* and the grinding platform. This platform, or *nongo,* into whose surface two grindstones are let, also has a semicircular shape. The wall against which it stands, or more particularly the area right above it, is often incised with a series of lozenge-shaped motifs framed by a ridge that forms a square on the wall surface. The lozenge motifs (which picture the calabashes and *zono,* a fiber net to be described next) are filled with perpendicular and oblique cross-hatchings that represent guinea corn (P.86; see similar designs

157

P.73. Inside a *diga*. From right to left: the semicircular wall *(galséga)* facing the *diga* entrance; an adobe platform *(bimbim)* for sitting or resting; the serrated *chira yuga;* another low wall defining the entrance area leading to the adjacent cooking space, or *diyu;* the grinding platform.

on the outer walls, P.67, P.71, P.76). Next to the grinding platform hangs a braided string construction, or *zono*, extending almost the full height of the room and used to store calabashes. When not stacked up in this *zono*, calabashes used every day are also hung on nails in the decorated wall area above the grindstones, displaying thereby a variety of colors ranging from a milky white-yellow to a rich ocher or sienna brown (P.74). A sealed grain bin, or *zuin* (P.74, D.28), also standing near the grinding platform and sometimes bearing the same incised motifs as those described, finally closes the sequence of related structures that characterizes a woman's *diga*.

The six features described (the *bimbim*, the *chira yuga*, the *diyuma cuño*, the *nongo*, the *zono*, and the *zuin*) are pivotal points around which the dweller's existence is ordered. In addition to their functional value, they symbolize the woman as life-giver and nurturer. Like the organs of a body, they form an integral whole and their designs physically express their interdependence. All built-in constructions are curved and connected to each other; they are also carefully maintained and uniformly surfaced, like the interior walls, with a lustrous finish that appears black or dark burnt sienna, depending on the light of the day. The pots and calabashes are closely related to the grindstone, grain bin, and incised wall motifs, for their size and quality are indicators of a woman's ability to support a larger or smaller number of dependents, her domestic status, social prestige, and reproductive powers.

The close association of a woman with her *diga-diyu* and the objects surrounding her is such that they become personal extensions of herself and her activities. Two of the skillfully crafted pots displayed on the *chira yuga*, for example, figure

159

among her prime possessions. One will be buried with her when she dies. Its contents remain secret as long as she is alive, and her eldest daughter, who will ceremonially look into it after her death, must not on any account do so before then, for fear of "becoming blind." The other, the *sogo*, has a domed cover and usually stands on top of a pile. It is used for the "breaking" ceremony performed at the close of the funeral celebration. The *sogo* is carefully carried to the crossroads leading to the home of the deceased's mother and shattered in front of witnessing family members. During the ceremony, the participants will not make a sound, for the soul of the deceased is considered to have frequented the pot during her lifetime, and uttering a sound before its final departure will most likely result in illness.[2] While the body of the deceased still lies in her *diga*, her face must be turned toward the sideboard and the pots, hence the term *chira yuga*, or "the face of the deceased."

The final departure of a woman is marked not only by shattering the pot, but also by knocking a piece off the top of the low wall, or *galséga*, which delimits the threshold of the *diga*. The rough texture of the exposed broken part acts as a constant reminder of her definitive passage to another world. The demarcation between the worlds of the living and the dead is the same as that of the outside and the inside, the familial and the communal. The act of coming in and going out takes on, thereby, all its significance, and a doorway is both the mouth and the sexual organ of its owner. *Digani*, the name of the entrance to the *diga*, means "mouth of the house"; its access, as one may recall, is selective—usually reserved for the woman's close female friends, her husband and children. Entering the womb of the *diga* may be seen as equivalent to introducing food into a body. The earlier description of the six features contained in the *diga* shows, indeed, that they all cooperate with the

160

P.74. Inside a *diga*. From right to left:
the grinding platform above which
everyday calabashes are hung; the
woman's grain bin; the braided string
construction *(zono)* used to store
calabashes.

diyu in the alimentation process, referring to food as a life-giving force. It also indicates that their shapes, as well as the fetal form of the coupled spaces, establish the womb image of the house through the nest-like powers of their curves. As a symbol of fertility and haven of refuge and regeneration, the *diga-diyu* further supports the hypothesis developed earlier on the spiritual meanings of semi-underground and semi-sunken dwellings (see Chapter 7). The assumption that constructions on the ground represent an evolved stage of underground habitations also seems correct when one realizes that the *diga-diyu*, whose floors are lowered as in several other Gurunsi dwellings, has its "mouth," or *digani,* opening onto a semicircular court named *kuñkolo,* which means "big calabash" and is a metaphor for "the vault of heaven" (D.28).[3]

The construction of a dwelling requires that its plan be traced first on the ground. Attaching a stick to a peg with a rope, the men draw a circle and then erect the wall of a *diyu,* the curvilinear *diga* and *kalgungu* leaning afterward on this "head of the house." The masonry technique is similar to that of the Lela. Clods of puddled earth mixed with cow dung (about 15 centimeters in diameter) are molded, then flattened out, each next to the last and slightly overlapping it, until they form a row completing the circumference of the room. The clods of the following row are embedded into the first by positioning them so as to fill the intervals between the round tops of the previous clods and pressing them downward until they overlap again on their sides. With such a tight connection between clods, cracks are unlikely to develop along the walls, whose homogeneity also facilitates the adhesiveness of the final coating.

Prepared and applied to the wall by the women, the coating is

P.75. Painted designs on the outer walls of a woman's dwelling unit.

made by combining ground earth, cow dung, and a viscid solution in which special grass has been macerated. To this water-resistant mixture, one usually adds finely crushed laterite, which gives the outer walls their orange-red terra-cotta color. While the coating is still wet, the women even out all asperities of the surface with flat pebbles having rounded edges and proceed to the mural decorations.

Wall designs are either painted, incised (with a pebble), or molded as bas-reliefs. Incised motifs, like the nested-V imprints of Lela and Nuna habitations, break the flow of rain into smaller streamlets to prevent a localized erosion of the walls. They often cover façades looking out to the courts, or *kuħkolo*, but are almost always found around the frame of doorways and on interior walls and furnishings. Painted motifs usually come in two colors: black and white. The black pigment is tradi-

tionally obtained from ground black schists, although it tends to be replaced nowadays by asphalt. This new material cannot, obviously, yield the same results, since the coarse, dripping designs achieved through its use lack the precision of lines applied with chicken feathers and the textural harmony of black schist on red laterite (P.64, P.65). The white color, employed mainly for filling in the designs, is produced by rubbing a kaolin stone on the specific area.

Four patterns prevail in the decorations of women's dwelling units. They usually come in horizontal bands with different widths and vary from one façade to another. The first, frequently found around roof parapets, doorways, and outdoor granaries, consists of two parallel lines whose interval is filled with a zigzag line (often emphasized by a double or triple line). The design may simply be incised (P.68); it may also be painted

163

alternately black and white or with black lines against a white background. In the first instance, the painting offers a simultaneous reading of two serrations of different colors (P.64, P.71); in the second, a dual reading of an upward and downward serration (P.67). The latter presentation is said to bear the name "neck of the dove."[4] A variant of this first pattern is the "broken calabashes,"[5] whose design remains almost the same but differs in size—three or four times larger—and in the alternate oblique hatchings that fill in the two denticulations (P.64). The "broken calabashes" motif may be cut into the surface or painted. It is sometimes replaced on the side of the wall that faces the *kuħkolo* by an incised series of lozenges filled with oblique or perpendicular cross-hatchings (P.67, P.71, P.76). These lozenges, commonly encountered on interior walls and built-in furnishings, also come with a vertical split in the middle which, when added to the different combinations of color, further increases the superimposed layers of readings that their first design already conveys (P.71, P.76). The fourth pattern is a horizontal herringbone pattern composed of two adjacent rows of black oblique hatchings running in opposite directions. Like the double serration motif, it appears not only on the outer wall of women's dwelling units but also on the outdoor granaries (P.65).

Decorations of men's *dra* remain within the domain of women's creations. Among the painted patterns that differentiate a man's façade from his wife's, one recognizes: (1) oblique cross-hatchings around the roof parapets; (2) vertical stripes of nested-V motifs within a horizontal register; (3) black lozenges against a white background or vice versa (P.64, P.65); and (4) a regular zigzag line filling in the interval between two horizontal parallels, with verticals issuing from the points of the zigzag. This last pattern is referred to as "men's cloth."[6]

Several observations may be made concerning the above examples of motif identified in mural decorations. The descriptions given are deceptive, for they reveal only an observer's view, which is that of a spectator and not of the drawer. The reading of a design motif naturally denotes a way of retracing the drawing process, but the pattern in its completed form always lends itself to more than one interpretation. This is further enhanced by the equal treatment given to the motif and its background, which enables the looker to reverse their respective roles to his or her liking. Thus, the "neck of the dove" pattern, for example, can be seen as black lines on a white surface or white fillings-in between black traits. The lozenge

P.76. Design motifs on the façade of a *diga*. The horizontal bas-relief commonly girds the center of the wall surfaces of dwellings.

165

motif may sometimes appear as (vertical stripes of) X motifs or as a juxtaposition of two triangles with their apexes meeting.

If the form of a design gives rise to several readings, so does its content. Different significations attributed to a particular motif are not uncommon among the inhabitants of the compounds. The double serration motif framing roof parapets and doorways (P.67, P.68, P.64, P.71) may resemble a "neck of the dove" when it is read upward, with the apexes pointing toward the sky or toward the wall surface for openings. With a downward reading it looks more like a row (or two overlapping rows) of filed teeth, an image which corresponds to its frequent application around entrances, or "mouths of the houses." Each triangle formed by the serrated motif further represents the triangular amulet that contains a magical substance and is widely worn on the body for protection by the people. When drawn vertically on the lower part of the wall that touches the ground, the zigzag shaping of these triangles also evokes running water.[7]

Each design motif has its own repertoire of significations whose articulation depends on the context in which it is situated. The house as a human body is beautified by adornment marks and paintings, or dressed with a finely designed cloth. Exterior wall patterns, like the weaving of women's loincloths, are applied in horizontal bands extending around the circumference of dwellings. For a man's façade, these bands may consist of vertical stripes of diverse motifs, or of alternating black and white surfaces, which bear names like "men's cloth" or "cloth strips" *(tana),* as among the Nankani.[8] Such names clearly indicate the parallel between wall designs and the woven narrow strips that are sewn together to make a man's smock.

The house modeled after the human body traditionally has no angularities (as seen in the *diga-diyu-kalgungu* combination). Its curvilinear outlines—including those of its built-in furnishings—are set off by the rectilinear decorative figures that may also stand for body paintings and tattoos. Round designs are scarce in wall motifs but they sometimes appear in the lower border of the lozenge pattern. This combination projects onto another plane the female fertility symbol expressed through the six associated features described earlier that characterize the interior of a *diga*. The same holds true for the entire composition of a façade decoration. Thus, the lozenge motif, which represents the *zono*, or braided string construction serving to store calabashes, is bordered by a semicircular motif portraying either the calabash itself, a piece of pottery (*yie* in Nankane), or the handle of a cane (*dogona*, also in Nankane).[9] Both motifs are filled with perpendicular and oblique cross-hatchings which stand for guinea corn (P.71). The diamond shape formed by the outline or strings of the *zono* is also called "broken calabash piece" *(wanzagese)* among the Nankani (this is a perfect example of simultaneous negative and positive readings of the same motif). This pattern, as we have already suggested, is as widely shared among the inhabitants of the area as the other "broken calabashes" pattern, which consists of triangles filled with alternate oblique hatchings (P.64). When apprehended in their totality, all these motifs, triangular amulets, running water, *zono*, calabashes, pottery, guinea corn—to mention just a few—converge to insist upon the life-giver image of the body, or the house.

9 NANKANI

The Nankani, the majority of whom reside in northeastern Ghana, occupy an area east of the Kassena territories in Upper Volta. Nankani is the name given them by their Kassena neighbors; the people also refer to themselves as Gurensi or Frafra, a British appellation based on their traditional greeting, "fara fara."[1] According to several sources, the Nankani originally emigrated from the region of Dagombaland. The territories they now occupy in Upper Volta were occupied five centuries ago by the Bussansi. Their ancestor Kabonga, who lived then in Gambaga (Ghana), came with his men to drive the Bussansi out, thereby compelling them to settle further north. The land Kabonga conquered was known for its fertility, and the people he chased, for the large size of their cattle herds. Kabonga thus established his home in Nembarongo, a quarter of Toungou where his numerous descendants still reside today.[2]

Two accounts, further research on which may help establish the missing link, have been given on the founding of the village of Ziou. A local elder of Mossi origin states that the first settlers were the Sia, a Nankani family that emigrated from Ghana around 1800 and has since then remained custodian of the earth of Ziou. The village was then named Zimtenga, meaning "blood everywhere," for, upon their arrival, the newcomers had slain pregnant women to identify the sex of their unborn children[3] and stained the site with the blood shed. Zimtenga later evolved into Ziou, a name that is now used to designate a district consisting of forty-five small villages.

Another local elder of Nankani origin relates that the first man to set foot on the site came from Fada Ngourma (225 kilometers east of Ouagadougou, in the Gurmantche area).[4] Having had quarrels of chieftainship with his peers, he left the

P.77. Southeast view of Adono's compound.

town, accompanied by his men, to go south and make his way to Gambaga. His older family members, who were Nankani, refused, however, to follow him all the way and settled down instead in Ayinorgo. Lanzuré, the founder of Ayinorgo, later left this village and moved to the site of Ziou, where he drove away the older Bussansi inhabitants, compelling them to emigrate to the left bank of the White Volta River. His two brothers, Simbindé and Pané, founded the villages of Apinia and Yelbissi, both considered quarters of Ziou. Lanzuré had four sons, Kumbala, Bua, Natirga, and Anaro, who founded in their turn the villages of Youka, Gou, Zanzé, and Tampélaga. These four villages belong nowadays to the conglomeration of Mouma, one of the two groupings that form Ziou, the other being Bongo.

Adono's compound stands within the limits of Mouma, whose hilly landscape is populated with habitations widely dispersed along the banks of a large depression. The main locus of social interaction in the area is the weekly market of Ziou, located on the west bank, near the dispensary and the primary school—two models of standard construction recently built with concrete blocks and corrugated-metal roofs.

Like most Kassena and Nankani habitations, Adono's compound is erected on a site sloping downward from west to east, and positioned so as to have its main entrance on the higher point of the slope facing west and its oldest dwelling unit—usually the senior woman's, hence the most important—on the lower point of the slope, directly opposite this entrance. Such an entrance orientation, common to the inhabitants of the region and often encountered among the Gurunsi, is due to the high northeast trades and harmattan, and the heavy rains that

169

beat east, often with hurricane force. The incline of the compound further prevents the active erosion of the bases of its walls by facilitating the outflow of rainwater, which smoothly drains off through holes from the internal packed-earth courts instead of stagnating around the constructions.

Nankani habitations are in many aspects similar to those of the Kassena of the east. Their descriptions may, therefore, be considered complementary. Adono's compound (D.30) strikes one above all by its precise use and naming of outdoor spaces. The homestead is surrounded by a semi-public sphere, the *poka dapurè* (which is similar to the *kara* among the Western Kassena), within the limits of which women grow okra, sorrel, beans, or millet. Beyond the *poka dapurè*, the inhabitants also identify the *dapurè*, or area behind the compound, and the *tampuré*, or refuse area, situated slightly off the compound front. The space preceding the entrance and spreading within the *poka dapurè* is named *talanga*.[5] It constitutes, as in most Gurunsi habitations, the males' area inside which stands the senior man's reception shelter, or *poñga*, and the ancestral shine, or *bagèrè*[6] (against the wall of the *zongo* on the left of the entrance, D.30). Access to the compound is, again, gained only after acknowledgment by the successive family guardians.

Two conical earthen pillars define the entrance *(yanga)* of Adono's compound (P.79). Upon entering, one is met on both sides with circular thatch-roofed constructions called *zongo* (D.30). Serving as an animal shelter (goats, sheep, and donkeys in the *bonga zongo*), the *zongo* also shares an important role in funeral customs with the *talanga* and the two ancestral pillars. Here, special attention has been given to the *zongo* immediately to the left of the entrance, which is painted with black markings

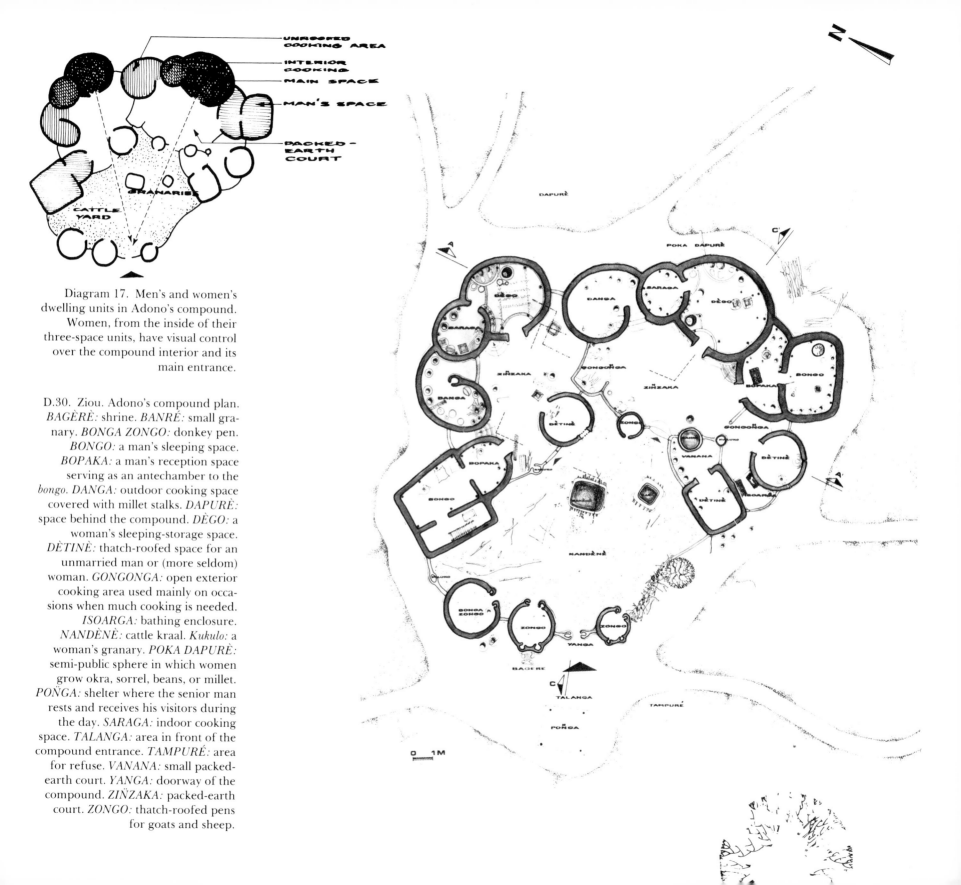

Diagram 17. Men's and women's dwelling units in Adono's compound. Women, from the inside of their three-space units, have visual control over the compound interior and its main entrance.

D.30. Ziou. Adono's compound plan. *BAGÈRÈ:* shrine. *BANRÉ:* small granary. *BONGA ZONGO:* donkey pen. *BONGO:* a man's sleeping space. *BOPAKA:* a man's reception space serving as an antechamber to the *bongo. DANGA:* outdoor cooking space covered with millet stalks. *DAPURÈ:* space behind the compound. *DÈGO:* a woman's sleeping-storage space. *DÈTINÈ:* thatch-roofed space for an unmarried man or (more seldom) woman. *GONGONGA:* open exterior cooking area used mainly on occasions when much cooking is needed. *ISOARGA:* bathing enclosure. *NANDÈNÈ:* cattle kraal. *Kukulo:* a woman's granary. *POKA DAPURÈ:* semi-public sphere in which women grow okra, sorrel, beans, or millet. *POÑGA:* shelter where the senior man rests and receives his visitors during the day. *SARAGA:* indoor cooking space. *TALANGA:* area in front of the compound entrance. *TAMPURÉ:* area for refuse. *VANANA:* small packed-earth court. *YANGA:* doorway of the compound. *ZIÑZAKA:* packed-earth court. *ZONGO:* thatch-roofed pens for goats and sheep.

D.31. Section AA' and southwest elevation of Adono's compound.

and white fillings (P.79, D.34) and will serve as a sleeping room for the senior man (Adono) when he grows old. During a funeral, the *talanga* is full of people from all parts of the area who gather to attend the ceremony. One of the rituals performed before the burial of an old man's corpse consists of having the oldest son climb on the wall of the *zongo* entrance—in the case of a woman, he climbs on a flat roof—and call his father's name to inquire about his death. Should a new grave be dug, a cow is slaughtered and placed at the main entrance, in the *talanga*. When the deceased is a senior member of a village section (a group of homesteads whose inhabitants are descendants of a common ancestor), his body is carried outside, not through the compound entrance, but through an opening made in the wall of the *zongo*.[7]

The custom of removing a corpse through an opening made in the wall of the deceased's own room instead of through the compound entrance has been given several interpretations. One of them lays emphasis on the sacred value of the main doorway, whose threshold has been purified by special ceremonies and must not be polluted by death. This accounts for the immediate blocking up of the wall opening after burial, which prevents death from re-entering the homestead, and for the "washing" of the compound entrance with a pot of beer at the close of a woman's funeral (after the "breaking" ceremony).[8] The "mouth" (*yanga*, or doorway) of the compound, like the "mouth" of each dwelling inside it, lies under the protection of the ancestor's spirits. The site of entrance and exit rites, it constitutes the point of transition not only between the external world and the familial world but also between the man's domain (the *talanga*) and the woman's domain (the inside

172

P.78. The woman is just stepping out of the outdoor cooking space *(danga)*, above which are laid bundles of millet stalks. Next to it on the right are the *saraga* and the *dègo*.

of a compound). Its access is, as we have seen, successively guarded by the senior man in the *ponga,* the spirits of the *bagèrè* shrine, and the two ancestral earthen pillars erected on its sides, which represent the viability of the family.[9] The house as a life-giving womb[10] thus cannot, once it has borne death, continue to grow without going through a purification process to mark its rupture with all life-destroying forces.

Piercing a hole in the wall and closing it after the corpse's passage as a measure to bar death from the living realm may also be interpreted as a symbolic act of destruction. The identification of the house with the human body and its dweller has been discussed in the two preceding chapters. The partial breaking of a wall can have the same significance as the destruction of the top of the low semicircular wall (the *galséga* among the Kassena and *zaño kungo* among the Nankani) facing the entrance of a woman's *dègo* (*diga* in Kassena). It is also equivalent to the destruction of objects considered to be personal extensions of the deceased—the breaking of a woman's pot and calabash and the burning of a man's bow and quiver—which allow him or her to be incorporated among the ancestors instead of wandering homelessly between the world of the living and that of the dead.

In some cases, the necessity for admission into the society of the afterlife through a clean break with one's previous surroundings is expressed by the complete demolition of the deceased's room or homestead. Thus, "when a man dies and leaves no 'sons' (or brothers), his compound is broken down and tobacco or corn is planted within the ruined walls, because the yard is rich in manure (having been a cattle kraal). When a man has no children, he is sometimes laughed at, and told,

P.79. Southwest view of Adono's compound showing the senior man's shelter, which faces the entrance framed on its sides by two conical earthen pillars. Immediately to the left of this entrance is a decorated *zongo* with the ancestral shrine in front of it.

'What are you, if you were to die, they would break down your house and plant tobacco in it.'"[11] The indispensability of an afterlife home accounts for the strong interdependence of the dead and the living. The house as an extension of the body dies with its dweller's death and lives on only through rebirth or procreation. To have progeny is, then, to have proper funerals, and vice versa. Both children and ancestors are commonly referred to as "builders up of compounds."[12] After a man's death, his son, upon sacrificing a beast, will say, for example, "Receive this sheep and keep this house and join your father and grandfather in guarding it properly, for in a house where even a few still remain, they will not plant tobacco."[13]

The position of the *zongo* next to the site of ancestral guardianship and at the boundary separating life from afterlife may explain why the senior man of the family often prefers to sleep there when he grows old. His dwelling unit stands otherwise next to his wife's (D.30) and can be reached only by crossing the *nandènè*, or cattle kraal, and the *ziħzaka*, or small packed-earth court. Access to the *ziħzaka* is gained, as in Kassena habitations, through a dip (80 centimeters high) in its enclosing walls (1.5 meters high or more). The man's unit generally comprises a *bopaka* and a *bongo*, two flat-roof constructions. Sometimes equipped with a storage space, the *bongo* is always preceded by a *bopaka*, or "small *bongo*," which serves as an antechamber in which to receive guests, to take one's meals, and to sleep during warm nights. Young unmarried men and women dwell in the *dètinè* (*deo:* "grass"), which are all erected with conical thatched roofs, more adapted to single rooms than to composite spaces such as the coupled *bongo-bopaka*.

The woman's dwelling unit is usually composed of an out-

D.32. Adono's compound. Axonometric cutaway of the senior woman's dwelling unit directly facing the compound entrance. *BOPAKA:* antechamber to the man's space *(bongo). DANGA:* outdoor cooking space. *DÈGO:* sleeping and storage space. *Bimbina:* stairs, also used as benches for drying grain and sitting. *Dèzañorè:* "mouth of the *dègo*," or doorway. *Ebraga* and *barga:* grindstones let into the surface of a platform. *Habina:* movable grindstone. *Kimanenga,* or "the face of the deceased": serrated "sideboard" holding a woman's collection of pots. *Zalanga:* braided string construction for storing calabashes. *Zaño kungo:* semicircular wall facing the entrance to the *dègo. GONGONGA:* open exterior cooking area. *Songo:* millet stalks; term also used to designate the woven mats. *NANDÈNÈ:* cattle kraal. *Bèsenga:* enclosing wall lowered on the right of the *zongo* to permit access to the packed-earth court, or *ZIÑZAKA. Zongo:* sheep pen. *SARAGA:* indoor cooking space.

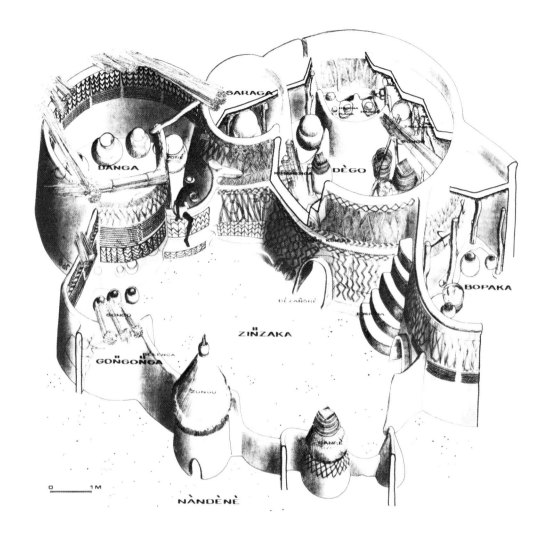

door cooking space covered with millet stalks, the *danga,* an indoor cooking space, the *saraga,* and a storage-sleeping space, the *dègo* (D.32, D.30), Two features that immediately differentiate the exterior of this unit from those of Kassena dwellings are the built-in semicircular adobe staircases generally situated at the curved junction between two spaces—the woman's *dègo* and the man's *bopaka,* or the *dègo* and the *saraga* (P.82, P.87, P.93)—and the access to the *danga.* Rectangular adobe staircases leading to second-floor rooms are frequently encountered in Nuna and Ko habitations, but semicircular staircases extending the packed-earth courts (*ziñzaka*) to the terrace roofs are rarely seen in areas other than the Nankani's. Carved with larger bottom stairs that also serve as benches for sitting and drying grains, these staircases are named *bimbina,* a term used by the Kassena to designate a sitting or resting platform (*bim-*

bim). Unlike the Kassena *kalgungu,* the *danga* is erected with its wall partly coiled to enclose the cooking area while creating a small entrance area that looks directly out onto the *ziñzaka.* Entry and exit from this area are gained by climbing over a medium wall that connects it to the *saraga* (D.30, D.32, P.78).

The mode of access defines, as we have seen, the degree of intimacy of a space. The composite act of entering that involves both stooping down and climbing up is, here, associated only with the more personal realm of the *dègo* (P.82, P.87). Even the man's *bopaka,* which is equipped like the *dègo* with a low arched doorway (P.93), is of easier access since it has no *zaño kungo,* or semicircular wall, at the entrance (D.31). To penetrate inside it, one needs only to stoop down, a reverse situation of that encountered in the *danga.*

The peculiar system of entry formed by the low arched door-

175

P.80. Entrances to a woman's *dègo*
(left) and a man's *bopaka* (right).

P.81. Entrance to a man's *bopaka*.
Next to it, on the right, is a *dètinè*.

way and the small semicircular wall facing it has been described in the preceding chapter, mainly as part of the intimacy gradient established in the transition from outdoor to indoor space and as a means of delaying access to a private realm. Other related explanations concerning the presence of the *zaño kungo* are available. Of equal importance, for example, is its function as a rain screen: the flow of water streaming down the outer wall surface is not only diverted to the sides of the entrance by the ridge that frames the doorway and often protrudes beyond it, but also prevented from leaking inside the room by the *zaño kungo*, which acts as a small dam during heavy rainfall. The *zaño kungo* also helps to keep marauding beasts out, a precaution which is reinforced by blocking the compound entrance with logs at night.

None of the practical reasons given, however, fully justify the use of the *zaño kungo*. The few functional advantages it presents are in most cases canceled by its disadvantages when compared to the flexibility of the widely used woven mat that people in other areas hang on their doorways at night and slide aside when they wish. The partition wall may, as some observers have noted, "keep outsiders from looking in without blocking ventilation"[14] or "keep out drafts."[15] One can, however, achieve the same result by positioning the woven mat in question accordingly (a practice not unknown to the Kassena and Nankani; see P.67). If the *zaño kungo* does protect the inhabitants from drafts during cold nights, it is also a strong drawback (discussed in Chapter 2) during the day when the sun is high and during hot nights, compelling those whose observances temporarily forbid them to go outside (a mother and young child, for example[16]) to remain in the heat. Moreover, in neighboring areas where habi-

177

P.82. Access to a woman's *dègo*.

tations are also equipped with similar doorways, these inner partitions can hardly be viewed as effective barriers to rain penetration. Among the Builsa, they sometimes do not close off the entrance space but leave narrow openings on the sides so that one can step around it—instead of stepping over it—when entering the room. Among the Nuna in Valiou, some older circular dwellings, which are thought to be of Mossi influence, also carry an inner partition at the entrance area. This partition is, however, 1.5 meters high—as high as the doorway—and positioned to block only half of the view from the opening. Such a setting reveals, aside from the problem of ventilation, the unequivocal function of the partition as a shield or a bulwark.

The *zaño kungo* combined with the low doorway appears indeed most effective as a defensive structure. It has been said by a European observer, A. W. Cardinall, to serve "to prevent a foe from carrying out a vendetta murder at night."[17] Such a statement may sound overly dramatic nowadays, but the explanation of the partition as protection against a surprise attack by intruders can in several aspects be justified. The *zaño kungo* of the *dègo* is, as in Eastern Kassena habitations, usually situated so as to look through the dip of the *ziñzaka* (packed-earth court) into the cattle kraal. It provides the inhabitants with a vantage point from which they can observe their adversaries without being visible. (It is worth noting here that, as in other Gurunsi habitations, the men in Adono's compound used to share, in the past, the same unit with their wives. The *bongo* and *bopaka* have been added at a later date; see D.47.) The lowered floor level of the *dègo* also allows a wider aiming angle, and the inhabitants squatting behind the *zaño kungo* can easily point their

D.33. Northeast elevation of Adono's compound.

D.34. CC′ section of Adono's compound.

arrows at the invaders. The reverse is not possible, for the latter can neither see into the dark openings nor shoot back and hit the target in a standing position.[18]

This highly defensive doorway gives the inhabitants a feeling of security, especially at night, when they are more vulnerable to unexpected attacks. An intruder would most likely consider the risk of entering a room in a defenseless position, thrusting his bent head forward in the dark without knowing what to expect from behind the partition wall. Once in the room, he still risks the danger of being trapped inside by family members of other dwelling units, for the doorway thus created is bound to slow down all entries and exits. To reinforce its defensive purpose, the *saraga,* or indoor cooking space, which can only be reached through the *dègo,* is also equipped with a similar entrance (D.34, P.73), although the partition wall facing it is gen-

erally lower than the *zaño kungo* of the *dègo* doorway. The lateral position of the *saraga* arched opening situated toward the back of the *dègo* maintains the intimacy of the cooking space. The *saraga* is thus often hidden from view from the *dègo* entrance and its access, designed to delay further penetration of the private realm, constitutes an additional step for the intruder to go through.

The presence of a similar system of entry leading to the *saraga* clearly indicates that the *zaño kungo* does not only serve to protect the inhabitants from rainwater, drafts, and animals, but also functions as a defensive structure delaying access to the interior. As we shall see, it is also a demarcation between the different realms of a dwelling and a physical expression of the life sequences of a human being. Penetration of the compound, from its most public outdoor spaces (the *tampuré*) to its most

P.83. One of the woman's prime possessions, the *zalanga,* hanging next to a shrine.

intimate indoor spheres (the *saraga*), is divided into four main stages marked by the crossing of four thresholds: those of the entrances leading inside the compound to the *nandènè* (cattle kraal), the *ziħzaka* (packed-earth court), the *dègo* (or the *danga*), and the *saraga*. The act of entering or exiting is renewed in each stage and reemphasized in different ways.

Upon approaching the main entrance of the homestead, for example, one becomes aware of the transition of realms through a slight change of physical and mental behavior: one prepares oneself to greet the senior man of the family first if he is in the *talanga* (male area immediately outside the entrance), or the senior woman before him if he happens to be inside the compound (female area). When passing through the doorway of the *dègo,* however, one is made conscious of the shift to a personal realm by the involvement of one's entire body in the

P.84. A man's *dètinè*.

act of crossing. Here, the change is reflected not only in a series of different positions—standing, bending, stooping, crawling, halfway standing, climbing—but also through touch—the smooth varnished surface of the *zaño kungo*—and through visual adaptation. Entry during the day is usually made from full sun; the eyes thus need time to adjust and the transition from bright to dark constitutes in itself an immaterial threshold that separates the social from the personal realm.

Each entrance is a site of the rites of passage. Knocking off the top of the *zaño kungo* facing a *dègo* doorway to mark the death of its owner has been discussed in the preceding chapter. This same *zaño kungo* also represents the different stages of childhood in a person's life. In some Nankani compounds, a child cannot, for example, be taken out of its mother's *dègo* until it can crawl out by itself. Not wanting to leave it alone, the

mother is thus confined to her room for a period of time and forced to sleep in the heat if that period falls in the hot season.[19] In other cases, the child is allowed in the yard but not outside the main entrance of the compound. To bypass this custom, which is decisive in the child's incorporation into the family group, the mother, seeing that her child "learns how to sit up, crawl around the walls, but as yet still does not know outside, . . . will resort to a plan. She will arrange secretly with a *poy-ablega* (a woman from her own village) to come on purpose to take the child outside. The mother no sooner sees that this woman has one leg across the threshold, but when too late to stop her, than she cries, 'Don't go out, Don't go out,' but the child is already outside. The reason for all this is that a spirit (*kyima*) cannot quarrel with a mistake made by a *poyablega* and not any fault of the mother. It is as if the spirits had done it

P.85. Nankani woman.

P.86. The grinding platform. The pounded grain is first roughly ground on the *ebraga* with a granite stone *(habina)*, then on the *barga* for a finer texture. The flour obtained is retrieved in the two hollow receptacles.

themselves. Should this (subterfuge) not be done, the child continues thus (crawling about the hut and yard). The mother will sit by it in the *nandènè* (cattle kraal), and one day the child will crawl outside itself. That is a sign that the spirits have agreed, and have themselves taken the child out."[20]

The interior of a woman's *dègo* is similar to that of the *diga* among the Eastern Kassena. The only difference seems to lie in the counterclockwise orientation of the fetal shapes of the coupled *saraga-dègo* in the compound layout. Thus, the six connected features that characterize the woman's personal realm are, here, all situated on the left of the *dègo* entrance. Upon entering, one recognizes the raised platform *(koaka)*, which, among the Nankani, is merely a shelf for storing a ground-nut bin; the *kimanenga,* "the face of the deceased" or serrated "sideboard" displaying several piles of varnished pots; the low

wall facing the *saraga* doorway; the grinding platform, above which hang everyday calabashes in their rich, varied color tones; and the *zalanga,* or braided string construction, which holds the woman's collection of calabashes.

The *zalanga* filled with calabashes (P.83) is an important female symbol that often recurs in wall design motifs. Three objects kept in it are, indeed, said to be of prime importance to a woman. The first is the *kumpio,* a special calabash in which she keeps her valuables and certain things to be used in connection with her funeral rite—"dried fish, dried okra, dried meat of a hare, a large bead called *pera nifo* (ram's eye)." The *kumpio,* considered the shrine of her soul *(sia)* during her lifetime (that of a man resides in his grain store or leather bag), is placed in the *zalanga* between two large calabashes and covered with a *wula,* a small calabash made only for that purpose and not for

P.87. The façade of a *dègo* varnished with a decoction of locust-bean pods. Note the bent stick molded on the side of the doorway and the painted designs on the ridge girding the wall surface.

P.88. The fireplace of a *saraga*, or indoor cooking space.

eating or drinking from. "A woman does not permit anyone else to touch her *kumpio* or look inside; should anyone do so and the owner, or even her child, sicken and die, the one who did so is accused of being a witch. She will be caught and have to undergo the ordeal of arrows *(perma lua)*." The third object contained in the *zalanga* is a red pot named *kalena*, which is also used at the owner's funeral rite.

The *kumpio, wula,* and *kalena* are carried by the deceased's eldest daughter to her late mother's home. When taking them thither the daughter may not speak or allow the things to shake about. . . . [At the crossroads] a branch of a shea butter tree with three forks at the end is set down exactly where the paths converge. The *kumpio* is set upon this branch and smashed, then the *wula* is broken up, and last of all the *kalena* pot, and the fragments are heaped together and left there.

The taking away and shattering of these calabashes and pot

P.89. A compound
interior.

after their owner's death is necessary, for "her soul is living inside [the *kumpio*] during her life and when she dies is still living there until they have finished the funeral rite, after which it departs to 'its going place.'"[21]

The building technology is the same as that of Eastern Kassena habitations. A few details, which are more evident in Nankani dwellings, need to be added. The lower constructional courses of the wall are usually built in a bell-mouthed form one and a half times thicker than those of its upper part (P.77, D.34). Besides reinforcing the stability of the wall, this well-marked slope also helps to prevent the rain that beats invariably from the east from eroding the base of the construction. The round *saraga* (indoor cooking space), erected first, is the central building against which lean the oval-shaped *danga* and *dègo*. The ceiling structure of the *saraga* and the *dègo* make use of

both the load-bearing-wall and post-and-beam systems. In the *saraga* it is simply composed of parallel beams propped up by forked posts. In the *dègo*, it becomes more complex: two or three beams resting on the wall shared with the *saraga* (above the built-in *kimanenga*, or "sideboard") radiate in a fan shape toward the other end of the room, where they are supported by forked tree trunks; two other, shorter lateral beams forming the sides of the fan rest entirely on posts. For drainage purposes, the ceiling is always slightly inclined.

In Nankani compounds, the wall is covered first with a layer of adobe called *zika*, which contains laterite gravel, then with a mixture of finer adobe called *bolè* and cow dung. The terrace, the inside floor, and the *ziħzaka* (court) make use of the same materials. The *zika* is smeared on their surfaces and tamped smooth; the *bolè* (sometimes mixed with cow dung) is, however,

P.90. A *bopaka* preceding a woman's *dègo*. This unusual combination is not encountered elsewhere in Nankani habitations; it may, however, be compared to the Kassena antechamber, the *napóro*.

added only to the terrace roof. Unlike the Kassena practice, the red laterite pigment is not incorporated into the coating but prepared separately and painted on with brushes made from blades of grass gathered in bundles. In some cases the entire façade of a dwelling is finished with a decoction of locust-bean pods *(Parkia biglobosa)*, which gives the red-orange color a shaded tint.

Mural decorations and their significance were discussed in the preceding chapter. Besides the incised and painted design motifs, a few figurative reliefs are also encountered on the inner and outer walls of both men's and women's spaces. These reliefs may appear singly or in pairs; they usually portray human beings, canes or walking sticks, and kin animals associated with the dwellers. The latter two are often seen above or on the side(s) of the doorway (P.68, P.87). One of the motifs most

P.91. Detail of the entrance.

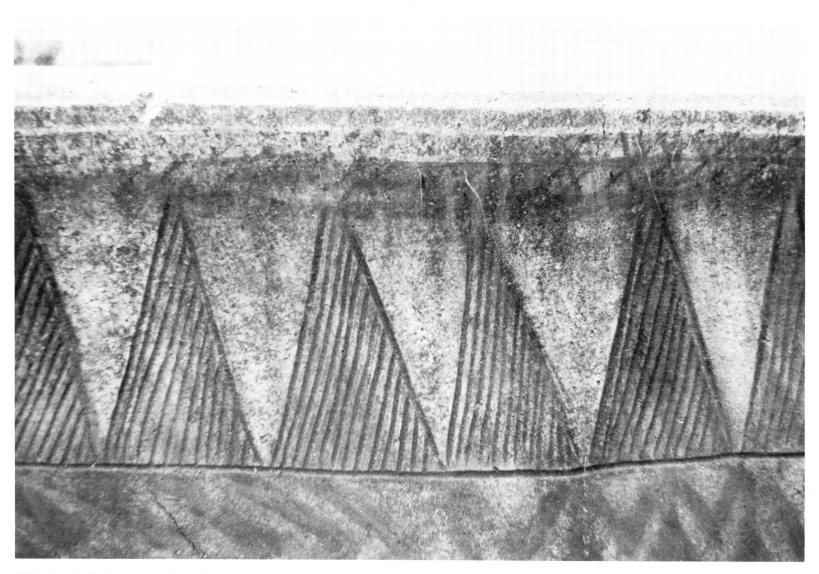

P.92. Details of a design motif widely
seen around the parapets of a
woman's dwelling spaces.

P.93. Doorway of a man's *bopaka*.

commonly used is the horizontal line that girds the center of the wall surfaces and either extends around the circumference of an individual dwelling space *(dètinè)* or flows from one façade to another, creating thereby a continuity between the *dègo, saraga,* and *danga* (P.78). This motif may come in the form of a well-marked ridge (P.78, P.82, P.87) or in rows of incised lines which divide the main ridge into smaller ones (P.76, P.78, P.93). Among the Tallensi (a neighboring group residing east of the Nankani in Ghana), the latter representation is often referred to as "the long eye," a symbol of longevity;[22] among the Nankani, it is called *yidoor,* or "lines running straight," a term also used to designate "rows in a cultivated field" or "parallel sticks on the bottom of a woman's carrying basket."[23]

The horizontal relief described above may be considered a practical wall motif that interrupts and disperses the flow of rainwater on the wall. This and the structural function that outsiders sometimes attribute to their presence do not, however, appear to be prime reasons for its widespread use. When observed more carefully, this motif presents a few revealing variations that seem to relate better to its interpretation as "rows in a cultivated field" or as "the long eye." On some *dètinè,* the horizontal relief encircling the outer wall surface forms a ridge whose ends, situated in the back of the room, portray two hoes meeting (the horizontal relief terminates in two curves or crescents with their backs almost touching). Furthermore, the motif recognized until now as a cane is sometimes molded like a bent stick, but other times more like a hoe (the bend has a sharper angle or deviates to a T shape with curved angles).[24] A variant of this cane motif, which usually stands on the sides of women's doorways, shows, indeed, two parallel vertical lines intercalated between two bent sticks (hoes). The combination of hoes with horizontal or vertical lines conveys more explicitly the image of a furrowed or cultivated field that has been cleaned (purified), sowed, and watered, and is capable of producing an abundant crop. As another symbol of fertility, this image meshes with the network of female signs expressed in mural decorations.[25] One notices, on the other hand, that rows of horizontal lines girding the outer and often also the inner wall surface of dwelling spaces[26] do not always form a continuous pattern. They are, instead, very frequently divided into two, four, or six sections, each section representing a long serpent coiling back on itself indefinitely (P.94). This motif, common to many parts of West Africa, is a variant of the widespread image of the circular snake swallowing its own tail, and usually comes in pairs to symbolize immortality and eternity.

P.94. Decorations on the interior wall of a man's space. The reliefs, which also appear on the facades of dwellings, represent a long snake coiling back on itself.

One of the most interesting aspects of these mural decorations, besides their spiritual, social, and other aesthetic functions, lies in their ability to vary the perception of this architecture with each change of light intensity and sun orientation. The combination of paintings, incisions, and reliefs largely accounts for the expressiveness of the dwellings, whose nuanced looks are as subtle and diverse as those of a human face. Thus, when the sun is veiled, all the black and white painted motifs stand out against the red tone of the walls, and when the sun is high, the incised and molded motifs come into relief, their shades altering with the light.

10 KUSASI

The original Kusasi are thought to have formed a comparatively small group who, in Upper Volta, were concentrated in the southern area between the Red and White Voltas and claimed descent from the inhabitants of three sections: Zawga (Zoaga), Biengu (Bingo), and Yuinga (Youga). Since the beginning of the century, however, the name Kusasi has been extended to include a significant number of immigrants, among whom figure followers of Mamprusi chiefs from Gambaga. In the past, the latter invaded part of the Kusasi land through which passed a trade route that they wished to keep open. This route was indeed very important because it allowed them to carry out exchanges with great caravans of Hausa and Mossi who used to stop in Tenkodogo on their way to Salaga.[1]

The village of Youga was founded by a Kusasi named Gogo Nanga, who came with three other men from Gambaga. It is situated 4 kilometers from the border of Ghana and comprises forty-five compounds scattered over a length of 2 kilometers. A line of mature trees, planted by the colonial administration along a path immediately north of Youga, spreads its shade over a market area where people gather once a week. This market and the two-classroom primary school erected nearby constitute the most obvious loci of community interaction.

Bako's compound is located in Youga and, like many other dispersed habitations of the region, follows a circular layout (D.35). Upon approaching its western-facing entrance, one immediately notices the presence of adobe granaries (boré) outside the compound. To the right of these granaries stands the senior man's shelter (paa) with its roof of millet stalks resting on seven poles.[2] Slightly to their left is the winn shrine, a small flat-topped circular mound above which lie two varnished earthen

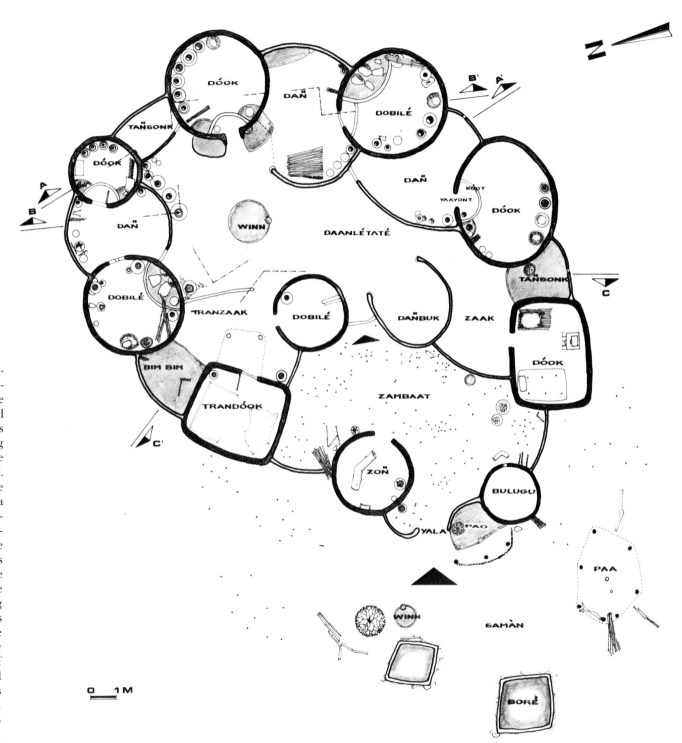

D.35. Youga. Plan of Bako's compound. *Bimbim:* adobe sitting platform. *Bulugu:* fowl house. *Boré:* adobe granary. *Daanlétaté:* communal packed-earth court. *Dañ:* a woman's private court and outdoor cooking space. *Dañbuk:* uncovered area for the preparation of guinea-corn beer. *Dobilé:* indoor cooking space; the *dobilé* opening onto the *tranzaak* is a guest room. *Dóok:* sleeping and storage space. *Kóot:* semicircular wall facing the doorway. *Paa:* shelter where the senior man rests and receives his visitors during the day. *Pao:* adobe platform. *Samàn:* area in front of the compound entrance. *Tañsonk:* bathing enclosure. *Trandóok:* senior man's space. *Tranzaak:* senior man's private court. *Winn:* shrine. *Yaayont:* doorway of a dwelling space. *Yala:* entrance of the compound. *Yimpon:* area behind the compound. *Zaak:* here, a man's private court. *Zambaat:* cattle kraal. *Zoñ:* multipurpose space, also used as a goat or sheep pen.

0   1M

D.36. AA′ and BB′ sections of Bako's
compound.

pots. The larger pot is used to cover an animal horn filled with
earth, which represents the *winn* of the dead father and,
through him, all the ancestors. The Kusasi consider each human being to be the physical expression of a *winn* created by
God, Widnam. The *winn* plays an important part before birth
and becomes, at a certain stage of a human's life, one with the
mortal body. Thus, a young man does not live in unison with
his *winn* until he reaches marriage age, a time when he will have
to build a shrine, or *bagr*, for his own *winn*, who then acts as his
intercessor in God's house.[3]

The *winn* shrine, the reception shelter *(paa)*, and the
granaries, which are intimately related to the senior man's existence (a man's soul, as we have seen among the Kassena and
Nankani, resides either in his grain store or in his leather bag),
all stand within the limits of the *samàn*. The *samàn* may be
compared to the Puguli *boña*, the Kassena *kara*, or the Nankani
talanga; it is the male area immediately in front of the compound entrance, where "one sits down with a stranger to con-
verse." Before reaching this entrance *(yala)*, one also notices on
its right a small built-in adobe platform *(pao)* protected from
exposure by a woven mat forming a screen in front of it and
built exclusively for the use of the senior man, who prefers to
sleep there on warm nights.

Once the compound entrance has been crossed, one steps
into the *zambaat*, or cattle kraal, and immediately meets with
two circular grass-roofed constructions, the *bulugu*, or fowl
house, on the right, and the *zoh*, or goat pen, on the left. The
zoh, like the Nankani *zongo*, not only shelters the goats at night
or provides the male elders of the family with a place to sit and
talk during the rainy season; it also serves as a transitional space

194

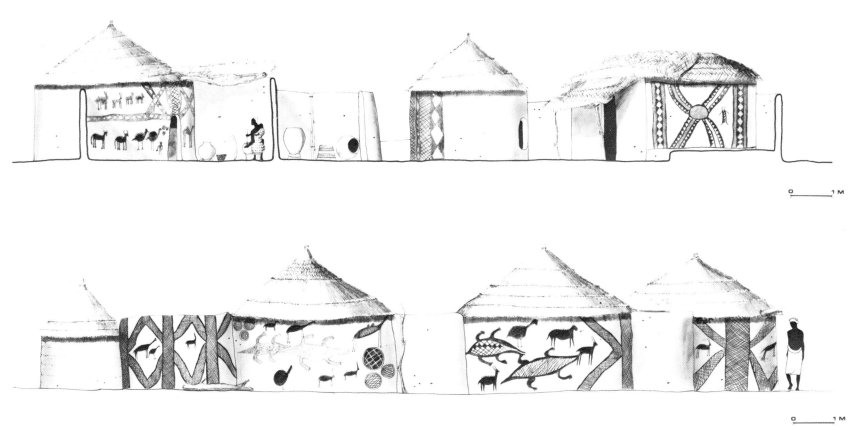

D.37. CC′ section and southeast elevation of Bako's compound.

where many rites of passage are performed. When a man or woman dies, for example, the corpse is bathed, then removed to the *zoħ*, where the head is shaved and the body rubbed with shea butter and dressed—in a goatskin with a belt of *sug* and *bea* fiber for a man; in *biug* fiber for a woman[4]—before it is carried out through a small second doorway of the *zoħ* that opens onto the outside of the compound.

Should the dead woman be a spouse of a polygamous man, he is not allowed to have intercourse with his other wives until her final obsequies have been held; this may mean a year or more after her departure. The widower will then have to undergo an ordeal to reveal whether he has observed his sexual abstinence or not, which will be "to pass through the door of the *zoħ*." A similar test exists for a female widow, who, on the other hand, is "made to pass through the doorway of the main entrance to the compound. One who has been unchaste during the period of her widowhood will refuse to do so and will struggle. She will then confess the name of the adulterer."[5] Such a woman is said to "go out from her compound" and must be purified before she is allowed to return. The same principle underlies the treatment reserved for any unfaithful wife in general, which consists of cutting her hip belt and uncovering her in front of the *zoħ*. A chicken is next sacrificed over its threshold and the woman is forced inside with a whip. There, water is poured over her to remove her potential to bring bad luck to the family. The woman so treated still cannot bear children until the name of the culprit is known, after which the compound entrance is washed with a pot of beer and another chicken sacrificed over a hole dug near it. With the blood and feathers inside it, the hole is then covered and the debt buried.[6]

195

P.95. Mural decorations of a compound.

P.96. Two men's spaces looking out onto the communal packed-earth court. The lowered wall on the left leads to a woman's dwelling unit.

The customs that have evolved around the compound entrance and the *zoħ* provide evidence of the close interaction between dwellings and dwellers, a concept that has been illustrated in all previous examples of Gurunsi architecture. They denote, above all, a dynamic and spiritual perception of space in which every single human-made object, every piece of land, every environmental presence vibrates with life and is likely to act upon a human's existence. The significance given to doorways and transitional spaces brings into play, with each particular situation, the sacredness of the living realms. Situated in the entrance zone and at the boundary between the outside and the inside, the *zoħ*, as a space for rites of separation and (re)incorporation, remains well separated from the block of dwelling units by the cattle kraal. It is usually positioned so as to look into the access (a dip in the enclosing wall) of the packed-earth court

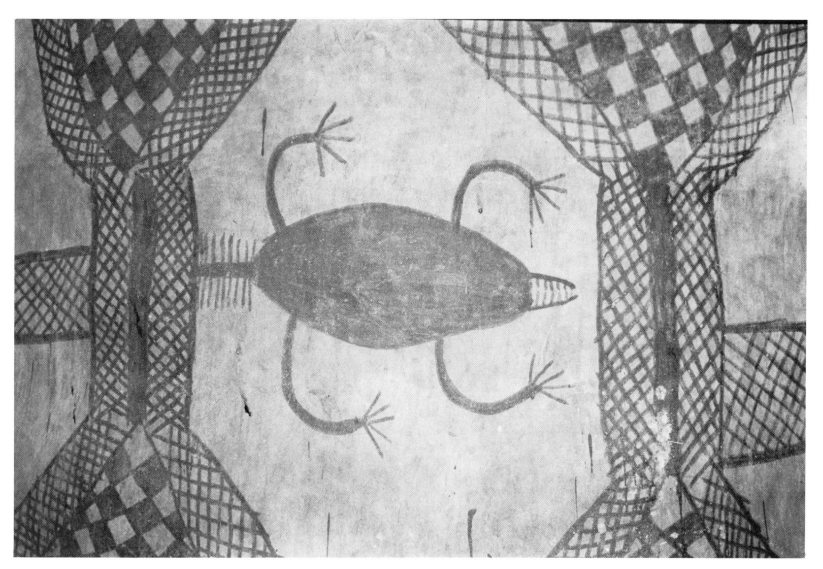

P.97. Mural decorations.

P.98. A senior woman's *dóok* facing the communal packed-earth court. The opening in the wall on the right gives access to her outdoor and indoor cooking spaces, the *daň* and the *dobilé*.

(*daanlétaté*, D.34). The *zoħ* and the senior woman's spaces constitute the prime points of reference for the building of a compound. In Bako's homestead, the *zoħ* is erected first (D.48), whereas in other homesteads it is constructed third, after the senior woman's indoor cooking space (*dobilé*) and sleeping room (*dóok*).

The gradient of outdoor spaces leading to the dwellings progresses from the *samàn* (area in front of the compound entrance), to the *zambaat* (cattle kraal), to the *daanlétaté* (communal packed-earth court supervised by the senior woman of the compound). Serving a distributive function, this court gives access to all the dwelling units of Bako's compound (D.35) but is shared only among Bako's wives and daughters-in-law, the men having their own smaller courts, the *zaak*. Two features standing within the *daanlétaté* denote its communal character: a large

shrine also named *winn*, which faces the senior woman's sleeping room (*dóok*) and remains visible to the other two women from their outdoor cooking spaces (*daħ*), and a partly walled area for the preparation of guinea-corn beer, the *daħbuk*, on the right of the court access.

Each woman's dwelling unit comprises two independent circular constructions surmounted by conical thatched roofs, the *dóok* and *dobilé*, whose intervals are enclosed by curved walls above eye level to form a third space, the *daħ*. These walls, spanning like two protective arms, maintain the privacy of both the *dóok* and the *dobilé* by hiding from view their doorways, which can therefore be reached only through the *daħ*. The exception to this setting is the senior woman's *dóok*, which looks out to the entrance of the court (*daanlétaté*), and is directly accessible (P.98). Her status inside the compound may be detected through the mediate position of her room and the elaborate shape of its doorway (D.36, section AA'). Low and arched, it is brought into relief by a protruding collar that frames its contour and terminates on each side in the form of a curved bench. On top of the right bench, two covered pots bearing signs of sacrifices are kept.

All doorways of women's *dóok* are equipped, as among the Eastern Kassena and the Nankani, with a low semicircular wall *(kóot)* that one must climb over upon entering. Two curved adobe platforms leaning against the extremities of this low wall constitute the only built-in interior furnishing of the space. They function as both a sitting and a temporary storage place. Of more permanent storage use are the large jars and baskets set against the wall on the periphery of the room. The *dóok* is connected to the *dobilé* by the *dañ*, which serves as a small pri-

vate court and outdoor cooking area, protected from the sun by loose bundles of millet stalks laid across its walls. A much lower partition than that found in the *dóok* also faces the entrance of the *dobilé*. Easily stepped over, it is sometimes not included in more recent constructions. The *dobilé* usually contains a woman's grinding platform and operates as her indoor cooking space.

Bako's room *(trandóok)* and that of his son *(dóok)* are situated opposite each other, at the boundary between the packed-earth court and the cattle kraal. Like the *zoñ* and the *bulugu* (fowl house) that guard the sides of the compound entrance, the men's rooms close off the ring of dwelling units defining the court. They differ from the women's spaces in their rounded square shapes and their easily accessible doorways devoid of the low semicircular partition that emphasizes the act of entering

199

P.99. A man erecting a conical pillar in front of the entrance of his compound.

P.100. The *daïbuk,* or space where millet beer is prepared.

and exiting. Bako, who is the senior man of the compound, not only has an enclosed smaller court for himself, the *tranzaak,* but has also built a small porch in front of the doorway of his room (dotted line in D.35). This porch, also found preceding women's spaces in other homesteads, is said to indicate the dweller's status, for only elders of the family may erect one in front of their rooms.

A woman having no offspring usually possesses only one room. As soon as she gives birth to a child, however, she may expect to have a second room built at the beginning of the next dry season. In some instances, this means that the space in which she lives, the two neighboring spaces, and their connecting walls will be demolished and four new constructions erected in their place.[7] This custom makes even more obvious the common expression that refers to children as "builders up of a compound." Thus, the general building sequence starting with a woman's *dobilé,* her *dóok,* the *zoh,* then the man's *dóok,* may continue with each new wife and each new daughter-in-law who joins the family and spread further as they become mothers of the compound.

The Kusasi build their dwellings with the same technique as that used by the Kassena and Nankani. The red laterite pigment is painted on top once the walls have been coated and carefully evened out. One of the most striking aspects of Kusasi habitations lies in their rich mural decorations composed of both geometric and figurative design motifs. The main color used in the area is the black pigment, set off against the red laterite background. All designs are painted; the interplay of colors, incisions, and moldings widely encountered among their Nankani and Eastern Kassena neighbors is absent here. A

P.101. Wall paintings of a man's space.

painting may come singly, in pairs, or in a series. The latter instance is particularly true for geometric motifs, which either spread along the entire height of the wall (P.101, P.100, D.36, D.37) or stretch out in a smaller series along the two horizontal registers that divide the outer wall surface of a dwelling (P.102).

Kusasi wall paintings have been compared to the modern mural decorations of the Konkomba (eastern neighbors of the Dagomba). Both are believed to be recent adaptations dating back only a few decades. The Konkomba's archaic style, as noted by several observers in the past, consisted of exclusively geometric, incised motifs to which color was added.[8] The evolution from colored engravings to paintings and from pure geometric to predominantly figurative designs, illustrating humans and the animals of their surroundings, seems to be widespread throughout West Africa. This process of transformation

is, indeed, already noticeable in the Kusasi's neighboring Kassena and Nankani areas, where wall engravings, like facial and body adornment marks, slowly disappear and seldom appear other than on façades of elder women's dwellings. The shift of emphasis from abstract or semi-abstract to highly figurative designs naturally also entails a change in the image of the house and perception of space. Instead of being carried out as usual by women, who share in this domain the role of perpetuating tradition, the designs are, nowadays, also executed by young boys who learn drawing at school and do not necessarily relate it to their cultural background or understand its significance in the traditional architectural context.

P.102. A man's rounded square *dóok*
(left) next to a woman's circular *dóok*
(right).

AFTERWORD

The Gurunsi houses of Upper Volta represent in themselves an argument on behalf of a vernacular architecture[1] that is developed by the people beyond the confines of the market and its manipulative industrial ware. They argue for preserving subsistence economies at a time when we have begun to realize that attempts to substitute universal commodities for vernacular values have led, not to equality, but to a worldwide form of poverty defined by standards that technocrats may modify at will.

The recovery of vernacular domains does not necessarily suggest a return to tradition; nor does this study of the architecture of the Gurunsi people aim at preserving the traditional houses and their inhabitants as if they were artifacts to be studied by experts and gazed at with wonder. It may be important to record a disappearing architecture whose wealth of constructions belongs to a culture in rapid transition and remains widely unknown. Our general intent is, however, to retrieve the value, not of tradition for its own sake, but of the people's autonomy in their traditional way of building.

The preceding texts, drawings, and photographs contribute to the body of works that aim at undermining the cult of progress lying at the root of our market-dependent society (a task that may sound outdated nowadays but continues nonetheless to be essential to those of us who believe in a lifestyle based on mutual reciprocity instead of exchange or vertical distribution). They lay emphasis on the necessity for a subsistence-oriented way of life in which the relation of men, women, and their buildings is not one of oppression or submission, but one of a mutual vulnerability. In Gurunsi villages, maintaining one's house is part of the rhythm of life; the period just before the rainy season, for example, is regularly devoted to refinishing and mending walls and roofs. A house in this society is not merely an enclosure to live in, but an environment to live with. It acknowledges the inevitability of decay and assumes that the containment of space is a means to an end, not an end in itself.

A number of problems generated by industrial production in Western societies are reflected in many "modern" schemes. The absence of territoriality and natural surveillance, the lack of transition from public to private space, the inadequacy of space for a majority of people—the very young and the very old—are among the visible symptoms of a decaying environment. Identical processes are observable in African urban areas and in an ever-growing number of rural settlements. Low-rise buildings within high-density developments, interior private courtyards, expandability, self-help, and passive energy systems are concepts now studied and praised in the West which have been used for centuries in African, Middle Eastern, and Southeast Asian architectures. But few of these studies have been used to improve new African towns or rural settlements. What, other than military and sanitary concerns, can we trace in the French colonial planning of towns in Senegal, Mali, or Upper Volta? In what way is the present use of square-grid planning, wide streets for cars, and high-rise or middle-rise housing adapted to African patterns of living? Standardization continues its relentless course, and one can easily foresee an invasion by its ubiquitous models of even the remote African countryside.

The condescension implied by such words as "primitive," "mud" houses, and "hut" is so deeply rooted that the very fact that a traditional African architecture exists almost never fails to astonish people, including African city dwellers. In the remote villages of Africa, schools are still based on European models and European textbooks, and are particularly efficient in identifying progress with affluence and technical sophistication. Modernization in Africa, as elsewhere, requires people to become suppliers and consumers. It implies high-rise apartments, suburban-style housing, unused communal spaces, and rigid zoning regulations that account for isolated shopping centers, recreational areas, and light industries. Aside from the long-term material drawbacks, the social and psychological side effects are bound to be at least as great as in the West since the gap between tradition and modernism is larger in Africa and the time for adaptation to change much shorter.

Traditionally, the sub-Saharan adobe house is built and maintained by the whole family—or by the entire village in the event of fire—during the dry season, when no farming is done. That task is also a social regulator: it strengthens the coopera-tive spirit, stimulates creativity, and performs an educational function. But Western countries have by now introduced a whole new set of materials, and with them the need for training, schooling, and specialization indispensable to their use and maintenance. The replacement of adobe by concrete blocks and corrugated-metal roofs gives the illusion of permanence, but the long-range consequence is the dissolution of a way of life. With their adoption the villagers give up their autonomy by becoming dependent on a chain of production beyond their control: the transportation of material, the services of the master builder for the construction, and the need for wages to acquire the money to meet the overall cost.

The last requirement accounts for the depopulation of the countryside and the spread of what Ivan Illich calls planned or modernized poverty. In the dry season, the villages are left populated only by old people, middle-aged women, and children; in the absence of young males, they are compelled gradually to abandon their traditional ways of building and maintenance. As "durable" material appears on the scene, neglect of the house becomes commonplace. On the one hand, it is more difficult to keep hand marks, cooking smoke, and other stains from appearing on whitewashed walls than on dark varnish-like or sand- or earth-colored walls. On the other hand, people do not have the same feelings about purchased objects as they do about self-made ones—human values differ from market values; the sense of creativity and responsibility is not at issue when housing becomes a consumer mass product. Not having participated in the process of their making, people expect houses to last without being cared for, and since maintenance involves more costs, it is usually overlooked.

"A house is at the same time the most visible and the most personal of ethnic traits."[2] Architecture as a reflection and projection of social and spiritual life plays, indeed, such an essential role in traditional societies that it leads Jean Capron, who studied the tightly knit fabric of Bwa habitations, to the following observation: "The Catholic missionaries are not unaware that the preservation of house forms inherited from the ancestral past fosters, as much as it translates, respect for the most profound values of Bwa culture. By their own admission, any long-lasting evangelical action requires 'the dismantling of dwelling blocks' and the constitution of a 'well-spaced' ['aéré'] habitation."[3] Such an observation presents a powerful argument against a state of mind unaware that architecture is not mere building and traditional habitation not a synonym for a lower building technology. Each case study presented here constitutes a storehouse of information. In contrast to the platitudinous and sterile repetition of some of our industrialized housing, these houses display an infinite range of variations on a theme, the theme here being simply a practice carefully transmitted from one generation to another to provide, not a rigid framework for conformity, but basic tools for creativity. Its flexibility leaves ample room for the mind to grow, and its limits depend largely on a self-defined preference. Consideration of the elements of this architecture gives us access to the accumulated experience and wisdom of generations, a wisdom that challenges our conceptual habits and calls for the re-examination and reorientation of our present environment.

APPENDIX

Phonetic symbols
Graphic conventions
Occupancy, kinship mapping, and
building evolution

Phonetic Symbols

The following phonetic symbols have been used in transcribing vernacular African words. The vowel symbols are elastic in their values; it is to be noted also that in many cases the pronunciation of words varies from one native speaker to another.

	English	French		International Phonetic Alphabet
a as in		pas; cas		(a)
à	art; car	sable; âge		(a:)
e or é	take	été; donner		(e)
ë		feu; noeud	Ger. schön	(ø)
è	pen; get	mettre (short)		(ɛ)
		maître (long)		
i	bit; physic	vite		(i)
in		vin (short)		(ɛ̃)
		ceindre (long)		
o	lot (short)	donne (short)		(ɔ)
	all (long)	fort (long)		
ó		dos; chaud		(o)
u	put (short)	tout (short)		(u)
	shoe (long)	cour (long)		
ch	sham; dish	chose		(ʃ)
g or gu	go; ghost	garde; guerre		(g)
j	closest equivalent would be dy in dieu (French)			
dj	rage; edge			(dz)
ñ	pinion; onion	campagne	Span. ñ	( ) (nj)
ṅ	bang; sing			( )
x	loch	Span. j in	jabón	(χ)
z	zinc; buzz	cousin; zéro		(z)
Z	pleasure; vision	jour; gilet		(ʒ)

The spelling of village names corresponds to the spelling used by the governmental administration of Upper Volta.

Graphic Conventions

Symbols are placed inside the spaces where people sleep. Those located outside of the compound indicate that the person either travels, resides elsewhere, or is deceased.

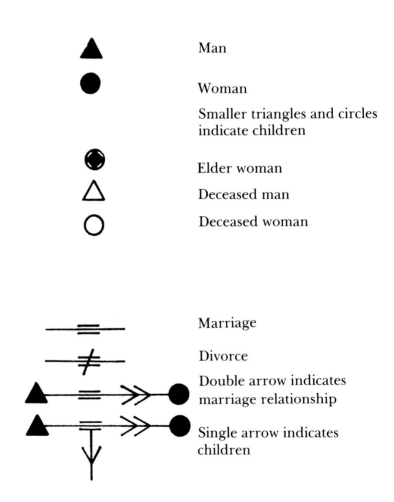

Man

Woman

Smaller triangles and circles indicate children

Elder woman

Deceased man

Deceased woman

Marriage

Divorce

Double arrow indicates marriage relationship

Single arrow indicates children

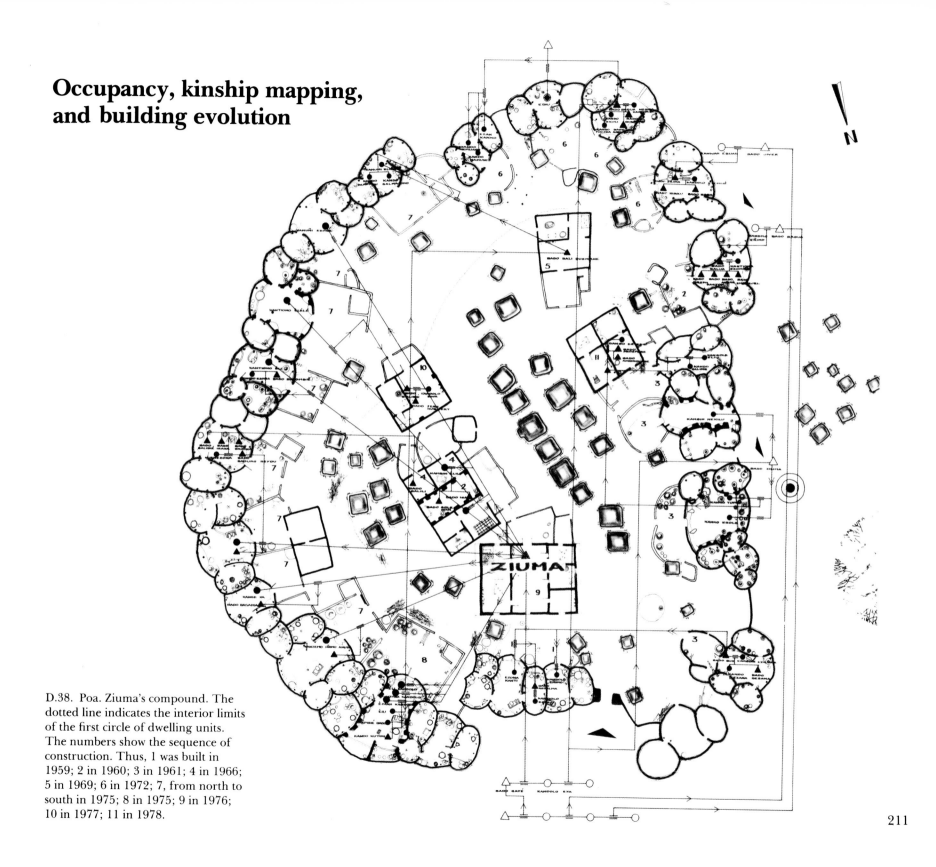

Occupancy, kinship mapping, and building evolution

ZIUMA

D.38. Poa. Ziuma's compound. The dotted line indicates the interior limits of the first circle of dwelling units. The numbers show the sequence of construction. Thus, 1 was built in 1959; 2 in 1960; 3 in 1961; 4 in 1966; 5 in 1969; 6 in 1972; 7, from north to south in 1975; 8 in 1975; 9 in 1976; 10 in 1977; 11 in 1978.

D.39. Pouni. Badu's compound. Badu is represented here inside his storage spaces on the first floor; his *dibi* is built on top of the room immediately north of where he is shown.

BADU

ÉLILITIÈNÈ

AZILA   AYA   BÈKAYÈ

ÈYÈ TIÈNÈ   ÈBU TIÈNÈ

ZILA ÈLUBIÈ   DIALA ZÈNA

HURUIN TIÈNÈ

GUADO

ONGO ZONGO

DIO

NÈGDÈ WENDÈ   ZÒNGO

AZILA AYA

AWAMBIÈ   TIÈNÈ

WA NIBIÈ   MARIAM NIBIÈ

VOUBIÈ   AYÀN   PIÈN   POMA

AWAMBIÈ   DIO

ZILA   BILÈ É   BADU

ÈKOBIÈ   NÈA

NÈKALDIÈ

0   1M

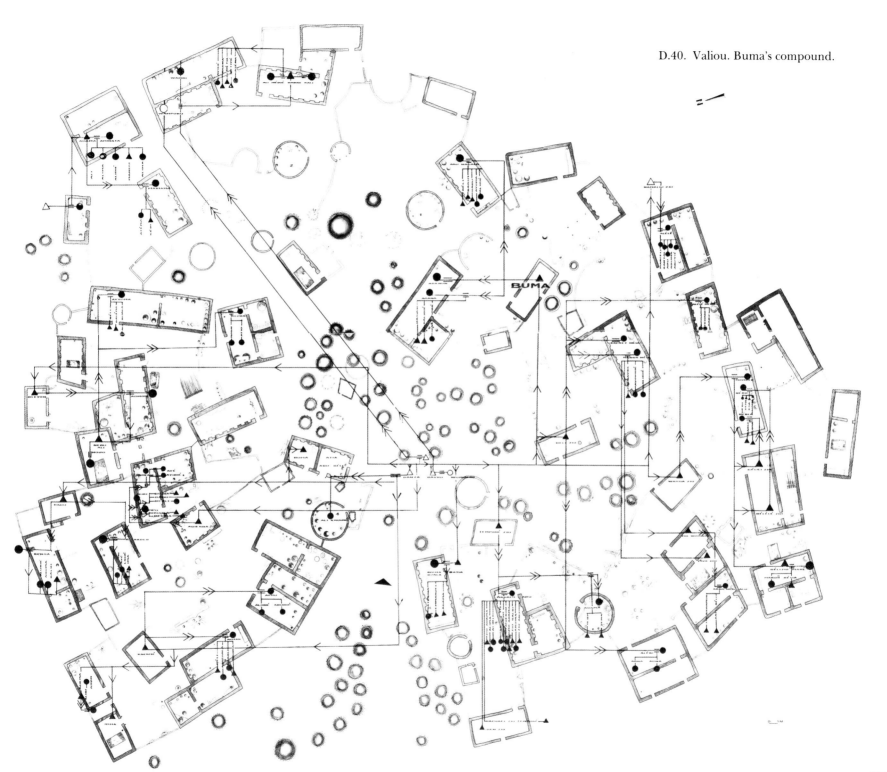

D.40. Valiou. Buma's compound.

213

D.41. Koena. Okano's compound.
The numbers indicate the chronology
of the construction, which started
forty years ago. Okano's *djanibiè*
stands on top of the spaces where his
name is indicated.

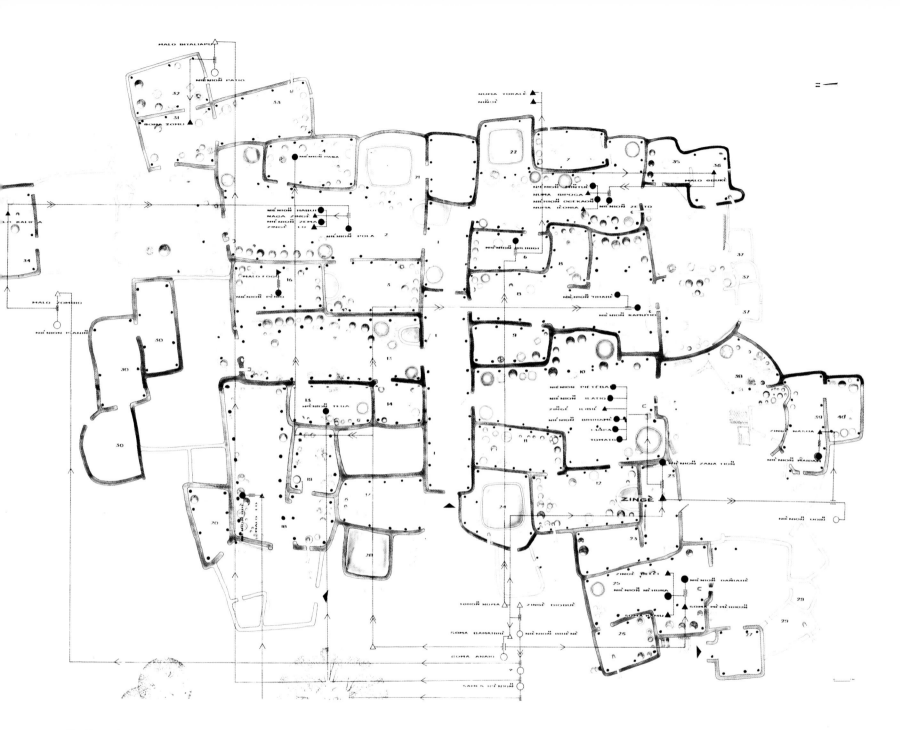

D.42. *Nyiémé.* Zingè's homestead. Phases of construction: from 1 to 20, 1950; 21 to 24, 1953; 25 to 28, 1957; 29 and 30: 1958; 31 to 34, 1964; 35 to 37, 1964; 35 to 37, 1972; 38, 1976; 39 and 40, 1978. The previous head of the family built an upper-story unit above spaces 13 and 14 and a filled-in room that functions as a support (it is left blank on the drawing).

D.43. Outoulov. Dakui's compound.

D.44. Koumbili. Atiga's homestead.

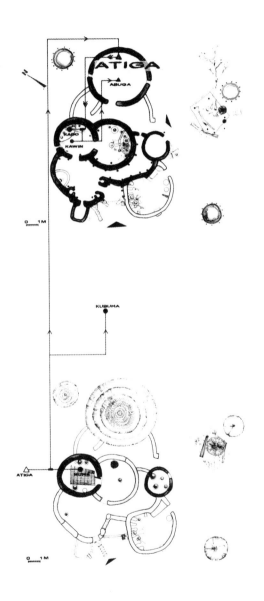

N

D.45. Tangassoko. Tanga's compound.

0   1M

217

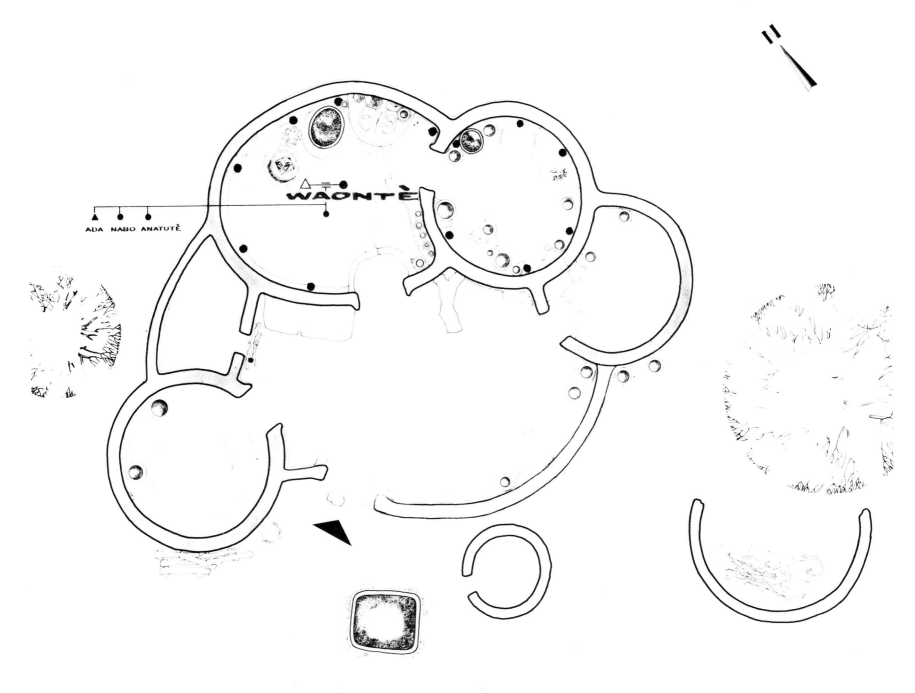

WAONTÈ

ADA   NABO   ANATUTÈ

D.46. Kolo.   Waonte's homestead.

218

0 ——— 1M

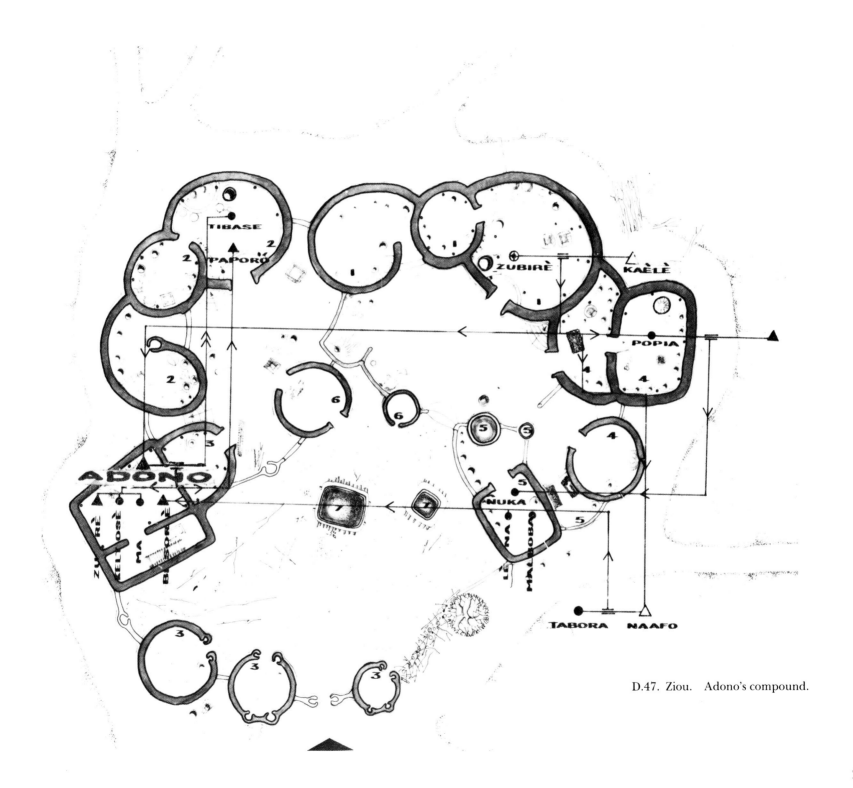

D.47. Ziou. Adono's compound.

219

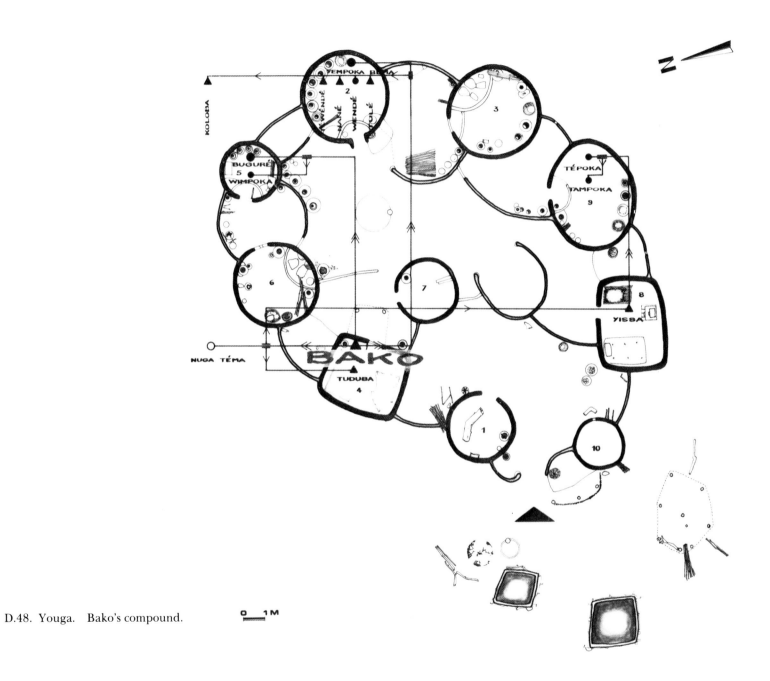

KOLOBA

TEMPOKA BEMA

2

KWÉNDÉ
NABÉ
WÉNDÉ
OLÉ

3

TÉPOKA

TAMPOKA

9

BUGURÉ
5
WIMPOKA

6

7

8

YISSA

NUGA TÉMA

BAKO

TUDUBA
4

1

10

D.48. Youga. Bako's compound.

0   1M

220

NOTES

Introduction

1. Anne-Marie Duperray, "Les Gourounsi de Haute-Volta: Conquête et colonisation, 1896–1933," thèse de 3ème cycle (Paris: Ecole des Hautes Etudes en Sciences Sociales, 1978), p. 16.

2. A term used to designate the aggregate number of languages distributed into two main groups: Tem in eastern Ghana and central Togo and Gurunsi, or Grusi in the nomenclature of most authors (Westerman, Bryan, Lavergne de Tressan, Zwernemann, Bender-Samuel), extending along both sides of the northern Ghana border and, in Upper Volta, beyond the Volta (see D.2). Gabriel Manessy, *Les Langues Gurunsi* (Paris: Selaf, 1969), I, 12–13.

3. *Ibid.,* II, 83.

4. A. Prost, "Deux langues gourounsi, le Kasem et le Nuni," *IFAN,* XXXIII, No. 2 (April 1971), 434, and F. J. Nicolas, "Glossaire L'élé-Français," *Mémoires de l'IFAN,* No. 24 (1953), p. 135. Both are cited in Duperray's dissertation.

5. Duperray, p. 19.

6. *Travels and Discoveries in North and Central Africa, 1849–1855* (1857; rpt. London: Frank Cass, 1965), III, 643.

7. Louis Tauxier discussed at length "La Question Gourounsi" in his *Nouvelles Notes sur le Mossi et le Gourounsi* (Paris: Emile Larose, 1924), pp. 35–54. He attributed Koelle's Guresa-speaking people to the Sissala, pp. 37, 191. B. S. Guggenheim also includes a summary of "The Grunshi Problem" in her "Aspects of the Portal and Portal Decoration in Northeastern Ghana," Ph.D. dissertation, Columbia University, 1976, pp. 46–55.

8. A. W. Cardinall, on the other hand, wrote that "Grunshi has come to be particularly used for the Kassena." *The Natives of the Northern Territories of the Gold Coast* (1920; rpt. New York: Negro Universities Press, 1969), p. viii. J. Zwernemann reached the same conclusion in "Shall We Use the Word 'Grunsi'?" *Africa,* XXVIII, No. 2 (April 1958), 124. These accounts may, in turn, explain why the Kassena designate their neighbors by the name Nankani.

9. Information given by Nama Pitié, "Les Gourounsi de Léo," Cahier de l'Ecole William Ponty, unpubl. ms., 1940, and Drissa Diakité, "Les Funérailles

au Gourounsi," Cahier de l'Ecole William Ponty, unpubl. ms., 1942–1944. The first meaning is given by Pitié and his sources, the second by Diakité.

10. Tauxier, pp. 35–36.

11. Cardinall, p. viii; Meyer Fortes, *The Dynamics of Clanship among the Talensi* (London: Oxford University Press, 1945), p. 16.

12. Duperray, p. 31. R. S. Rattray in *The Tribes of the Ashanti Hinterland* (1932; rpt. London: Oxford University Press, 1969), I, 232, also saw the word Gurunsi as "equivalent of the word 'Kaffir'—unbeliever, eater of dogs—as bestowed by Mohammedans on those who do not follow the Prophet."

13. Bruce T. Grindal, "An Ethnographic Classification of the Sissala of Northern Ghana," *Ethnology*, XI, No. 4 (October 1972), 411.

14. The "Paleonigritic" civilizations traced by Jean-Claude Froelich on a map he includes in *Les Montagnards "Paléonigritiques"* (Paris: ORSTOM, 1968), p. 248.

15. According to Duperray, the term *pyo*, used by the other groups to designate the administrative chief of a village, exists among the Lela only as a name for the chiefs chosen at the time of groupings for land cultivation. The Ko, on the other hand, have no term to designate such a chief and have borrowed from their Dyula neighbors the word *diamanatigi* (p. 48).

16. Distinction made by Jean Capron, *Communautés villageoises Bwa* (Paris: Institut d'Ethnologie, 1973), I, 55–56, who took his information from J. L. Boutillier, "Rapport sur les structures foncières en République de Haute-Volta" (Paris: ORSTOM, 1963). For an analysis of both systems of power, see Kunz Dittmer, "Die sakralen Häuptlinger der Gurunsi im Obervolta-Gebiet, Westafrika," *Mitteilungen aus dem für Völkerkunde im Hamburg*, Vol. XXVII (1961).

17. Rattray, I, xv.

18. In *Transactions of the Historical Society of Ghana*, VI (1962), 80.

19. A term used by Capitaine Binger, *Du Niger au Golfe de Guinée* (Paris: Hachette, 1892), I, 433–434. The older type of habitation still existing nowadays in Koumbili is not an "underground," or "semi-underground," but, more precisely, a "semi-sunken" dwelling. See note 9 of Chapter 7.

20. The Puguli (Chapter 5), like their Birifor neighbors, see no contradiction in clan and lineage membership traced through women, although they are also primarily organized on the basis of agnatic descent. They may, with the Sissala, be classified as "semi-matriarchal" (Tauxier).

21. The Bwa are the Gurunsi's western neighbors, who, in the past, have been included in the generic name Bobo. Called Bobo-Oulé by the Dyula, the Bwa also number among the oldest inhabitants of the region. For more details on the Bwa, and for a general picture of the Gurunsi's other western neighbors, see Capron, I, 24–69.

22. See, for example, Binger, I, 430–433; II, 35.

23. The history of Mossi kingdoms has been traced by M. Izard, *Introduction à l'histoire des Royaumes Mossi*, Recherches Voltaïques, XII and XIII (Paris: CNRS–CVRS, 1970). Information on the history of the Gurunsi is mainly based on Duperray's dissertation, which proves to be (in our opinion) the most complete study on the subject up to date.

24. *Ibid.*, pp. 153, 273.

25. *Ibid.*, p. 16.

26. Duperray, p. 70.

27. For more information on the Karantao movement, see *ibid.*, pp. 70–76; Louis Tauxier, *Le Noir du Soudan* (Paris: Emile Larose, 1912), pp. 410–412;

and N. Levitzion, *Muslims and Chiefs in West Africa* (London: Oxford University Press, 1968).

28. Spelled Gandiari by Binger.

29. See both Georges Savonnet, "Notes sur quelques ruines situées dans la région de Léo," *Notes Africaines*, No. 71 (1956), pp. 65–67, and Duperray, p. 80.

30. It is worth noting that a small number of Muslims in Sissalaland and Kassenaland, for example, are former inhabitants of the area who were captured by the Zabarima, sold, and taken away from their country. They have returned home, having converted to Islam during the period of their captivity. Tauxier, *Le Noir du Soudan*, pp. 332, 359. See also note 32.

31. Binger, I, 481, 446 (our translation).

32. From the West African coastal regions to Chad. Babatu is said to have brought back Gurunsi slaves to work along the Niger River. J. Rouch, *Colloque sur les cultures voltaïques*, p. 166 (cited by Duperray, p. 85). See note 30.

33. Nazi Boni, *Histoire synthétique de l'Afrique résistante* (Paris: Présence Africaine, 1971), p. 205. The statement, as Duperray pointed out, is valid for the neighborhoods of Leo, not for those of the Kassena and Nankani, who consider Hamaria more an oppressor than a liberator.

34. For more details on Hamaria and his revolt, see Savonnet; Pitié; Duperray, pp. 83–89; and J. J. Holden, "The Zabarima Conquest of Northwest Ghana," *Transactions of the Historical Society of Ghana*, VIII (1965), 60–86.

35. For an analysis of the problems that arose in Gurunsiland under the colonial administration, see Duperray's dissertation.

36. Tauxier, *Le Noir du Soudan*, pp. 168–69 (our translation).

37. *The Scope of Anthropology*, trans. S. Ortner Paul and R. A. Paul (London: Jonathan Cape, 1967), p. 44.

Chapter 1

1. Names have been changed to protect, whenever possible, the inhabitant's identity.

2. A local fermented drink very popular in Upper Volta. Details for the preparation of this drink can be found in Edward A. DeCarbo, "Artistry among Kasem-speaking Peoples of Northern Ghana," Ph.D. dissertation, Indiana University, 1977.

3. *Tiogo: Etude géographique d'un terroir Léla*. Atlas des Structures Agraires au Sud du Sahara, II (Paris: Mouton, 1968), 41–43.

Chapter 2

1. See Denis Paulme, ed., *Women of Tropical Africa* (Berkeley: University of California Press, 1963), p. 10.

2. It is nevertheless difficult to prove that the use of the terrace roof for sleeping at night is due solely to the loose assemblage of the dwelling units, whose exposed walls tend to retain more of the heat. This use among the Nankani and the Kassena may simply relate to the design of the entrance into their living units. The built-in low wall in the doorway does not, obviously, have the same flexibility as a door (although it presents many advantages in other respects) that can be entirely shut or opened for ventilation.

3. Ruth Eaton, "Mud," *Architectural Review*, No. 1016 (October 1981), p. 222.

4. C. A. Diop, *Nations nègres et culture* (Paris: Présence Africaine, 1955; rpt. 1979), and *Antériorité des civilisations nègres: Mythes ou vérité historique?* (Paris: Présence Africaine, 1967). Both studies have been partly translated into English in Mercer Cook, ed., *The African Origin of Civilization: Myth or Reality?* (Westport, Conn.: Lawrence Hill, 1974).

5. In traditional Gurunsi societies, house building is done by the family members with the assistance of a local group of helpers who offer their services on the principle of reciprocity. They are generously provided with meals and beer during the days of work but receive no monetary payment. They may be called "masons," after L. Tauxier, only in the sense that they have experience in masonry.

Chapter 3

1. Buma, as mentioned in the Introduction, is not exactly the senior man of the compound but the eldest among the active men.

2. Marcel Griaule, *Dieu d'eau: Entretiens avec Ogotemmêli* (Paris: Fayard, 1966), pp. 27–33. English version: *Conversations with Ogotemmêli* (1965; rpt. New York: Oxford University Press, 1975).

3. Jean-Paul Lebeuf, *L'Habitation des Fali* (Paris: Hachette, 1961), pp. 369–370, 459–461, 153, 543.

4. Nama Pitié, "Les Gourounsi de Léo," Cahier de l'Ecole William Ponty, unpubl. ms., 1940.

5. See Griaule, pp. 24, 136, 201, and Lebeuf, p. 461.

6. Other combinations are also seen: the split motifs come, for example, in fours with a round motif in the middle which separates them in twos.

7. See Griaule, pp. 16–18; 24, 130–31, and Lebeuf, p. 383.

8. F. J. Nicolas, "Mythes et êtres mythiques des L'éla de la Haute-Volta," *Bulletin de L'IFAN*, XIV, No. 4, (October 1952), 1355.

9. See plans of a Mossi compound in Gérard Remy, *Donsin: Les structures agraires d'un village Mossi de la région de Nobere*, Recherches Voltaïques, XV (Paris: CNRS–CVRS, 1972), 54; or Junzo Kawada, *Le Zitenga*, Recherches Voltaïques, VI (Paris: CNRS–CVRS, 1967), hors texte 1.

Chapter 5

1. This statement gives credence to Henri Labouret's hypothesis. The latter assumes the term Puguli was first used by the LoWiili, the Dagaba (or Dagari), and the Birifor to designate a group of people who call themselves Pwa (or Pwo in the singular). Later on, it was adopted by the French administration, whose Mande-Dyula informants "did not bother searching for the true name of their neighbors." The Pwa consider themselves akin to the Dea and claim a common linguistic background with the Isala or Sissala. See *Nouvelles Notes sur les tribus du rameau Lobi, leurs migrations, leur évolution, leurs parlers et ceux de leurs voisins*, Mémoires IFAN, No. 54 (Dakar: IFAN, 1958), pp. 28–31, 49–50.

2. See Henri Labouret, *Les Tribus du rameau Lobi* (Paris: Institut d'Ethnologie, 1931), p. 151. For another example, see Plan 24 in Georges Savonnet, *Les Birifor de Diepla et sa région insulaires du rameau Lobi (Haute-Volta)*, Atlas des Structures Agraires au Sud du Sahara, XII (Paris: ORSTOM, 1976), 79.

3. Labouret, *Les Tribus*, p. 152, and Savonnet, p. 79.

4. The use of the terrace has been extensively described by scholars working in the area. See, for example, Jack Goody, *The Social Organisation of the LoWiili* (London: Oxford University Press, 1967), p. 39; Labouret, *Les Tribus* p. 152, Pl. IX; and the photographs in Babar Mumtaz, "Villages on the Black Volta," in Paul Oliver, ed., *Shelter and Society* (London: Barrie & Jenkins, 1969), pp. 84–85.

5. Savonnet, p. 80; Mumtaz, p. 88; Christian Pradeau, "Kokolibou (Haute-Volta) ou le pays Dagari à travers un terroir," *Etudes Rurales*, Nos. 37–39 (January–September 1970), p. 88.

6. The technique of having a filled space supporting the upper floor is also found among the Dagari. See G. Savonnet, *Pina: Etude d'un terroir de front pionnier en pays Dagari*. Atlas des Structures Agraires au Sud du Sahara, IV (Paris: Mouton, 1970), 24.

7. Matriclan and patrilineage memberships equally define the social role of a Puguli. Nyiémé is composed of five clans recognizable through their names and avoidances (referring to certain animals that should not be eaten or killed by clan members).

8. Gurunsi societies, as mentioned in the Introduction, are predominantly patrilineal.

9. "At the beginning cowries were exchanged for strips of woven fabric, that is to say, for the Word of the ancestors, and especially that of the seventh ancestor, the master of Speech. These cowries came from Lébé, himself offspring of the eighth ancestor, whose number was that of the Word." In Marcel Griaule, *Conversations with Ogotemmêli* (1965; rpt. New York: Oxford University Press, 1975), p. 204. For a more detailed analysis of these numbers, see Marcel Griaule and Germaine Dieterlen, *Le Renard pâle* (Paris: Institut d'Ethnologie, 1965), Vol. I.

Chapter 6

1. Reproduced in Georges Savonnet, *Pina: Etude d'un terroir de front pionnier en pays Dagari*, Atlas des Structures Agraires au Sud du Sahara, IV (Paris: Mouton, 1970), p. 18.

2. Bruce T. Grindal, "An Ethnographic Classification of the Sissala of Northern Ghana," *Ethnology*, XI, No. 4 (October 1972), 409–423.

3. Pina is an example of such segmented communities. Here, according to Savonnet, the two groups, Dagari and Sissala, try to ignore and interfere as little as possible with each other.

4. See Grindal; John W. Nunley, "Sissala Sculpture of Northern Ghana," Ph.D. dissertation, University of Washington, 1976, pp. 15, 25–29; and Labelle Prussin, *Architecture in Northern Ghana* (Berkeley: University of California Press, 1969), pp. 67–68.

5. For other examples, see R. S. Rattray, *The Tribes of the Ashanti Hinterland* (1932; rpt. London: Oxford University Press, 1969) II, Figs. 134, 135, p. 489.

6. The wall surrounding Yoro was meant only to enclose the Zabarima's and Sissala's properties. The one in Sati, on the other hand, was built to resist the attacks of these same Zabarima. Georges Savonnet, "Notes sur quelques ruines situées dans la région de Léo (Haute-Volta)," *Notes Africaines*, No. 71 (July 1956), pp. 65–67.

7. Our research does not support Prussin's observations on the haphazard and indiscriminate placing of tapered buttresses in Sekai and Larabanga, or the exclusively functional interpretation of engaged buttresses

she gave in *Architecture in Northern Ghana*, pp. 74–75, 86–87.

8. See photographs and descriptions of Dyula habitations of Bondoukou in Louis Tauxier, *Le Noir de Bondoukou* (Paris: Ernest Leroux, 1921), Pls. V, VI, VII, XIII, XV, XVIII, and pp. 76, 219. The Dyula's role in the spread of the mosque style has been discussed by P. Ferguson in "Mosques and Islamization Process in the 19th Century among the Eastern Dyula" (unpubl. ms., cited in R. W. Hull, *African Cities and Towns before the European Conquest* [New York: W. W. Norton, 1976], pp. 68, 72), and mentioned by Prussin (see note 9).

9. Labelle Prussin, "Pillars, Projections, and Paradigms," *Architectura* (Munich: Deustcher Kunstverlag, 1977), pp. 65–81. These earthen pillars may be seen on the terrace roofs of Nuna and Kassonfras habitations. Louis Tauxier in *Le Noir du Soudan* (Paris: Emile Larose, 1912), p. 168, simply noted that they were erected to the divinity of the Ancestors or the Sky. See also Fig. 136 in Rattray, p. 491.

Chapter 7

1. Information given by the chief of the district of Pô in Jean Cremer, *Matériaux d'ethnographie et de linguistique soudanaise* (Paris: Paul Geuthner, 1924), II, ii.

2. Louis Tauxier, *Le Noir du Soudan* (Paris: Emile Larose, 1912), p. 201. In *Nouvelles Notes sur le Mossi et le Gourounsi* (Paris: Emile Larose, 1924), pp. 45, 48–49, Tauxier raises the question of whether the Fra are truly Kassena or not, but he still classifies them with the Kassonbura under the denomination "Kassouna." In "Les Notions du dieu-ciel chez quelques tribus voltaïques," J. Zwernemann distinguishes the Occidental Kassena or Kassena Fra from the Oriental Kassena or Kassena Bura and the Meridional Kassena. *Bulletin de l'IFAN*, XXIII, series B, Nos. 1–2 (January–April 1961), 259–262.

3. Also called Koumoullou by Capitaine Binger in *Du Niger au Golfe du Guinée* (Paris: Hachette, 1892), II, 4–5.

4. This version is said to come from the chief of Koumbili and has been set down by Tauxier in *Le Noir du Soudan*, p. 224. The interpretation of the name is Tauxier's.

5. Cited by Captain R. S. Rattray in *The Tribes of the Ashanti Hinterland* (1932; rpt. London: Oxford University Press, 1969), I, 260.

6. Another version, which differs in many details from ours and is said to come from Kampedegue (Kampiriki?) or the father of the present chief of Kolo, may be found in Bernard Saint Jalmes, "Aspects historiques et sociologiques d'un village Kasséna de Haute-Volta" unpubl. ms. (Ouagadougou: CVRS, n.d.).

7. The pacific coexistence of both forms of power, discussed in the Introduction, has also been noted by Rattray, who considered it to belong to "an elaborate system of decentralized administration" (pp. xv–xvi, xx). His distinction between secular and spiritual leaderships is, however, questionable.

8. Binger, II, 4–5.

9. G. Le Moal, "Les Habitations semi-souterraines en Afrique de l'ouest," *Journal de la Société des Africanistes*, XXX, fascicule I (Paris: Musée de l'Homme, 1960), 198. The half-sunken dwelling, which Le Moal designates as *habitation en sous-sol* (literally translated as "basement habitation"), is to be distinguished from the entirely sunken dwelling with its roof on ground level, *habitation semi-souterraine* or semi-underground habitation.

10. Binger, I, 433–434.

11. Le Moal, p. 197.

12. A series of cylindrical openings on the ground may still be seen in the circle of Ziniare. Each widens out toward the interior to form a habitable space that communicates with the neighbors' space. These dwellings are now unused and partly filled with earth. They were occupied by the Nyonyose, the first inhabitants of the area before the Mossi's arrival, whom Tauxier considered remote kin of the Gurunsi. More details on the Nyonyose may be found in R. Pageard, "Recherche sur les Nioniossé," *Etudes Voltaïques*, No. 4 (1963), pp. 5–71.

13. Habitations in the first three villages were described by Binger, I, 402–403; those in the last three by Le Moal, pp. 196–197.

14. L. Frobenius, *Das unbekannte Afrika* (Munich: C. H. Becksche, 1923), p. 92.

15. Binger, I, 403. The quoted passage is our translation.

16. Le Moal, p. 199.

17. Jean Cremer, *Matériaux d'ethnographie et de linguistique soudanaise*, IV (*Les Bobo*), 26–33.

18. *Ibid.*, pp. 92–95.

19. Pageard, pp. 24, 28.

20. Marcel Griaule, *Conversations with Ogotemmêli* (1965; rpt. New York: Oxford University Press, 1975), p. 26.

21. *Ibid.*, pp. 28, 42.

22. Drissa Diakité, "Les Funérailles au Gurounsi," Cahier de l'Ecole William Ponty, unpubl. ms., 1942–1944. See also the drawings of Lela graves by F. J. Nicolas in "Les Surnoms-devisés des L'éla de la Haute-Volta," *Anthropos*, XLIX (1954), 94.

23. In the Dogon dwelling, whose rooms symbolize male and female and their union, the "head of the house" also refers to the end room with the hearth, which symbolizes the head of the woman lying on her back, the smoke being her breath, the large central room her body, the storerooms on each side her outstretched arms, and the communicating door her sexual organ. Griaule, pp. 94–95.

Chapter 8

1. An example illustrating the choice of space as a form of language may be found in Aboya's account of a man's attitude when he approaches, for the first time, his future wife and her mother. The man will inquire about the dwelling quarter of the girl's mother and "he will climb down to the place [the private court] where they sit. When he sees a comfortable place to sit down, he will not sit there, but sits down at the foot of the ladder which he had descended. When the people nearby see him, and if they like his looks, they will say, 'A-a-a, don't sit there, that is not a sitting place.' He will remain silent, sitting there, in his fine attire. If the girl likes him, she will quickly spread a mat and tell him to pass inside. He will rise up, remove himself, and go to where they have allowed him a mat." Captain R. S. Rattray, *The Tribes of the Ashanti Hinterland* (1932; rpt. London: Oxford University Press, 1969), I, 142.

2. Similar accounts may be found among the Nankani. See Rattray, I, 203, 291, 166–167. E. A. DeCarbo, in "Artistry among Kasem-speaking Peoples of Northern Ghana," Ph.D. dissertation, Indiana University, 1977,

pp. 65, 114, also gives a few details on the *sogo*. See also the description of the *kumpio* in the following chapter.

3. See also J. Zwernemann "Les Notions du dieu-ciel chez quelques tribus voltaïques," *Bulletin de l'IFAN*, XXIII, series B, Nos. 1–2 (January–April 1961), 260.

4. B. S. Guggenheim, "Aspects of the Portal and Portal Decoration in Northeastern Ghana," Ph.D. dissertation, Columbia University, 1976, p. 93.

5. DeCarbo, p. 117.

6. Guggenheim, p. 93.

7. Information given by a local informant who compared the triangular designs to photographs. Their role, he said, is to speak to the children of younger generations and remind them of their ancestors.

8. The name *tana*, which translates as "cloth strips," is given by Fred T. Smith in "Gurensi Wall Painting," *African Arts*, XI, No. 4 (July 1978), 40.

9. All Nankane names are Fred T. Smith's. *Ibid.*, p. 41. The cane, according to one local account, is what a young man carries with him when he goes to his fiancée's home.

Chapter 9

1. Local information, which confirms that given by Captain R. S. Rattray, *The Tribes of the Ashanti Hinterland* (1932; rpt. London: Oxford University Press, 1969), I, 232.

2. The information was given by a resident of Léo, M. Bouchot, and cited by Louis Tauxier in *Le Noir du Soudan* (Paris: Emile Larose, 1912), p. 262. Local accounts, according to Tauxier, have confirmed this information (p. 246).

3. This account is a historical legend of the Gurunsi. It has also been recorded among the Nuna of Sapouy, the Lela of Poun, and other ethnic groups. J. Zwernemann, "La Querelle pour l'enfant pas encore né," *Notes Africaines*, No. 101 (1964), pp. 26–27.

4. A detail which, according to the informant, gives credence to this version is the similarity between Nankani and Gurmantche facial scarifications.

5. The *zenore* in Rattray's study.

6. Details on the *bagèrè* are given in Rattray, pp. 215–221.

7. For more details, see the accounts of Aboya (a Nankani writer) in Rattray, pp. 194–195, 186–187, 210.

8. *Ibid.*, p. 203. The "breaking" ceremony has been discussed in the preceding chapter.

9. A symbol mentioned in Chapter 6.

10. See the two preceding chapters for the womb image of the house.

11. Rattray, p. 196.

12. *Ibid.*, pp. 131, 146, 182.

13. *Ibid.*, p. 196.

14. Herta Haselberger, *Bautraditionen der westafrikanischen Negerkulturen* (Vienna: Herder, 1964), II, 70, cited by B. S. Guggenheim, "Aspects of the Portal and Portal Decoration in Northeastern Ghana," Ph.D. dissertation, Columbia University, 1976, p. 82.

15. Rattray, p. 251.

16. According to Aboya, a child "is left in the room until it can crawl and go out itself. . . . The bringing up of such children is difficult, for in hot weather it is hard not getting outside. The sun descends hotly and everyone wants to sit where the wind casts itself, but behold it is taboo for the child to go out, and mother and child are forced to remain in the heat, and they do not know what to do." Rattray, p. 134.

17. *The Natives of the Northern Territories of the Gold Coast* (1920; rpt. New York: Negro University Press, 1969), p. 99.

18. Compare with the low loopholes in semi-sunken habitations of Koumbili (see Chapter 7).

19. See note 16.

20. Aboya's account in Rattray, p. 134.

21. Aboya's account; the extracted passage is Rattray's, pp. 166–167, 291.

22. Guggenheim, p. 107.

23. Fred T. Smith, "Gurensi Wall Painting," *African Arts*, XI, No. 4 (July 1978), 40.

24. Among the Dogon the bent-stick shape also corresponds to a graphic sign named *inewala*, or hoe. For more details, see Marcel Griaule and Germaine Dieterlen, *Signes graphiques soudanais* (Paris: Hermann, 1951), pp. 25, 14.

25. See Chapters 3 and 8.

26. More particularly the walls of men's spaces (*dètinè* or *bopaka*); can the rows of horizontal lines separated in pairs—but without the snake's head—and often found on the walls of women's spaces, be considered the same motif?

Chapter 10

1. For precise details, see T. E. Hilton, "Notes on the History of Kusasi," *Transactions of the Historical Society of Ghana*, VI (1962), 79–86.

2. Ernst Haaf, in *Die Kusase* (Stuttgart: Gustav Fischer, 1967), p. 43, notices the same fixed number of poles.

3. Additional information on *Widnam* and the *winn* may be found in Ernst Haaf's *Die Kusase*.

4. Captain R. S. Rattray, *The Tribes of the Ashanti Hinterland* (1932; rpt. London: Oxford University Press, 1969), I, 391, 394.

5. *Ibid.*, pp. 395–396; 393–394.

6. Haaf, p. 79.

7. *Ibid.*, p. 46.

8. Herta Haselberger, "Quelques Cas d'Evolution du décor mural en Afrique occidentale," *Notes Africaines*, No. 101 (January 1964), pp. 14–16.

Afterword

1. The word "architecture," which denotes a perception of building by the specialist architect, may be considered contradictory to the term "vernacular." We find no other word, however, that conveys the sense of the totality of designing (basically, the arrangement of elements that make up the house), building, inhabiting, living, and spiritualizing. "Vernacular dwelling" as an alternative is not, in our opinion, an adequate solution, since "dwelling" in today's language tends to reduce the house to a mere shelter.

2. A. Leroi-Gourhan, *Milieu et techniques* (Paris: Albin Michel, 1945), p. 254 (our translation).

3. *Communautés villageoises Bwa* (Paris: Institut d'Ethnologie, 1973), I, 246 (our translation).

SELECTED BIBLIOGRAPHY

Adamou, Aouba. "Le Vêtement au Gourounsi." Cahier de l'Ecole William Ponty. Unpubl. ms., 1942.

Alexander, Christopher, Sara Ishikawa, et al. *A Pattern Language.* New York: Oxford University Press, 1977.

Archer, Ian. "Nabdam Compounds, Northern Ghana." In *Shelter in Africa.* Ed. Paul Oliver. New York: Praeger, 1971. Pp. 46–57.

Armitage, Captain C. H. *The Tribal Markings and Marks of Adornment of the Natives of the Northern Territories of the Gold Coast Colony.* London: Royal Anthropological Institute, 1924.

Arnheim, Rudolf. *The Dynamics of Architectural Form.* Berkeley: University of California Press, 1977.

Bachelard, Gaston. 1969. *The Poetics of Space.* 1958; rpt. Boston: Beacon Press, 1969.

Barral, Henri. *Tiogo: Etude géographique d'un terroir Léla.* Atlas des Structures Agraires au Sud du Sahara, II. Paris: Mouton, 1968.

Barth, Henry. *Travels and Discoveries in North and Central Africa, 1849–1855.* 3 vols. 1857; rpt. London: Frank Cass, 1965.

Barthes, Roland. *Camera Lucida.* Trans. Richard Howard. New York: Hill and Wang, 1981.

————. *Empire of Signs.* Trans. Richard Howard. New York: Hill and Wang, 1982.

Baumann, H., and D. Westermann. *Les Peuples et les civilisations de l'Afrique.* Paris: Payot, 1957.

Beguin, J. P. *L'Habitat au Cameroun.* Paris; Editions de l'Union Françaises, 1952.

Bellour, Raymond, and Catherine Clément, eds. *Claude Lévi-Strauss.* Paris: Gallimard, 1979.

Bendor-Samuel, John T. "The Grusi Sub-Group of the Gur Languages." *Journal of West African Languages,* II, No. 1, 47–55.

Binger, Capitaine. *Du Niger au Golfe de Guinée par le pays de Kong et le Mossi.* 2 vols. Paris: Hachette, 1892.

Bon, G. *Grammaire Lélé.* Mémoire IFAN, No. 24. Dakar: IFAN, 1953.

Bowdich, Edward T. *Mission from Cape Coast Castle to Ashantee.* 1819; rpt. London: Frank Cass, 1966.

Briffault, Robert. *The Mothers*. New York: Atheneum, 1977.

Calame-Griaule, G. "Notes sur l'habitation du plateau central Nigérien." *Bulletin IFAN*, XVII (B), Nos. 3–4 (1955), 477–499.

Capron, Jean. *Communautés villageoises Bwa*. Vol. I. Paris: Institut d'Ethnologie, 1973.

———. "Univers religieux et cohésion interne dans les communautés villageoises Bwa traditionnelles." *Etude Voltaïques*, No. 4 (1963), pp. 73–124.

Cardinall, Allen W. *The Natives of the Northern Territories of the Gold Coast*. 1920; rpt. New York: Negro Universities Press, 1969.

Champagne, Emery P. "Traits de la vie paienne dans la préfecture apostolique de Navrongo." *Annali Lateranensi*, VIII (1944), 147–154.

Chang, Amos Ih Tiao. *The Tao of Architecture*. Princeton: Princeton University Press, 1956.

Chappel, T. J. H. *Decorated Gourds in North-eastern Nigeria*. London: Ethnographica, 1977.

Charles, Léon. "Les Lobi." *Revue d'Ethnographie et de Sociologie*, II (1911), 202–220.

Church, Harrison R. J. *West Africa: A Study of the Environment and of Man's Use of It*. 1960; rpt. London: Longmans, 1965.

Clapperton, Hugh. *Journal of a Second Expedition into the Interior of Africa*. London: Murray, 1829.

Cockburn, Charles. "Fra-Fra House." *Architectural Design*, XXXII (1962), 299–300.

Coutouly, François de. "Enquête sur l'habitation Gourounsi." *Revue Anthropologique*, XLI (1931), 244–254.

Cremer, Jean. *Matériaux d'ethnographie et de linguistique soudanaise*. Vol. I. Paris: Emile Larose, 1923.

D'Azevedo, Warren L., ed. *The Traditional Artist in African Societies*. Bloomington: Indiana University Press, 1973.

DeCarbo, Edward A. "Artistry among Kasem-speaking Peoples of Northern Ghana." Ph.D. dissertation, Indiana University, 1977.

Delafosse, Maurice. *Vocabulaires comparatifs de 60 langues ou dialectes parlés en Côte d'Ivoire ou dans les régions limitrophes*. Paris: Leroux, 1904.

Denyer, Susan. *African Traditional Architecture*. New York: Africana Publishing Company, 1978.

Derrida, Jacques. "Structure, Sign, and Play in the Discourse of the Human Sciences." In *The Structuralist Controversy*. Ed. Richard Macksey and Eugenio Donato. Baltimore: Johns Hopkins, 1972. Pp. 247–272.

Diakité, Drissa. "Les Funérailles au Gourounsi." Cahier de l'Ecole William Ponty. Unpubl. ms., 1942–1944.

Diasso, Goliou A. "Les Rêves au Gourounsi." Cahier de l'Ecole William Ponty. Unpubl. ms., 1946.

Dickson, Kwamina B. *A Historical Geography of Ghana*. Cambridge: Cambridge University Press, 1969.

Dieterlen, Germaine. *Essai sur la religion Bambara*. Paris: Presses Universitaires de France, 1951.

Diop, Cheikh Anta. *The African Origin of Civilization: Myth or Reality?* Ed. Mercer Cook. Westport,. Conn.: Lawrence Hill, 1974.

———. *Nations nègres et cultures*. 2 vols. Paris: Présence Africaine, 1979.

Dittmer, Kunz. "Die sakralen Häuptlinge der Gurunsi im Obervolta-Gebiet und die feudalen Fürstentümer im Sudan." *Tribus*, IX (1960), 68–80.

———. "Die sakralen Häuptlinge der Gurunsi im Obervolta-Gebiet, Westafrika." *Mitteilungen aus dem für Völkerkunde im Hamburg*, Vol. XXVII (1961).

Duperray, Anne-Marie. "Les Gourounsi de Haute-Volta: Conquête et colonisation, 1896–1933." Thèse de 3ème cycle. Paris: Ecole des Hautes Etudes en Sciences Sociales, 1978.

Dyson-Hudson, Neville. "Structure and Infrastructure in Primitive Society: Lévi-Strauss and Radcliffe-Brown Comments." In *The Structuralist Controversy*. Ed. Richard Macksey and Eugenio Donato. Baltimore: Johns Hopkins, 1972. Pp. 218–246.

Eyre-Smith, St. J. *A Brief Organization of the History and the Social Organization of the Peoples of the Northern Territories of the Gold Coast*. Accra: Government Printers, 1933.

Fortes, Meyer. *The Dynamics of Clanship among the Tallensi*. London: Oxford University Press, 1945.

Foucault, Michel. *Discipline and Punish*. New York: Vintage Books, 1979.

Fraser, Douglas. *Village Planning in the Primitive World*. New York: Braziller, 1968.

Frobenius, Leo. *Und Afrika sprach*. 3 vols. Berlin: Vita, 1912–1919.

———. *Das unbekannte Afrika*. Munich: C. H. Becksche, 1923.

———. *Kulturgeschichte Afrikas*. Zurich: Phaidon, 1933.

Froelich, Jean-Claude. *La Tribu Konkomba du Nord-Togo*. Mémoire IFAN, No. 37. Dakar: IFAN, 1954.

———. *Les Montagnards "paléonigritiques."* Paris: ORSTOM, 1968.

———, Pierre Alexandre, and Robert Cornevin. *Les Populations du Nord-Togo*. Paris: Presses Universitaires de France, 1963.

Funke, E. "Vokabular der Kussassi: Sprache im Westsudan." *Mitteilungen der Seminars für orientalische Sprachen*, XXIII–XXV (1922), 88–98.

Gardi, René. *Indigenous African Architecture*. New York: Van Nostrand Reinhold, 1973.

Girault, Louis, R. P. "Essai sur la religion des Dagara." *Bulletin IFAN*, XXI (B), Nos. 3–4 (1959), 329–356.

Glück, Julius F. "Afrikanische Architektur." *Tribus*, VI (1956), 65–82.

Gnankambary, Blami. "La Révolte Bobo de 1916 dans le cercle de Dédougou." *Notes et Documents Voltaïques*, III, No. 4 (1970), 55–87.

Goody, Jack. *The Ethnography of the Northern Territories of the Gold Coast West of the White Volta*. London: Colonial Office, 1954.

———. *Death, Property and the Ancestors*. Stanford: Stanford University Press, 1962.

———. *The Social Organisation of the LoWiili*. London: Oxford University Press, 1967.

———. *Technology, Tradition and the State in Africa*. London: Oxford University Press, 1971.

Griaule, Marcel. *Dieu d'eau: Entretiens avec Ogotemmêli*. Paris: Fayard, 1966. English version: *Conversations with Ogotemmêli*. 1965; rpt. New York: Oxford University Press, 1975.

——— and Germaine Dieterlen. *Signes graphiques soudanais*. L'Homme, No. 3. Paris: Hermann, 1951.

——— and ———. *Le Renard pâle*. Vol. I. Paris: Institut d'Ethnologie, 1965.

Grindal, Bruce. *Growing Up in Two Worlds: Education and Transition among the Sissala of Northern Ghana*. San Francisco: Holt, Rinehart and Winston, 1972.

———. "An Ethnographic Classification of the Sissala of Northern Ghana." *Ethnology*, XI, No. 4 (October 1972), 409–423.

Guggenheim, Barbara Sue. "Aspects of the Portal and Portal Decoration in Northeastern Ghana." Ph.D. dissertation, Columbia University, 1976.

Haaf, Ernst. *Die Kusase*. Stuttgart: Gustav Fischer, 1967.

Hall, Edward T. *The Hidden Dimension*. New York: Anchor Books, 1969.

Haselberger, Herta. "Wandmalerei, Gravierter und modellierter Wandschmuck in den Savanen von Togo und Obervolta." *International Archives of Ethnography*, XLIX, No. 1 (1960), 201–223.

———. "Essai de classification de différents styles du décor mural en Afrique occidentale." *Notes Africaines*, No. 106 (1965), pp. 47–49.

———. "Le Décor gravé chez les Boussansé." *Notes Africaines*, No. 105 (1965), pp. 26–31.

———. "Quelques Cas d'évolution du décor mural en Afrique occidentale." *Notes Africaines*, No. 101 (1964), pp. 14–16.

Hebert, Jean. "Révoltes en Haute-Volta de 1914 à 1918." *Notes et Documents Voltaïques*, III, No. 4 (1970), 3–54.

Hilton, T. E. "Notes on the History of the Kusasi." *Transactions of the Historical Society of Ghana*, VI (1962), 79–86.

Holden, J. J. "The Zabarima Conquest of Northwest Ghana." *Transactions of the Historical Society of Ghana*, VIII (1965), 60–86.

Hull, Richard W. *African Cities and Towns before the European Conquest*. New York: W. W. Norton, 1976.

Illich, Ivan. *Tools for Conviviality*. New York: Harper & Row, 1973.

———. "Vernacular Values." In *The Schumacher Lectures*. Ed. Satish Kumar. New York: Harper & Row, 1980.

———. *Shadow Work*. Boston: Marion Boyars, 1981.

———. "Vernacular Gender." *CoEvolution*, No. 33 (1982), pp. 4–23.

Izard, Françoise. *Bibliographie générale de la Haute-Volta*. Recherches Voltaïques, 7. Paris: CNRS–CVRS, 1967.

Izard, Michel. *Introduction à l'histoire des royaumes Mossi*. Recherches Voltaïques, 12 and 13. Paris: CNRS–CVRS, 1970.

Kawada, Junzo. *Le Zitenga*. Recherches Voltaïques, 6. Paris: CNRS–CVRS, 1967.

Koelle, Sigismund. *Polyglotta Africana*. London: London Missionary House, 1854.

Labouret, Henri. *Les Tribus du rameau Lobi*. Paris: Institut d'Ethnologie, 1931.

———. "Afrique occidentale et equatoriale." In *L'Habitation indigène dans les possessions françaises*. Paris: Société d'Editions Géographiques Maritimes et Coloniales, 1931. Pp. 23–43.

———. *Nouvelles Notes sur les tribus du rameau Lobi*. Mémoires IFAN, No. 54. Dakar: IFAN, 1958.

Lacan, Jacques. "Of Structure as an Inmixing of an Otherness Prerequisite to Any Subject Whatever Discussion." In *The Structuralist Controversy*. Ed. Richard Macksey and Eugenio Donato. Baltimore: Johns Hopkins, 1972. Pp. 186–200.

Lebeuf, Jean-Paul. *L'Habitation des Fali*. Paris: Hachette, 1961.

Leiris, Michel. *Cinq Etudes d'ethnologie*. Paris: Denoël/Gonthier, 1969.

Le Moal, G. "Les Habitations semi-souterraines en Afrique en l'ouest." *Journal de la Société des Africanistes*, XXX (1960), 193–203.

Leroi-Gourhan, André. *Milieu et Techniques*. Paris: Albin Michel, 1945.

Lévi-Strauss, Claude. *Race et Histoire*. Paris: Gonthier, 1961.

———. *The Scope of Anthropology*. Trans. Sherry Ortner Paul and Robert A. Paul. London: Jonathan Cape, 1967.

Levitzion, Nehemia. *Muslims and Chiefs in West Africa*. London: Oxford University Press, 1968.

Manessy, Gabriel. *Les Langues Gurunsi*. 2 vols. Paris: Selaf, 1969.

———. *Les Langues Oti-Volta*. Paris: Selaf, 1975.

Manoukian, Madeleine. *Tribes of the Northern Territories of the Gold Coast*. London: International African Institute, 1951.

Marc, Olivier. *Psychology of the House*. London: Thames and Hudson, 1977.

Marchal, Monique. "Les Paysages agraires de la Haute-Volta: Analyse structurale par la méthode graphique." Dissertation. Paris: Ecole des Hautes Etudes en Sciences Sociales, 1978.

Marchant, Paul. "Ghana." In *Shelter II*. Bolinas: Shelter Publications, 1978. Pp. 6–9.

Monteil, Charles. "Le Village africain de l'ouest." *Bulletin IFAN*, XXVII (B), Nos. 3–4 (1965), 706–714.

Mekkawi, Mod. *Bibliography on Traditional Architecture in Africa*. Howard University, Washington, D.C.: Mekkawi, 1978.

Mumtaz, Babar. "Villages on the Black Volta." In *Shelter and Society*. Ed. Paul Oliver. London: Barrie & Jenkins, 1969.

Newman, Oscar. *Defensible Space: Crime Prevention through Urban Design*. New York: Collier Books, 1973.

Nicolas, J. F. "Les Surnoms-devisés des L'éla de la Haute-Volta." *Anthropos*, XLV (1950), 81–118; XLIX (1954), pp. 83–102.

———. "La Question de l'ethnique 'Gourounsi' en Haute-Volta." *Africa*, XXII (1952), 1013–1040.

———. "Sept Contes des L'éla de la Haute-Volta." *Anthropos*, XLVII (1952), 80–94.

———. "Un Conte à refrain chanté par les L'éla de la Haute-Volta." *Anthropos*, XLVIII (1953), 158–170.

———. "Onomastique personelle des L'éla de la Haute-Volta." *Bulletin IFAN*, XV (B), No. 2 (1953), 818–847.

———. *Glossaire L'élé-Français*. Mémoire IFAN, No. 24, 2. Dakar: IFAN, 1953.

Noll, Ned. "Les Français au Gourounsi." *A Travers le Monde*, III (1898), 21–23.

Norberg-Schulz, Christian. *Intentions in Architecture*. Cambridge: MIT Press, 1965.

———. *Existence, Space and Architecture*. New York: Praeger, 1971.

Nunley, John W. "Sissala Sculpture of Northern Ghana." Ph.D. dissertation, University of Washington, 1976.

Oliver, Paul. "Introduction." In *Shelter in Africa*. Ed. Paul Oliver. New York: Praeger, 1971. Pp. 7–24.

———, ed. *Shelter, Sign and Symbol*. Woodstock: The Overlook Press, 1977.

Pageard, Robert. "Recherches sur les Nioniossé." *Etudes Voltaïques*, No. 4 (1963), pp. 5–71.

Paulme, Denise. "Que savons-nous des religions africaines?" In *Les Religions africaines traditionnelles*. Paris: Editions du Seuil, 1965. Pp. 13–32.

———, ed. *Women of Tropical Africa*. Berkeley: University of California Press, 1963.

Péron, Yves, and Zalacain Victoire. *Atlas de Haute-Volta*. Paris: Editions Jeune Afrique, 1975.

Pieper, Jean. "An Outline of Architectural Anthropology." *AARP*, XVII (March 1980), 4–10.

Pitié, Nama. "Les Gourounsi de Léo." Cahier de l'Ecole William Ponty. Unpubl. ms., 1940.

Poewe, Karla O. *Matrilineal Ideology*. New York: Academic Press, 1981.

Ponton, G. L. "Les Gourounsi du groupe voltaïque." *Outre-Mer*, Nos. 2–3 (1933), pp. 99–118; No. 4 (1934), pp. 315–337.

Pradeau, Christian. "Kokolibou (Haute-Volta) ou le pays Dagari à travers un terroir." *Etudes Rurales*, Nos. 37–39 (January–September 1970), pp. 85–112.

Preiswerk, Roy, and Dominique Perrot. *Ethnocentrism and History*. New York: Nok Publishers, 1978.

Problèmes d'enseignement en Haute-Volta: Monographie de village Mossi. Bordeaux: Institut des Sciences Humaines Appliquées, n.d.

Prost, André. *Contribution à l'etude des langues voltaïques*. Mémoires IFAN, No. 70. Dakar: IFAN, 1964.

————. "Deux Langues Gourounsi: Le Kasem et le Nuni." *Bulletin IFAN*, XXII (B), No. 4 (1970), 975–1082; XXXIII (B), No. 2 (1971), 343–434.

————. *Enquête sommaire sur le Ko, langue Gourounsi de Haute-Volta*. Dakar: Faculté des Lettres, 1972.

Prussin, Labelle. *Architecture in Northern Ghana*. Berkeley: University of California Press, 1969.

————. "Pillars, Projections, and Paradigms." *Architectura, Journal of the History of Architecture* (Munich: Deutscher Kunstverlag, 1977), pp. 65–81.

———— and David Lee. "Architecture in Africa: An Annotated Bibliography." *Africana Library Journal*, IV, No. 3 (1973), 2–32.

Rapoport, Amos. *House Form and Culture*. Englewood Cliffs, N.J.: Prentice-Hall, 1969.

Rattray, Captain R. S. *The Tribes of the Ashanti Hinterland*. 2 vols. 1932; rpt. London: Oxford University Press, 1969.

Remy, Gérard. *Donsin: Les structures agraires d'un village Mossi de la région de Nobere*. Recherches Voltaïques, 15. Paris: CNRS–CVRS, 1972.

Rouamba, Paul T. "Terroirs en pays Mossi, à propos de Yaoghin (Haute-Volta)." *Etudes Rurales*, Nos. 37–39 (January–September 1970), pp. 129–149.

Rudofsky, Bernard. *Architecture without Architects*. New York: Doubleday, 1964.

Saint Jalmes, Bernard. "Aspects historiques et sociologiques d'un village Kasséna de Haute-Volta." Ouagadougou: CVRS, n.d.

Savonnet, Georges. "Notes sur quelques ruines situées dans la région de Léo." *Notes Africaines*, No. 71 (July 1956), pp. 65–67.

————. *Pina: Etude d'un terroir de front pionnier en pays Dagari*. Atlas des Structures Agraires au Sud du Sahara, IV. Paris: Mouton, 1970.

————. *Les Birifor de Diepla et sa région insulaires du rameau Lobi (Haute-Volta)*. Atlas des Structures Agraires au Sud du Sahara, XII. Paris: ORSTOM, 1976.

Sieber, Roy. *African Furniture and Household Objects*. Bloomington: Indiana University Press, 1980.

Silva, Julio A. "Habitat traditionnel en Haute-Volta." N.p., 1970.

Skinner, Elliott P. *The Mossi of the Upper Volta*. Stanford: Stanford University Press, 1964.

Smith, Fred T. "Gurensi Wall Painting." *African Arts*, XI, No. 4 (July 1978), 36–41.

Tauxier, Louis. *Le Noir du Soudan: Pays Mossi et Gourounsi*. Paris: Emile Larose, 1912.

————. *Le Noir de Yatenga*. Paris: Emile Larose, 1917.

————. *Le Noir du Bondoukou*. Paris: Ernest Leroux, 1921.

————. *Nouvelles Notes sur le Mossi et le Gourounsi*. Paris: Emile Larose, 1924.

Traditional Sculpture from Upper Volta. New York: African-American Institute, 1978.

Turner, John F. C. *Housing by People*. New York: Pantheon, 1976.

Van Gennep, Arnold. *The Rites of Passage*. Chicago: University of Chicago Press, 1960.

Wenzel, Marian. *House Decoration in Nubia*. London: Gerald Duckworth, 1972.

Zahan, D. "L'Habitation Mossi." *Bulletin IFAN*, XII, No. 1 (1950), 222–229.

————. "La Notion d'écliptique chez les Bambara." *Notes Africaines*, No. 80 (1958), pp. 108–111.

Zevi, Bruno. *The Modern Language of Architecture*. New York: Van Nostrand Reinhold, 1978.

Zwernemann, Jürgen. "Shall We Use the Word 'Gurunsi'?" *Africa*, XXVIII, No. 2 (April 1958), pp. 123–125.

————. "Les Notions du dieu-ciel chez quelques tribus voltaïques." *Bulletin IFAN*, XXIII (B), Nos. 1–2 (January–April 1961), 243–272.

————. "Feldtypen und Speichertypen bei den Kasena in Obervolta." *Zeitschrift für Ethnologie*, LXXXVIII, No. 2 (1963), 310–317.

————. "Zur Sozialordnung der Kasena von Pô." *Tribus*, XII (1963), 33–103.

————. "Divination chez les Kasena en Haute-Volta." *Notes Africaines*, No. 102 (1964), pp. 58–61.

————. "La Querelle pour l'enfant pas encore né." *Notes Africaines*, No. 101 (1964), pp. 26–27.

————. "La Fondation de Po: Essai d'interprétation des traditions orales d'une ville Kasena." *Notes et Documents Voltaïques*, II, No. 2 (1969), 3–15.

INDEX

230